Captive Anzacs

AUSTRALIAN POWS OF THE OTTOMANS DURING THE FIRST WORLD WAR

During the First World War, 198 Australians became prisoners of the Ottomans. Captivity caused these men to question their position as soldiers and their role in the war, while living under the rule of a culturally, religiously and linguistically different enemy also proved challenging.

Overshadowed by the grief and hardship that characterised the post-war period, and by the enduring myth of the fighting Anzac, these POWs have long been neglected in the national memory of the war.

Captive Anzacs explores how the prisoners felt about their capture and how they dealt with the physical and psychological strain of imprisonment, as well as the legacy of their time as POWs. More broadly, it explores public perceptions of the prisoners, the effects of their captivity on their families, and how military, government and charitable organisations responded to the POWs both during and after the war.

Intertwining rich detail from letters, diaries and other personal papers with official records, Kate Ariotti offers a comprehensive, nuanced account of this little-known aspect of Australian war history.

Kate Ariotti is a historian of war and society and a lecturer in Australian history at the University of Newcastle.

OTHER TITLES IN THE AUSTRALIAN ARMY HISTORY SERIES

Series editor: Peter Stanley

Phillip Bradley *The Battle for Wau: New Guinea's Frontline 1942–1943*

Mark Johnston *The Proud 6th: An Illustrated History of the 6th Australian Division 1939–1946*

Garth Pratten *Australian Battalion Commanders in the Second World War*

Jean Bou *Light Horse: A History of Australia's Mounted Arm*

Phillip Bradley *To Salamaua*

Peter Dean *The Architect of Victory: The Military Career of Lieutenant-General Sir Frank Horton Berryman*

Allan Converse *Armies of Empire: The 9th Australian and 50th British Divisions in Battle 1939–1945*

John Connor *Anzac and Empire: George Foster Pearce and the Foundations of Australian Defence*

Peter Williams *The Kokoda Campaign 1942: Myth and Reality*

Karl James *The Hard Slog: Australians in the Bougainville Campaign, 1944–45*

Robert Stevenson *To Win the Battle: The 1st Australian Division in the Great War, 1914–1918*

Jeffrey Grey *A Soldier's Soldier: A Biography of Lieutenant-General Sir Thomas Daly*

Mark Johnston *Anzacs in the Middle East: Australian Soldiers, Their Allies and the Local People in World War II*

Mark Johnston *Stretcher-bearers: Saving Australians from Gallipoli to Kokoda*

Christopher Wray *Pozières: Echoes of a Distant Battle*

Craig Stockings *Britannia's Shield: Lieutenant-General Sir Edward Hutton and Late-Victorian Imperial Defence*

Andrew Ross, Robert Hall and Amy Griffin *The Search for Tactical Success in Vietnam: An Analysis of Australian Task Force Combat Operations*

William Westerman *Soldiers and Gentlemen: Australian Battalion Commanders in the Great War, 1914–1918*

Thomas Richardson *Destroy and Build: Pacification in Phuoc Tuy, 1966–72*

Tristan Moss *Guarding the Periphery: The Australian Army in Papua New Guinea, 1951–75*

Captive Anzacs

Australian POWs of the Ottomans during the First World War

KATE ARIOTTI

CAMBRIDGE
UNIVERSITY PRESS

CAMBRIDGE
UNIVERSITY PRESS

University Printing House, Cambridge CB2 8BS, United Kingdom

One Liberty Plaza, 20th Floor, New York, NY 10006, USA

477 Williamstown Road, Port Melbourne, VIC 3207, Australia

314–321, 3rd Floor, Plot 3, Splendor Forum, Jasola District Centre, New Delhi – 110025, India

79 Anson Road, #06–04/06, Singapore 079906

Cambridge University Press is part of the University of Cambridge.

It furthers the University's mission by disseminating knowledge in the pursuit of
education, learning and research at the highest international levels of excellence

www.cambridge.org
Information on this title: www.cambridge.org/9781107198647

© Kate Ariotti 2018

First published 2018

Cover designed by Anne-Marie Reeves
Typeset by SPi Global
Printed in China by C & C Offset Printing Co. Ltd, February 2018

A catalogue record for this publication is available from the British Library

A catalogue record for this book is available from the National Library of Australia

ISBN 978-1-107-19864-7 Hardback

CONTENTS

Illustrations	vii
Maps	viii
Preface	ix
Acknowledgements	xi
Note on terminology	xiv
Glossary	xv
Introduction	1
Chapter 1 Becoming prisoners of war	9
Chapter 2 The circumstances of confinement	31
Chapter 3 Shaping camp life	52
Chapter 4 Outside connections	71
Chapter 5 Reactions at home	90
Chapter 6 After the Armistice	115
Chapter 7 'Repat' and remembrance	134
Conclusion	158
Appendix 1: POWs by service	162
Appendix 2: POW deaths	169
Notes	174
Bibliography	199
Index	216

Illustrations

Frederick Ashton, pictured with other Australian POWs at their
prison camp at San Stefano, near Constantinople 3

HMAS *AE2* 15

Maurice George Delpratt, c. 1919 28

Message sent by Maurice Delpratt from Constantinople informing
his family of his capture, July 1915 29

Belemedik, base camp of the Berlin–Baghdad Railway project 37

Section of Berlin–Baghdad Railway line at Hadjikiri 39

Demobilised Ottoman Army troops being transported
away from the front 41

POW officer houses at Afyonkarahissar 54

Australian officers at Afyonkarahissar 67

POW graves in the Christian cemetery at Belemedik 69

Medically repatriated POW Patrick O'Connor with an Australian
POW of the Germans, Philip Warburton Symonds 77

The staff of the Australian Red Cross Prisoner of War Department
in London 86

The founder of the Australian Branch of the British Red Cross
Society, Lady Helen Munro Ferguson 98

Memorial card produced by Esther Curran to commemorate
the death of her son David as a POW in the Ottoman Empire 113

Haidar Pasha Cemetery, Istanbul, the cemetery of concentration
for prisoner-of-war graves from around the Constantinople region 125

Headstone of Air Mechanic Francis Adams, Baghdad North Gate
Cemetery, 2009 128

Maps

Map 1 Key sites of capture for Australians in the Middle East   xvi

Map 2 The main Ottoman prison camps in which Australian
POWs were held   xvii

PREFACE

The Australian Army has a long and admirable record in fostering serious research and publication about its history. For more than a century the army has seen the value of history to its future. From its outset 'military history' was part of the formal education of officers at the Royal Military College, Duntroon, and for a time officers' promotion depended upon candidates being able to give a coherent analysis of 'Stonewall' Jackson's Shenandoah Valley campaigns in promotion exams. An understanding of the army's history and traditions remains central to its *esprit de corps*, in its most literal meaning.

From the 1970s (as a consequence of educating officers at university level) the army has produced several generations of educated soldiers, several of whom became historians of note, including John Coates, Robert O'Neill, David Horner, Peter Pedersen, John Mordike, Bob Hall, Jean Bou, Bob Stevenson and Craig Stockings. The creation of an Army History Unit in the late 1990s demonstrated the army's commitment to encouraging and facilitating serious history. Under Dr Roger Lee it exerted a profound influence on managing the army's museums, on supporting research on army history and on publishing its history.

One of the most impressive demonstrations of the army's commitment to history has been its long association with several major publishers, notably with Cambridge University Press. This has been a productive relationship, brokered by Roger Lee and the former long-standing general editor of the Army History Series, Professor David Horner.

The Cambridge Army History Series brings to an academic and popular readership historical work of importance across the range of the army's interests and across the span of its history. The series, which I now have the honour to edit, seeks to publish research and writing of the highest quality relating to the army's operational experience and to its existence as an organisation, as a part of its contribution to the national narrative.

The Army History Unit has created a community of writers and readers (including soldiers in both roles), the product of whose questions, research, debate and writing informs the army's understanding of itself and its part in Australia's history. It is a history to be proud of in every sense.

Kate Ariotti's *Captive Anzacs: Australian POWs of the Ottomans during the First World War* constitutes the first full account of the experience of Australians captured on Gallipoli and in the Middle East. The doctoral thesis on which it is based was awarded the Army History Unit's C.E.W. Bean Prize, a reminder of how the army fosters historical talent. Dr Ariotti's book continues the recent move to redress the neglect from which prisoners of war (other than those of the Japanese) have suffered in our historical record. It reflects on an experience that, however much soldiers may wish to ignore it, can befall those who enter battle. It also takes the historical exploration of these Australian soldiers' experience into the heart of the Middle East, a region to which Australian troops were to return repeatedly in the course of the ensuing century. These men, who lived in the region and among its people, were the forebears of Australian soldiers who continue to forge relationships with them.

Professor Peter Stanley
General Editor, Australian Army History Series
UNSW Canberra

ACKNOWLEDGEMENTS

I am fortunate to have benefitted from the wisdom, encouragement, advice, and intellectual and personal support of many people during the course of producing this book. It is with the deepest gratitude that I formally acknowledge those who, in different ways, have helped bring *Captive Anzacs* to fruition.

This book is based on my PhD thesis, which was completed at the University of Queensland under the principal supervision of Associate Professor Martin Crotty. A supporter of my interests in the study of war and society since I was an undergraduate, Martin guided me through the PhD process with patience, humour, and generosity, and provided important advice as I finished the book. I greatly value his continued interest in my work and to him I extend heartfelt thanks.

I am privileged to work among an inspiring group of historians of the highest calibre at the University of Newcastle. For their support of this book and my other research interests, their advice on all aspects of academic life, and their enthusiasm for the practice and teaching of history I thank Dr James Bennett, Dr Kit Candlin, Professor Catharine Coleborne, Associate Professor Nancy Cushing, Dr Sacha Davis, Professor Philip Dwyer, Professor Victoria Haskins, Associate Professor Hans Lukas Kieser, Dr Julie McIntyre, Professor Roger Markwick, Associate Professor Wayne Reynolds, Dr Elizabeth Roberts-Pedersen and Professor Lyndall Ryan. Before I commenced my appointment at Newcastle I worked at the Australian War Memorial, and I will always be grateful for the insights into the world of military history offered during my time there by the dedicated group of historians and editors in the Military History Section.

Historical research of any kind is reliant on the expertise and assistance of hard-working archivists, librarians and curators, and thanks are due to the staff at the many museums, archives, memorials and libraries I visited in Australia and overseas during the course of my research. Here I also acknowledge the financial support provided by the Australian Academy of the Humanities in the form of a Travelling Fellowship, which enabled me to visit various archives and libraries in the UK. Many of these institutions kindly granted permission to reproduce material from their collections in the book. I thank the Australian Army History Unit for permission to cite from official files held in the Australian War Memorial, as well as the National Archives of Australia and the Commonwealth War Graves Commission for allowing me to use and quote from their records. The Australian War Memorial and the State Libraries of New South Wales and Queensland provided permission to reproduce material where appropriate. I also extend my sincere thanks to Jan Delpratt for providing me with photographs and other material related to her father. All efforts have been made to trace and acknowledge the copyright holders of other material quoted in the book; the author and publisher apologise for any errors or omissions and would be grateful to hear from any person who may have been overlooked or has further information that would redress this situation.

Parts of the book incorporate some material which appeared previously in the following articles and chapters: Kate Ariotti, 'Australian prisoners of the Turks: Negotiating culture clash in captivity' in *Other Fronts, Other Wars: First World War Studies on the Eve of the Centennial,* ed. J. Burgschwentner, M. Egger and G. Barth-Scalmani, pp. 146–66: Brill, 2014; Kate Ariotti, '"At present everything is making us most anxious": Families of Australian prisoners in Turkey' in *Beyond Surrender: Australian Prisoners of War in the Twentieth Century,* ed. J. Beaumont, L. Grant and A. Pegram, pp. 57–71: Melbourne University Press, 2015; Kate Ariotti, '"I'm awfully fed up with being a prisoner": Australian POWs of the Turks and the strain of surrender', *Journal of Australian Studies* vol. 40, no. 3 (2016) pp. 276–90, available online http://www.tandfonline.com/10.1080/14443058.2016.1199585; and Kate Ariotti, 'International encounters in captivity: The cross-cultural experiences of Australian POWs in the Ottoman Empire', ed. K. Ariotti and J. E. Bennett, *Australians and the First World War: Local-Global Connections and Contexts,* pp. 47–6: Palgrave Macmillan, 2017 (reproduced with permission of Palgrave Macmillan/Springer Nature). The author and Cambridge University Press thank the publishers for their permission to use this material.

I am so very thankful to those who helped make the book a reality: series editor Professor Peter Stanley, Vilija Stephens and Jodie Fitzsimmons at Cambridge University Press, Dr Andrew Richardson from the Australian Army History Unit, editor Cathryn Game and PhD candidate Bryce Abraham. I am indebted to Peter for championing this book and for ensuring it met his rigorous standards of analysis and writing, to Vilija and Jodie for expertly and patiently guiding me through the publication process, to Andrew for sourcing images and maps, to Cathryn for her close reading and editing, and to Bryce for his assistance preparing the manuscript for submission.

Numerous other people have offered comments on drafts, general advice, coffee and hugs. There are far too many kind souls to list here but special mention must go to Dr Gemmia Burden, Dr Romain Fathi, Dr Alexia Moncrieff, Dr Kerry Neale, Dr Aaron Pegram and Dr Jon Piccini. I am also immensely grateful to my family – Peter and Maxine, Helen and Sam, Robyn and Andrew, and all the Ariottis – who provided unwavering support as I completed the manuscript. While there are so many things to thank them for, their confidence in me and ability to keep my thinking in perspective helped me more than they probably realise.

Last, I acknowledge my husband Dr Nick Ariotti, who in many respects has been a captive of my research himself for some years. His patience, good humour, editorial critique, technological support and tireless encouragement made this book possible. To him I say love and thanks – for everything.

NOTE ON TERMINOLOGY

The nation known today as Turkey did not exist during the First World War. Technically, it was the Ottoman Empire against whom the Australians, British and other allies fought. The Ottoman Empire encompassed diverse territories and peoples, including Arabs, Kurds, Jews, and Greeks and Armenians. However, it was the ethnic Turks who dominated the political landscape and comprised the majority of Ottoman forces during the war. Contemporary accounts reflect this and generally refer to the Ottoman enemy as 'the Turks'. Indeed, the Australian POWs believed they were in the hands of the Turks, and that they were in captivity 'in Turkey'. In keeping with the correct terminology for the time periods discussed, however, the terms 'Ottoman Empire' and 'Ottoman Army/ soldier' are used throughout the book until after 1923, when 'Turkey' is used.

The book makes significant use of letters, diaries, postcards, memoirs and other sources produced by the prisoners and their families, as well as newspaper articles and government and aid agency reports from the time of the First World War. Quotations from these sources have been incorporated to provide insight into the thoughts, feelings, outlooks and attitudes of those directly and indirectly affected by captivity in the Ottoman Empire. These quotations might include language that is today deemed racist or offensive. Such language and views do not necessarily reflect those of the author.

GLOSSARY

AGS	Australian Graves Service
AIF	Australian Imperial Force
ANZAC	Australian and New Zealand Army Corps
ARC	Australian Red Cross
AWL	Absent Without Leave
AWM	Australian War Memorial
CPWC	Central Prisoners of War Committee
ICRC	International Committee of the Red Cross
IWGC	Imperial War Graves Commission
NAA	National Archives of Australia
NAK	National Archives, Kew
NCO	Non-commissioned officer
PITC	Prisoners in Turkey Committee
POW	Prisoner of War
RAN	Royal Australian Navy
RCPF	Red Cross Prisoner of War Fund
RSL	Returned and Services League of Australia
VD	Venereal disease
YMCA	Young Men's Christian Association

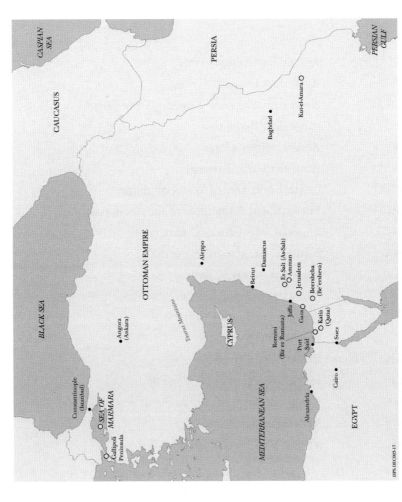

Map 1 Key sites of capture for Australians in the Middle East

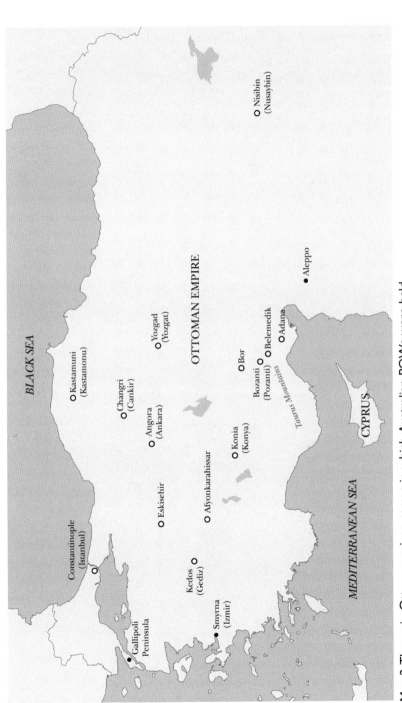

Map 2 The main Ottoman prison camps in which Australian POWs were held

INTRODUCTION

In the early hours of the morning of 25 April 1915, the first wave of Australian and New Zealand Army Corps (ANZAC) troops landed on the Gallipoli peninsula. Alongside the British and French, the landing of the Australians and New Zealanders signified the second allied attempt to penetrate the Dardanelles and seize the Ottoman capital of Constantinople. Within hours of the dawn assault the war was already over for hundreds of soldiers on Gallipoli, killed or wounded as they attempted to get off the beaches and ascend the sheer cliff faces with which they were confronted. By the end of the day the war was also over for Private Frederick Ashton, a young West Australian from the 11th Battalion, Australian Imperial Force (AIF) – but under very different circumstances. Ashton had joined the firing line near Shrapnel Gully after bringing ammunition to the troops, but was almost immediately tasked with finding a stretcher-bearer for a wounded soldier. As he picked his way through the disorienting landscape he became confused and, in his own words:

> When I looked around me I could see no sign of our former firing line, nor could I see anyone – they seemed to have vanished completely.
> I tried to get back to Shrapnel Gully ... but had lost all sense of direction altogether ... I heard a shout, and on looking up, saw about 8 or 10 Turks covering me with their rifles ... At the same time bullets were coming from the rear on the right. I immediately threw up my hands.[1]

Ottoman soldiers stripped Ashton of his weapon and personal effects, marched him behind their lines, and sat him in a tent under guard. A few hours later he was joined by three other Australians, Private Reginald Lushington, Lieutenant William Elston and Captain Ron McDonald, who were captured together near Pope's Hill. Together, these four men were the first Australians to be taken prisoner by their Ottoman enemy, and the first Australians taken prisoner in the war.

During the course of the First World War, an additional 194 Australians joined Ashton, Lushington, Elston and McDonald as prisoners of the Ottomans. Captured during the Gallipoli campaign and in the other so-called sideshow actions in Mesopotamia (Iraq) and Sinai–Palestine, these men from the infantry, Light Horse and Camel Corps, navy and Flying Corps were held in prison camps throughout the Anatolian heartland of the Ottoman Empire. Their experiences varied according to rank, the time and place of their capture, and the camp to which they were assigned. Some were able to live out captivity in relative comfort while others endured tough conditions and poor treatment. At the time of the Armistice in late 1918, fifty-five lay in graves scattered throughout the empire.

The extended imprisonment of Australian servicemen in the Ottoman Empire during the First World War was unprecedented. The South African Boers had taken a limited number of colonial troops prisoner during the Boer War of 1899–1902, but the guerrilla-like nature of that conflict, especially in its latter stages, made administration of prisoners of war (POWs) difficult for the mobile Boer commandos, and most men they captured were stripped of their weapons and horses and left to find their own way back to their lines.[2] Captivity in the Ottoman Empire was also challenging. Men taken prisoner by the Ottomans suddenly found themselves thrust into a new position – captive rather than combatant – and living under the rule of a culturally, religiously and linguistically different enemy in a crumbling empire riven by internal disunity and ethnic tension. In these constrained circumstances, ensuring the provision of aid to the prisoners and maintaining connections between prison camp and home proved difficult, while, when the war ended, the aftermath of captivity – dealing with the dead and with the physical and psychological effects on the living – also posed certain challenges.

Despite the novelty and intrigue of their story, the POWs have long remained on the margins of Australian history and memory of the First World War. This is partly because captivity in the First World War was, for Australians, a minority experience. During the four years of the war, 412 000 Australians enlisted in the AIF, of whom nearly 60 000 died while more than 150 000 were wounded. In contrast, fewer than 4000 were taken prisoner: 198 by the Ottoman Army and the remainder by the

Frederick Ashton, captured on 25 April on Gallipoli, was one of the first Australians taken prisoner by the Ottomans. Here he is pictured with other Australian POWs at their prison camp at San Stefano, near Constantinople. Standing left to right: Ashton, David Boyle, Reginald Lushington, Thomas Chalcroft and Keith Cahir. Sitting left to right: Martin Troy, Robert McColl and Harry Foxcroft. (AWM C01052)

Germans on the Western Front, particularly after the attacks at Fromelles in 1916, Bullecourt in 1917 and Dernancourt in 1918. After the war, in the face of such overwhelming grief, loss and hardship, the fate of a relatively minimal number of POWs was soon overshadowed.

This neglect of POW experiences was compounded by the developing mythology of the fighting Anzac that became central to public commemoration in the post-war period, and which left little room for those who failed to meet the idealised prescription of the battlefield hero. This included POWs, for surrender and imprisonment, and the sense of powerlessness and passivity that are often conflated with it, sat somewhat awkwardly against the triumphalist celebration of the supposedly innate soldiering qualities of the Australian soldier. Then, after the Second World War, the prisoners of the Japanese dominated Australian understandings of wartime captivity. The high death rates of many of the Pacific prison camps, the images of emaciated, brutalised men and women, and the stories of suffering and cruelty they so vividly told, coupled with the scale of numbers involved – 22 000 Australians were taken POW by the

Japanese from 1942 onwards – was, for Australia, one of the greatest tragedies of the Second World War. A keen scholarly interest in their experiences, first fostered by historians Hank Nelson and Joan Beaumont in the 1980s, has ensured that over time these POWs attained an almost legendary status in Australian war history, to the effective exclusion of those who endured captivity at the hands of different enemies in different wars.[3]

But shifting trends in the study of military history and the war and society nexus has led to a refocusing of scholarly and popular interest in marginalised voices and perspectives, including, more recently, First World War POWs. Influenced by a growing international literature that has explored the captivity experience through the lenses of violence and propaganda, forced labour, cross-cultural interactions, escape attempts and the psychology of surrender, Australian historians have also turned their attention to the experiences of those taken prisoner during the First World War.[4] Most focus has been directed to the POWs of the Germans, such as David Coombes' *Crossing the Wire* (2011) and Aaron Pegram's several book chapters and journal articles. The prisoners of the Ottomans have received some consideration, mainly from non-academic writers who have used the diaries and memoirs of several ex-POWs to produce accounts of their lives in captivity, such as Greg Kerr's *Lost Anzacs: The Story of Two Brothers* (1997) and Fred and Elizabeth Brenchley's *Stoker's Submarine* (2001) and *White's Flight* (2004). Academic studies are limited to a few book chapters and articles and one published monograph, Jennifer Lawless' *Kismet: The Story of the Gallipoli Prisoners of War* (2015).[5]

These publications, particularly Lawless' book, provide a solid basis for understanding what happened to the POWs; however, there is still much more to be said about the captivity of Australians in the Ottoman Empire during the First World War. Most of the existing literature centres on the experiences of those captured on Gallipoli, reinforcing the dominance of the peninsula in Australian war historiography and excluding the experiences of prisoners captured elsewhere in the Middle East. It also focuses on the specifics of imprisonment – locations and conditions of POW camps, interactions with captors, and escape attempts – but, as Michael McKernan, Janette Bomford and Christina Twomey have shown in their studies of Australians taken prisoner by the Japanese during the Second World War, wartime captivity affects far more than just the captive.[6] The role of external aid and welfare agencies, the reaction of those at home to servicemen being taken prisoner, the effects on family and friends, the commemoration of the dead, and the process of repatriation and return to civilian life are also significant factors in understanding the totality of captivity.

Captive Anzacs builds on the existing work on the POWs of the Ottomans and broadens the lens to examine these different elements of the captivity experience. It focuses on how Australians were affected by captivity in the Ottoman Empire, intimately and more broadly, and how they responded to the many challenges it posed. The book explores how the prisoners felt about their capture, how they negotiated the circumstances of their confinement, and how they dealt with the legacy of their time as POWs. It also details the provision of aid and support to men in the camps, how their captivity was represented in the Australian press, the strain felt by the prisoners' families, and the ways in which those who died in captivity were commemorated after the war. These important insights into the consequences of capture and imprisonment – and how those affected by this wartime reality managed, shaped, adjusted to and ultimately coped with its constraints and difficulties – reveal that despite being a minority experience, captivity during the First World War had widespread and, for some, long-lasting effects.

Such analysis relies on piecing together a rich, although fragmented, archive of personal, official and published records while remaining alive to their potential limitations and restrictions. Central to the exploration of any POW experience is the writings of the prisoners themselves, including diaries and letters. Prisoners were not supposed to keep diaries in the Ottoman prison camps, but a few men managed to maintain records of their daily lives. Letters sent by prisoners to family and friends at home, now found in service records, Red Cross reports and private collections, also offer interesting glimpses into camp life. While diaries and letters often convey the immediate feelings of the prisoner, they must be viewed with caution as they often contain elements of self-censorship and reflection that can skew the representation of events and experiences. Correspondence during the war was ritualised, formulaic and codified, often written more to mask the truth than reveal it.[7] For the historian, however, silences and gaps – the things that could not be said – still prove useful. Indeed, Michael Roper argues that often it is the silences in personal records that convey the most:

> We can learn to read the emotions of sons between the lines of letters home ... They dropped clues in their omissions, abrupt changes of topic, things alluded to but ultimately left unsaid, and contradictory comments about their spirits ... The result was a characteristically

oblique style of communication which can nevertheless reveal much about the emotional experience of Army life.[8]

Reading between the lines of POW diaries and correspondence, in similar fashion, can reveal much about the emotional impact of imprisonment.

Memoirs also offer a valuable window into the captivity experience. Eight Australian POWs wrote memoirs after the war, including former Flying Corps officers Ron Austin and Thomas White, and soldiers Reginald Lushington, George Handsley and John Halpin.[9] Several British prisoners also published accounts of their time in captivity after the war, such as renowned archaeologist Leonard Woolley.[10] While their stories are unique and evocative, they too must be approached with care. Based largely on memory, which can be subject to distortion, suppression or exaggeration, they are also generally written well after the events they describe and are given a specific, shaped narrative structure for the benefit of the audience. The motivations of the author must also be considered; as Robin Gerster suggests, POW memoirists often 'big-note' their experiences by overemphasising escape attempts or denigrating their captors in a form of 'belated revenge'.[11]

Corroborating these sources alongside other records can overcome some of these potential issues. This book has drawn on official records from the Australian Governor-General's office, the Red Cross, the Imperial (now Commonwealth) War Graves Commission and the Department of Repatriation or, as it was often referred to at the time, 'the Repat'. These files and papers offer important insights into the ways in which external parties provided aid and support to the POWs and their families at different stages of the captivity experience, from the moment of capture through to return and resettlement into civilian life. Again, however, care must be exercised, as official records can also promote a specific agenda. This is particularly the case with post-war Repatriation files, which, as historian Stephen Garton notes, are 'more likely to be a repository of complaint than compliment'.[12] Nevertheless, when read together with service records compiled by the Department of Defence, these official records reveal a detailed chronology of a man's imprisonment and the wider ramifications of his time in captivity.

Newspapers and family papers add another element to the story. During the war Australians relied primarily on newspapers for information – wireless was not introduced in Australia for news and leisure purposes until the 1920s – and it was in newspapers that casualty lists, letters from soldiers, advertisements for charitable fundraisers, and letters to editors were published. It is in newspapers therefore that one can learn how the POWs were represented and perceived at home during the war as well as the reception they received upon their return. Private collections of family material – correspondence, photographs, genealogical records and the like – also shed light on the effects of imprisonment on families, the ways in which former POWs settled into life after the war, and how captivity, and the war in general, were remembered as time went on.

This book is structured to present a comprehensive overview of captivity in the Ottoman Empire and its aftermath. The first three chapters focus on the prisoners themselves. Chapter 1 examines the transition the men made from combatant soldiers, sailors and airmen to captives, and demonstrates that becoming a POW was a process that began with capture and, after time spent journeying to sites of imprisonment, ended with the prisoners' reflections on their fate. It explores the preconceptions and perceptions the prisoners entertained about their captors, how they responded to their initial treatment behind enemy lines and en route to a prison camp, and their responses to their new status. Once a camp was reached the prisoners faced an indefinite time in imprisonment in a radically different environment. The circumstances of their confinement caused much anger and anxiety. Chapter 2 explores how cultural clashes over food, accommodation, travel, work and medical care were of immediate concern, while challenges to the Australians' sense of racial and cultural superiority and the generalised restrictions and constraints of captivity led to mental and emotional strain. Chapter 3 reveals how the prisoners negotiated and responded to these issues and implemented measures to normalise their conditions, emphasising that the captives were not passive recipients of imprisonment but that they actively worked to manage and shape their situation.

Chapter 4 marks a shift in the focus of the book to those outside the prison camps who were also affected by captivity in the Ottoman Empire. It examines the actions of the Australian, British and Ottoman governments, the role of neutral protecting powers and the efforts of the Red Cross and other aid organisations, and explains how these different parties worked together to manage the provision, implementation and administration of relief.

How Australians at home felt about, and responded to, the capture and imprisonment of Australian servicemen in the Ottoman Empire is the focus of chapter 5. It examines how captivity was represented in the press, how these representations shifted over time, and how the government and charitable associations drew on heightened public awareness of

Australians in enemy hands to encourage enlistment and fundraising. This chapter also reveals the effects of captivity on the prisoners' families, and how they felt about, and reacted to, the peculiar absence of their loved ones.

The Armistice with the Ottoman Empire in late October 1918 signalled the end of the war, and therefore the end of imprisonment. Chapter 6 details the POWs' reverse transition out of captivity. It also examines the fate of those who did not survive, and demonstrates the challenges faced by the Imperial War Graves Commission as they worked to identify and relocate POW graves, as well as the allies' attempts to prosecute the Turks for their actions during the war – including towards prisoners.

The final chapter addresses the legacy of imprisonment. Once the prisoners returned to Australia, they resumed civilian life, yet for many their time as POWs continued to resonate. The post-war health of the former prisoners is a key focus, including the longer-term physical and psychological effects of extended captivity, and the ways by which the men and their families interacted with 'the Repat'. The place of POWs in the memory of the war, and how and why captivity was eclipsed by other experiences, is also explored.

In marrying together battlefield, prison camp, home and aftermath, the chapters move beyond a simple narrative of Anzacs behind barbed wire to situate the POW experience in a wider and interconnected set of histories: the operational conduct of the war; the effects of the conflict in the Ottoman Empire; the rise of official and volunteer aid; the impact of war on families; the processes of return and repatriation; and the development of modes of commemoration. In doing so, *Captive Anzacs* offers a more rounded, nuanced appreciation of the POWs of the Ottomans, of how people responded to the challenges generated by their capture and imprisonment, and of the totality of this intriguing episode in Australian First World War history.

CHAPTER 1

BECOMING PRISONERS
OF WAR

In November 1918 Lieutenant Leslie Luscombe completed an official statement outlining the events that led to his capture on the Gallipoli peninsula three years earlier. Luscombe had led a group of men in an advance on an enemy position, only to become isolated with no promise of reinforcements and surrounded by Ottoman troops. With the majority of his party killed or wounded, Luscombe surrendered and he and several others were taken prisoner. Under the internationally recognised laws of war in operation at the time of the First World War, the Hague Convention of 1899 (revised in 1907), POW standing was granted immediately after surrender or capture. But the drastic change from combatant to captive was not as simple or as straightforward for the men involved. Rather, it was a transitional process that began with capture and, after moving behind the lines and journeying towards a prison camp, finished with a period of reflection and acceptance.

CAUSES OF CAPTURE

The Australians taken prisoner by the Ottomans were captured on various fronts throughout the war. The first were the infantrymen and submariners captured during the Gallipoli campaign. Conceived by the British as a way to break the deadlock into which the early fighting in Europe had descended, Gallipoli strategists rationalised that opening up a third front would increase the strain on the Central Powers and relieve the pressure on the Russian forces fighting the Ottomans in the Caucasus.

Defeating the Ottomans at Gallipoli would also allow for allied control of the Dardanelles, the narrow waterway that linked to the Black Sea, meaning more supplies could be sent to the Russians. Ultimately, however, Gallipoli was a disaster for the allies. Initial attempts to penetrate the Dardanelles in February 1915 using the British and French navies failed, and a second attack, using British, French, Anzac and colonial soldiers charged with crossing the peninsula and capturing the Ottoman capital of Constantinople, was launched in April. As we have seen, four Australians were taken prisoner on the very first day of the infantry landings on Gallipoli; less than a week later, the crew of the Royal Australian Navy submarine HMAS *AE2*, the first submarine to pass successfully through the Dardanelles into the Sea of Marmara, joined their ranks. More Australians fell into enemy hands as the fighting on Gallipoli dragged on – particularly during the August offensive, the allies' last big push to break the stalemate of trench warfare on the peninsula – until, by the time of the withdrawal in December 1915, a total of eighty Australians had been taken prisoner.

At the same time as allied soldiers were landing on Gallipoli, another group of Australian servicemen were en route to Mesopotamia. Concerns for the safety of British oil pipelines in the Persian Gulf necessitated the opening of another front against the Ottomans, and the Indian Government had requested help. The British secured the port city of Basra in late 1914 and set out north to clear the region with the ultimate goal of taking the city of Baghdad. The nature of the terrain meant that aerial reconnaissance was essential and more airmen were needed, so a detachment of Australian pilots and air mechanics from the newly formed Australian Flying Corps, known as the Half-Flight, were sent to assist. In total, eleven Australians were taken prisoner in Mesopotamia: two pilots, and nine air mechanics who were caught up in the capitulation of the Kut-el-Amara garrison in April 1916.

The majority of Australians taken prisoner by the Ottomans, ninety-four men, were light horsemen and cameleers captured on the Sinai–Palestine front from 1916 to 1918. After the withdrawal from Gallipoli, the AIF expanded to double its former size. The infantry joined the war on the Western Front, but the majority of the mounted units remained in the Middle East, operating first to assist in guarding the Suez Canal and then as part of the British offensive to push the Ottoman forces out of the Sinai Desert and up into Palestine. As the fighting continued, a Camel Corps was created to move deeper into the harsh terrain of the desert. Australian light horsemen and cameleers were captured sporadically during the three years of fighting in this region, but particularly during their major engagements at Romani in August 1916, Gaza in April 1917, and Amman and Es Salt in March and May 1918. Twelve Australian pilots were also captured in the region after the first full squadron from the Australian Flying Corps was attached to the British effort there as No. 67 (Australian) Squadron, Royal Flying Corps.

The exact circumstances of each man's capture depended on his location and his role in the services. Australians involved in the ground campaigns – members of the infantry, the Light Horse and the Camel Corps – were captured owing to three key factors: wounds; breakdown of communication; and confusion. Despite romantic notions that Australians always collected their wounded, the realities of battle meant that this was not always possible and, in the rush of withdrawal and retreat, wounded men were left on the battlefield and brought in by the enemy. Prisoners captured in this manner were typically wounded during full-scale attacks, such as the August offensive on Gallipoli or in the numerous operations across the Palestinian front. Just under half of those who became prisoners in these campaigns were in some way wounded at the time of capture, usually sustaining gunshot or shrapnel wounds to the limbs. Wounds of this type were not immediately fatal but were bad enough to immobilise the victim – those with more severe wounds (to the chest or abdomen) typically died on the battlefield while men with lesser injuries could make their way back to Australian lines.

In several cases Australian wounded were left because they were believed to be dead, or at least close to death. Checks for signs of life on the battlefield were often perfunctory, and wounded men were, as was the case with Sergeant John Halpin, sometimes assumed to be beyond help. Halpin's comrades from the 12th Light Horse believed he had been killed during the attack on Es Salt in May 1918 and left him behind when they withdrew, but he had actually been knocked unconscious after falling from his horse and was picked up by an enemy patrol several hours later.[1] Wounded men were also left because no one could get to them. Corporal Edward Picton of the 7th Light Horse, hit by shrapnel in both legs while taking a message from the front to his commanding officers at Amman, was left 'with no assistance' during the retirement of his unit.[2] According to his regiment's 1923 history, Picton's comrades saw him fall but reasoned he 'was in such an advanced position that he could not be rescued'.[3]

Other wounded were captured because there was no one around to render assistance. Private Martin Troy of the 16th Battalion – 'knocked senseless' after a particularly heavy bombardment at Pope's Hill on

Gallipoli in May 1915 – regained consciousness to find himself isolated between the lines and surrounded by the dead and other wounded, while Cameleer Charles Flatt, shot in the legs three times, was similarly marooned among the dead after his unit's attack at Gaza.[4] In many cases, men captured in these circumstances were not found by enemy patrols for hours, or sometimes days, after the battle ceased. The dangers of patrolling no-man's-land meant that areas between the lines were not regularly inspected by either side, and no doubt the Ottomans also assumed many of those remaining on the battlefield were dead or dying.

Communication problems were another factor that led to the capture of several Australians on Gallipoli and in Sinai–Palestine. In the heat of battle, effective communication between headquarters and frontline troops, the different units involved, officers and men, and the men themselves occasionally broke down. In Palestine, the fluidity of the fighting and the constant movement of troops meant sometimes orders to retire were not passed on, were received too late, or were unable to be carried out. Many of the men captured because they did not receive orders to retire were those in outpost positions who were effectively forgotten, leaving them isolated and vulnerable. A breakdown of communication like this led to Trooper Charles Carr's capture in the Jordan Valley in May 1918. Carr, on outpost reconnaissance duty, did not receive any indication that his comrades had withdrawn. He rode back to what had been his commanding officer's position to give his report, only to find it occupied by a party of Ottoman soldiers. They shot at Carr – he avoided being hit but was taken prisoner.[5] Groups of men were also captured because of lack of direction. Twelve members of the 4th Light Horse Brigade's Field Ambulance were taken prisoner after they found themselves stranded at Es Salt: Drivers D'Arcy Armstrong, Benjamin Briant, Henry Brockhurst, George Clarke, Herbert Hebbard, Francis Matthews, George Miller, Ernest Mitchell, Robert Seaton, Arthur Thompson and brothers Matthew and John Sloan were holding horses in a *wadi* (gully) fifty yards from the main ambulance during the May 1918 operation when, 'without issuing any orders', the Ambulance retreated. According to Armstrong, the group was completely surrounded 'before realising the seriousness of our position'.[6]

In some cases an order to retire was issued but was received too late for the men to act. Those captured in this fashion were predominantly from Light Horse units, which often delayed withdrawals and retreats until the last minute. Sergeant Harold Sullivan, Lance Corporal Percy Scroop and Troopers Charles Patten and Edwin Rose of the 9th Light Horse were captured together at Romani in this way; they had dismounted to assist a party of British machine-gunners when they received an order to retire, but were too far away from their horses to reach Australian lines in time. Sometimes an order was issued and received but nothing could be done. During the second attack on Gaza in 1917, for example, Australian camel-eers and about eighty British infantry – taking cover in an enemy trench they had won after an arduous battle accounting for the loss of more than three-quarters of their company – found themselves under heavy bombard-ment with limited remaining ammunition. The group reasoned they had 'no chance whatsoever' of surviving a withdrawal, and the highest-ranking soldier, a British lieutenant, raised a white flag in surrender.[7]

Confusion also accounted for the capture of Australians involved with the ground campaigns. As was the case with the wounded, men taken prisoner under these circumstances were usually captured during or imme-diately after large-scale attacks when ground quickly changed hands. Cameleer John Romaro, captured near Jaffa in December 1917, was taken prisoner after becoming confused and effectively walking behind enemy lines. Despatched at night to bring in two wounded men, Romaro had crossed through no-man's-land and into enemy territory before realising his error. 'First thing I was aware of,' he wrote in a post-war report, 'was being accused by an Officer who spoke English. I knew it was not one of our chaps so made a bolt for it. A pistol bullet passed through the fleshy part of my right elbow, which brought me to a halt.'[8] Confusion accounted for the capture of groups of men, too. During their withdrawal from the fighting on Gallipoli in August 1915, Lieutenant Stewart Stormonth and his party of three non-commissioned officers (NCOs) and twelve men became lost in the dark and confusing maze of gullies, and ended up veering off the edge of a spur. While attempting to find a new route and meet up with another party of Australians, Stormonth walked straight into a group of Ottoman soldiers. Realising he and his group had inadvertently fallen into enemy territory and were stranded, Stormonth immediately surrendered and the entire party was taken prisoner.[9]

The circumstances of capture differed for men involved in the aerial or naval branches of the forces. Pilots and submariners spent extended periods of time in enemy territory, and those who were captured were taken after the failure of their respective air or seacraft, or after successful attacks from the enemy. The first Australian pilot to fall into Ottoman hands was captured in Mesopotamia in September 1915. Lieutenant William Treloar was engaged in a reconnaissance mission over the Ottoman position at Es-Sinn, south of Kut, when his engine cut out and, amid 'a perfect hail of rifle fire', he was forced to bring down his plane near a network of Ottoman trenches.[10] Captain Muhammed Ali, an Ottoman officer who later became a POW of the British, saw Treloar's plane land. He reported that the plane came to a slow stop and Treloar and his observer ran from the aircraft. When they realised they were surrounded, however, they returned and raised their arms to indicate surrender.[11] One other Australian pilot, Captain Thomas White, was taken prisoner in Mesopotamia after his plane was irreparably damaged during a mission to cut telegraph wires near Baghdad in November 1915.

All other Australian flying officers held as POWs by the Ottomans were captured in Sinai–Palestine. Like Treloar, Lieutenant Leonard Heathcote was forced down by engine trouble, but the others were captured after being attacked by their German counterparts (although the Ottoman forces did have an airborne branch, flying missions over Palestine were conducted by German pilots). Lieutenant Claude Vautin was captured in July 1917 when a German airman shot out his controls and forced him down near Gaza, while Lieutenants Fred Hancock and Arthur Poole were taken prisoner after their plane was hit by anti-aircraft fire on a reconnaissance mission over Nablus in January 1918. Pilot Poole brought the wrecked plane down behind enemy lines and, as per protocol, set the machine alight. 'We were under heavy shell and machine gun fire,' Hancock later wrote, 'and within five minutes we were surrounded by a body of German and Turkish soldiers.'[12]

Naval submariners were also captured after direct attacks in enemy territory. The greatest number of Australian POW submariners came from HMAS *AE2*. Tasked with breaching the Dardanelles and penetrating the Sea of Marmara, the *AE2* successfully dodged submerged mines and nets for five tense days before it was attacked by the Ottoman torpedo boat *Sultanhisar* and scuttled on 30 April 1915. In his 1925 memoir, the captain of *AE2*, Henry Stoker, wrote of his ship's demise: 'BANG! ... A cloud of smoke in the engine-room. We were hit and holed! And again in quick succession two more holes. Finished! We were caught! We could no longer dive and our defence was gone. It but remained to avoid useless sacrifice of life. All hands were ordered on deck and overboard.'[13] The thirty-two submariners on board *AE2*, a mixed crew of British and Australians, safely abandoned their ship and were plucked out of the water by the crew of *Sultanhisar*.

Other reasons for capture cut across different divisions and locations. Several Australians fell into enemy hands after going to the aid of stricken comrades. Trooper Martin Brennan of the 11th Light Horse was taken prisoner after he stopped during his retreat across an exposed *wadi* at Es Salt to administer first aid to Sergeant John Merson, who was shot through

HMAS *AE2*. The first submarine to breach the Dardanelles and enter the Sea of Marmara, it was scuttled on 30 April 1915 and the crew taken prisoner. (Sea Power Centre, Australia)

both legs. Merson explained in a post-war report that Brennan 'worked very hard to save me ... under very heavy fire', but the two men quickly found themselves 'completely surrounded by the enemy with fixed bayonets and their belts full of hand grenades'.[14] Flying Corps officers were also captured after attempting to assist their fellows. In May 1918, four Australians were taken prisoner after a dramatic rescue attempt failed. Lieutenants Joseph McElligott, Douglas Rutherford, Ronald Challinor and Frederick Haig were on a tandem reconnaissance flight over the Es Salt region when they engaged a German aircraft. McElligott and Rutherford's escort plane was hit in the petrol tank, and the two men were forced to land. Haig and Challinor witnessed their landing and after again engaging the German – causing him, in Challinor's words, to 'splitarse' away from them – landed to pick up the two men.[15] But the German airman returned, firing upon the rescue plane and disabling it. The four men saw enemy troops advancing on their position and, 'under no obligation to commit suicide', they surrendered.[16]

Sheer bad luck also extended to men across the different fronts. Although arguably every POW could attribute his capture to misfortune, several men were taken prisoner under particularly unfortunate circumstances. Sergeant Maurice Delpratt was captured on Gallipoli when he sought cover in an enemy trench after being mistaken for an enemy soldier by Australian machine-gunners on his way to convey a message to advanced troops, while Private John Clarke of the 11th Light Horse was picked up by Ottoman soldiers after his horse kicked him in the groin during his unit's retirement from an Ottoman counterattack near Romani in August 1916, rendering him 'helpless'. In one particularly disastrous incident in Palestine in January 1918, Flying Corps officer Lieutenant Vincent Parkinson was captured after a British aircraft, attempting to outmanoeuvre a German plane, collided with Parkinson's machine and brought it crashing down. The two British airmen and Parkinson's Australian pilot were killed, and Parkinson was left with a fractured skull.[17]

BEHIND ENEMY LINES

Although the circumstances of capture varied, the ultimate outcome for each man was the same: he had been taken prisoner and was now at the mercy of his enemy. The majority of the captured men initially exhibited shock at the events that had befallen them. Australians who enlisted for 'the war to end all wars' and became POWs had not expected their fate. They were prepared to fight, be wounded and even to die, yet few were prepared for the possibility of sitting out the war in the hands of the enemy. In his memoir *Turkish Days and Ways* (1940), Lieutenant James Brown, an Australian doctor taken prisoner in 1916 while serving in a British yeomanry unit, reflected that he had not expected his capture and subsequent imprisonment. 'We used to talk about the uncertainties of war,' he wrote. '[A]lthough imprisonment may have been mentioned, it was never really contemplated as a probable personal experience. Either we would remain unscathed or be wounded and killed.'[18] John Halpin echoed these sentiments in a post-war piece for *Reveille*, journal of the New South Wales branch of the Returned Sailors' and Soldiers' Imperial League of Australia (the precursor of today's RSL). 'Captivity did not enter my mind,' he explained. 'Strange that of all possible eventualities, capture was never discussed in Palestine. It was a thing that simply could not come to pass.'[19]

The men of the AIF received minimal training regarding capture and captivity, except how to take prisoners themselves. The accepted rules and regulations regarding the humane treatment of POWs established in the Hague Conventions and the Geneva Convention of 1906 were set out in the officers' manuals of military law and disseminated among the men. Pamphlets addressing and outlining guidelines concerning treatment of captured enemy soldiers – how to accept a surrender, how to transport prisoners away from the front line, and what could and could not be taken from prisoners – were circulated in early 1915.[20] Although, as Aaron Pegram writes, the Australians might not have received much training in how to act if captured, they were, according to historian Dale Blair, aware of and appreciated the rights of the POW.[21] The extent to which Australian soldiers followed these laws and guidelines has been the focus of recent scholarship; however, their awareness of international regulation meant that their expectations – or, at best, hopes – of treatment after surrender were based on these principles.[22]

Some men, particularly those taken early in the war, were surprised that they had survived the act of surrender. The Australians who served on Gallipoli, in particular, were wary of their Ottoman enemy. Upon the outbreak of war, Australian ideas about 'the Turks' were based on Orientalist ideas of them as an inferior, uneducated people who remained tied to the land rather than embracing industrialisation. The ease with which the Ottoman attempt to cross the Suez Canal in February 1915 was repulsed, and the poor condition of the troops taken prisoner by British forces during the attack, reinforced these ideas. But when it became clear the Australians would face the Ottomans in battle, this indifference was replaced by references to the warlike nature of the early Turkic tribes, the alleged atrocities committed by Ottoman Turkish troops against the Armenians and Bulgarians during the latter half of the nineteenth century, and the Balkan Wars. Official war correspondent (later official historian) Charles Bean reported rumours swirling around the troops – based on the stories of army officers who had experience with 'less disciplined Turkish troops' – about the treatment the Turks supposedly meted out to stranded soldiers.[23] These stories aroused in the Australians a sense of anger and distrust toward their enemy, which was compounded by reports of the alleged crucifixion of British marines who had landed on Gallipoli after the first naval bombardments of the peninsula, and other tales of the suspected hamstringing and mutilation of wounded soldiers.[24] Writing after the war, Leslie Luscombe summed up the Australian soldiers' early cynicism about the enemy's approach towards stranded men, stating that, in his view, it was 'not customary for the Turks to take any prisoners'. He believed his party of POWs were an 'exception to this general rule'.[25]

Other captives expressed a sense of relief. For the wounded, capture meant the prospect of medical attention and assistance while, for the able-bodied, it signified the end of battle and promised the possibility of food, drink and rest. Several prisoners reported the kindness and generosity of their captors during and immediately after their surrender. John Wheat claimed that the crew of the *Sultanhisar* treated the *AE2* submariners with great respect and, although they confined the prisoners to the hold of the ship – the POWs actually outnumbered the crew who, according to the captain of the *Sultanhisar*, were alive to the possibility of being overrun by their new captives – they went to great lengths to ensure that the submariners were provided with dry clothes and tobacco.[26] Similarly, many of the airmen taken in Palestine commented on the decent treatment they received after their respective captures. To an extent, the good treatment of the submariners and the airmen can be attributed to an unwritten code of gallantry and sportsmanship between the naval and air forces during the war. After *AE2* was scuttled, the crew of the *Sultanhisar* observed a long-standing naval tradition and saluted the sinking vessel while, according to Frederic Cutlack, historian of the Australian Flying Corps, the opposing airmen on all fronts 'regarded each other with a curious mix of personal esteem and deadly hostility' and would often drink toasts to enemy pilots in their messes.[27] However, many of the ground troops captured on Gallipoli and in Palestine also commented on the compassionate way in which they were treated during and after their capture. For Private Harry Brown, 'the treatment immediately after capture [on Gallipoli] was not too bad', while one light horseman claimed that his party was 'fairly well treated' and another reported that 'the Turks into whose hands I fell treated me very kindly'.[28]

Captured Australians also felt relief because, for some, being taken prisoner meant protection. Several of the Australians captured in Palestine and Mesopotamia were first confronted by Arab and Bedouin people and, while some proved friendly, others were not. In some areas Arab tribesmen were promised rewards for capturing allied servicemen and, as a result, they were keen to detain any marooned men, even violently. Pilot Thomas White was one of several Australians effectively rescued by the enemy. White and his observer experienced a decidedly unhospitable welcome after they were stranded near Baghdad. Local Arab men attacked the two airmen with clubs and rifles – just as White was sure they were to be killed, a party of Turks arrived and escorted the two officers to their headquarters. For stranded POWs, then, the arrival of Ottoman troops could be seen as a blessing.

But not all those taken prisoner reported initial good treatment and feelings of relief after capture. The testimony of many Australians indicates that they experienced or witnessed abuses of POWs immediately after capture, and their overwhelming response was anger. Some were subjected to physical violence – Frederick Ashton, for example, was hit on the head with the butts of rifles and Private Robert Griffiths was allegedly 'punched and kicked and butted with a rifle several times'.[29] This kind of behaviour was mainly perpetrated by the lower ranks, and could be attributed to the heat of battle and as a way of restraining the new captives. Several prisoners were robbed. It was inevitable that weapons would be confiscated, but personal possessions were also taken. The plundering of prisoners was common among servicemen from all armies on the various fronts, including the Australians, who became notorious among the allies for 'souveniring' items from POWs.[30] This did not diminish the outrage of those, like Private Patrick O'Connor, who lost personal items during the process of surrender:

> The Turk touched me with his foot. Then he unbuttoned my tunic and saw a money belt I was wearing. Apparently he was unable to see how it unbuckled, for he seized hold of it and bumped me up and down by it until it snapped ... Another marauding Turk came along shortly and went through my pockets. He got a few cards and a letter, but missed my watch ... A third Turk came along. He was luckier than his predecessors for he found my watch and also robbed me of a ring I was wearing.[31]

Personal papers and photographs were often returned, presumably because they held little monetary value, but in many cases prisoners were relieved of everything, including their rations and, in one instance, a set of false teeth.[32] Lance Corporal Timothy Cahill was left with only his hat after his capture, while Matthew Sloan of the 4th Light Horse Field Ambulance was stripped of his entire uniform 'barring a steel helmet and a pair of sox [sic]'.[33] In return, as John Merson explained, the men were given their captors' garments:

> As soon as I was surrounded despite the fact my boots were full of blood, and my riding breeches saturated also, they roughly pulled my boots off and leggings which they put on straight away and seeing that my legs had swelled considerably, they ripped up the outside seam of my breeches with knives and then pulled them off, after which a Turk took off his ragged trousers, threw them at me, and put on mine.[34]

Good-quality uniforms and boots were scarce commodities for Ottoman troops, and prisoners' clothes and footwear were therefore a significant prize. The Australians recognised the poor state of their captors' uniforms and footwear, and correctly surmised that this was what drove them to take the prisoners' clothes. But acknowledging the condition of their captors did not lessen the prisoners' anger at being relieved of their uniforms and forced to wear threadbare cast-offs that left them with little protection against the terrain or the weather. Complaints, however, were ignored. John Halpin voiced his anger to the German commander of the Ottoman troops who took him prisoner, to no avail: '[H]e wagged his head in survey of our multi-coloured Turkish garb and moved off, doubtless too well versed on the "taking" ways of his Turkish allies.'[35]

The Australians' treatment continued to range between extremes as they moved further behind enemy lines. Privates John Beattie and Charles McLean had a fairly relaxed time on Gallipoli. Escorted by 'an easy going middle aged man', Beattie was taken to a dressing station where his wounded foot was bandaged and he met McLean.[36] The two men were marched in front of an English-speaking officer, who permitted them to rest while he searched their belongings. All their possessions were returned and, before the two men continued on their journey, a group of Ottoman soldiers approached offering cigarettes and food. Other wounded prisoners also commented positively about their treatment while being moved off the battlefield. Many were provided with makeshift crutches or were stretchered to aid posts and dressing stations – one light horseman was carried by an Ottoman soldier for half a mile before he was placed on a stretcher. The medical arm of the Ottoman Army consisted of Turkish medical officers, as well as Arab, Greek and Armenian doctors and orderlies conscripted into the military to serve the sick and wounded. German medical officers, sanitation inspectors and nurses also assisted the Ottoman Army as part of the German Military Mission and under the auspices of the German Red Cross. Several captives reported they were well looked after by enemy medical personnel. Cameleer Patrick Duffy stated that the wounded in his party received good treatment after their capture at Gaza in April 1917, with 'the bad cases' being sent immediately to field hospitals while the less seriously wounded were treated at aid posts.[37]

Not all prisoners were as fortunate, however. Many of the wounded and the able-bodied confronted different hazards as they moved off the battlefield. Escorts continued to rob and harass, they had to dodge the bombs and bullets of their own comrades who continued their attacks on the enemy, and they remained the targets of Ottoman troops unaware of their capture – Australians taken on Gallipoli, for example, were told to remove their distinctive hats as snipers would otherwise shoot at them. The prisoners were also, as was the case with POWs on both sides of the enemy divide and on all fronts, the victims of their captors' anger and frustration. Several Australians said they had been assaulted, spat at and verbally abused once behind Ottoman lines, and some wounded POWs were scathing of what they saw as the rudimentary and unhygienic medical treatment they received. Lance Corporal Francis Easton, captured severely wounded at Romani, reported that he was left unattended at a casualty clearing station and that fellow prisoners bound his wounds, while, after a bumpy journey to an aid post on a stretcher that was dropped every time his escorts heard a shell approaching, Private John Davern's gunshot wound was neither assessed nor cleaned before being bandaged, which eventually led to a serious infection. However, the prisoners generally accepted that their treatment was on par with that meted out to wounded Ottoman troops. That their own army's battlefield medical facilities were often equally basic, and that maintaining standards of hygiene was a difficult task for the medical officers and nurses of all belligerents, was seemingly forgotten by most.

Once behind enemy lines the POWs also had to contend with interrogations by Ottoman and German officers. Most were asked to provide only their personal details, although several were questioned on other matters, such as troop numbers and dispositions, weaponry, or the morale of those at home. Those who declined to answer met with a range of responses from their captors. Some earned their admiration for refusing to talk, but, in a reflection of the value of POWs as a source of intelligence, others were encouraged to provide information through a variety of coercive means.[38] Airmen captured in Palestine reported that they were treated to lavish meals and alcohol in an effort to persuade them to open up. Other prisoners claimed that they were detained in tents or huts with 'plants' – enemy soldiers masquerading as either fellow POWs or as locals who could not understand English. Commander Stoker of the AE2 was placed in a room with several others he believed were military prisoners who had been offered rewards for getting information out of him. More forceful means were also attempted. Trooper Duncan Richardson claimed he was 'thrashed' for refusing to answer questions while several men reported they were threatened with the denial of food and water.[39] One group of POWs, captured at Romani, were lined up as if to face a firing squad for their perceived lack of cooperation.

The first distinctions in treatment between officers and men become evident in the immediate post-capture period. Although not always a definite, clear-cut division, POW officers were, as historian Joan Beaumont notes, usually treated better and commanded more respect from their captors than the other ranks.[40] Charles Carr reported that he had been treated in exemplary fashion after his capture, but he soon realised this was because he had been mistaken for an officer. When Carr's real rank was discovered, his preferential treatment ended. This distinction became even more apparent to the prisoners as they travelled further into captivity.

TRAVELLING TO IMPRISONMENT

Once the process of capture was completed and new prisoners were organised behind Ottoman lines, their journeys into imprisonment began. Military historian Arthur Barker argues that, for the new captive, the experience of travel and temporary confinement while en route to a prison camp is 'an ordeal which may well be the worst he has to suffer during the whole course of his captivity'.[41] The main Ottoman prison camps were situated in Anatolia, meaning that these journeys could last months, depending on the prisoner's point of capture and condition. They were something of an initiation period in which the POWs were brought into extended close contact with their captors and gained an appreciation of what would await them in the camps. Such journeys marked significant moments in the transition from combatant to captive; they were, as John Halpin later wrote, 'the kindergarten of our captivity'.[42]

Prisoners captured in the Dardanelles were transported to the Ottoman capital of Constantinople, a journey undertaken either by boat across the Sea of Marmara or on a longer overland route through several small villages and towns. On the overland route, prisoners from the ranks were conveyed to a Constantinople-bound train in stages by bullock wagons, and were held in barracks and abandoned buildings along the way.[43] In an extension of their superior treatment, however, captive officers experienced a much more relaxed journey. Together with Stewart Stormonth, Leslie Luscombe travelled across the peninsula in a horse-drawn *araba* (carriage) assisted by an Ottoman officer who was 'wonderfully considerate and likeable in every way'.[44] Before they boarded the train bound for Constantinople, Luscombe and his fellow captive officers were accommodated in a luxurious hotel and given a three-course meal and beer, haircuts and shaves, and the opportunity to partake in a traditional Turkish bath.

Officers and other ranks captured in Palestine and Mesopotamia endured much longer journeys into captivity. Lack of transport infrastructure meant that those captured in these more isolated areas of the Ottoman Empire travelled in stages into Anatolia through such cities as Jerusalem, Nazareth, Damascus, Aleppo and Baghdad. Like their counterparts captured on Gallipoli, Australian officers captured in Palestine journeyed fairly comfortably. AFC officers Challinor, Haig, Rutherford and McElligott were transported from Amman to Nazareth, where they were entertained for a week at a German mess, then travelled to Damascus, where they lived with Ottoman officers, before continuing their journey to a prison camp. The other ranks, however, were transported via a combination of train trips and foot marches, often in trying conditions. Corporal Clyde Currie, captured at Gaza in 1917, travelled to Jerusalem in 'railway trucks that were closed in, 60 men to a truck, the one small window the guard kept closed'.[45] D'Arcy Armstrong and the other members of the 4th Light Horse Field Ambulance captured at Es Salt were marched for miles on what he called 'a goat track through the hills' to the city of Nablus. The majority of their party had been stripped of their boots and uniforms and undertook the march barefoot. The prisoners arrived 'all in a bad state', Armstrong explained in a post-war report, 'our feet were all torn and blistered'.[46] Other Australians told of similar experiences. After marching from Ottoman headquarters at Katia, roped together in groups of four, Trooper George Handsley and other POWs captured at Romani were put on a train bound for Jerusalem. 'The filth was indescribable', Handsley explained:

> We were packed so close together that it was impossible to sit down for rest. We just managed to crouch with our heads between our knees. We were given a bag of hard biscuits for the journey, and a few dates, which were promptly confiscated by our escort ... Most of us were suffering from dysentery, and as there was no sanitary arrangements in the cattle truck, we were soon in a filthy condition.[47]

Handsley and the other prisoners travelled under these conditions for two days before reaching their destination.

Perhaps the most distressing journey into captivity was endured by those taken prisoner after the fall of the Kut-el-Amara garrison in Mesopotamia in April 1916. Following an aborted attempt to take the city of Ctesiphon in late 1915, British Major-General Charles Townshend's 6th Indian Division was forced to retreat to Kut, approximately 160 kilometres south of Baghdad, where thousands of Ottoman troops laid siege to the British–Indian forces. After several failed attempts to reinforce the garrison and the rejection of a secret offer to pay the Ottomans for the release of the troops (Enver Pasha turned down the British deal), Townshend surrendered. On 29 April 1916, thousands of sick and starving troops, including several Australians, were taken prisoner.

The Australian contingent at Kut comprised seven air mechanics and two NCOs of the Australian Flying Corps: Francis Adams, David Curran, Keith Hudson, William Lord, James Munro, William Rayment, Leo Thomas, James Sloss and Thomas Soley. Soldiers from the garrison, already weak from the siege, were separated from the officers, formed into columns and force-marched more than a thousand kilometres north into Anatolia. Tied together and harassed by hostile Bedouin tribes along the way, the prisoners were robbed of their clothing, boots and personal possessions, or were forced to exchange them for food. With only limited rations, water, shelter or medical assistance, in their feeble state many suffered from dysentery, malaria, ulcerated feet and exposure.[48] Those who dropped from exhaustion or illness were left along the roadside; one Australian reported that he tied his wrists to the back of a supply cart so that he could not fall out and be left behind.[49] Major-General Charles Melliss, Townshend's second-in-command, followed the same route as the first column of other ranks three weeks later. 'I came across some heartrending scenes,' he wrote in a letter to British Prime Minister David Lloyd George in 1917. 'I found numbers of our men ... lying exhausted and nearly all desperately ill, and many in the extreme stages of dysenteric enteritis, mere living skeletons – uncared for – unassisted – without medicines ... selling their clothing and boots to the Arab villagers to purchase milk to keep life within them.'[50] Only two of the original group of nine Australians, Acting Flight Sergeant James Sloss and Air Mechanic Keith Hudson, survived to reach a main prison camp. Sloss later reflected that, in doing so, he 'suffered almost beyond human endurance'.[51]

Once the prisoners arrived in a staging city, they were confined according to their rank and their condition while awaiting transportation to a prison camp or the continuation of their journey. To reach sites of temporary confinement, they often marched through the streets in parades designed to boost the morale of local forces and civilians. Upon their arrival in Constantinople, the submariners of the *AE2* were given Ottoman military uniforms and were marched off the boat and through the city, as were those soldiers captured on Gallipoli during the August offensive.[52] Similar public parades occurred in the Middle East. Some prisoners reported that they were spat at, and claimed that local people in the crowds made threatening throat-cutting gestures. But others stated that the civilians they encountered appeared war-weary and disillusioned. John Wheat claimed 'very little notice was taken of us' as his group of POWs marched through Constantinople, while one light horseman reported that civilians in Jerusalem had repeatedly asked the prisoners when the British would be coming to relieve the city.[53] Historian Heather Jones attributes physical and verbal abuse of prisoners of war en route to imprisonment to the strength of war culture within the captor nation.[54] Such testimony from the Australian prisoners suggests that an aggressive war culture had not permeated all areas of the Ottoman Empire.

Fit POWs were usually detained in military barracks and civilian gaols in these cities while further transportation to a prison camp was arranged. For most of the Australian prisoners, their memories of temporary confinement were of squalid, vermin-ridden cells and rooms and meagre rations. Reginald Lushington was imprisoned in the basement cells of a military barracks in Constantinople before being transferred to a prison camp deeper in the countryside, and described his time in the barracks as 'hell – and a hell which got worse each day we stayed there'.[55] The cells were dirty and overrun with bugs, the prisoners received no food, and there was no opportunity for exercise. Similar stories were common among the Australians captured in Palestine. Upon their arrival in Damascus in 1916, one group of prisoners were confined to a 'verminous and filthy' barracks and locked into a small room rife with lice and which had only one barred window, used in place of a latrine.[56]

While, as we have seen, POW officers were typically accommodated in relatively comfortable conditions and permitted certain freedoms, rank did not always confer such privileges. In Mesopotamia, Thomas White spent nearly two months at a military barracks in Mosul in conditions he likened to those provided to prisoners during the Spanish Inquisition. Locked up with four other officers in a one-windowed cell and under constant armed guard, White and his fellow POWs slept on bug-infested grass mats and were allowed to bathe only sporadically. Sanitation at the barracks was far below the standard to which the officers were accustomed, and many contracted debilitating diseases. Upon his arrival White was surprised to find fellow AFC pilot William Treloar, but did not recognise him at first owing to the emaciating effects of malaria and dysentery Treloar had suffered since his capture some three months earlier.

Wounded prisoners journeying into captivity were admitted to hospitals in these staging cities, where they experienced a range of conditions and treatment. Many of the Australians captured wounded on Gallipoli were first hospitalised in the Harbie military hospital in

Constantinople, which one POW rather condescendingly wrote was 'quite as good as some English hospitals I have seen'.[57] However, as an act of reprisal against alleged mistreatment of Ottoman POWs in British hands, they were later transferred to Tashkishla Barracks Hospital, the site made famous during the Crimean War as the workplace of Florence Nightingale. The POWs were appalled by the primitive conditions at Tashkishla – upon arriving there Patrick O'Connor thought their escorts had 'pulled up at a livery stable'.[58] The wounded prisoners were herded into rooms with boarded-up windows and no lights, and slept on straw mattresses on the floor. Nurses were not permitted to visit, wounds were neglected, no clothes or bedding were supplied, and the prisoners received little in the way of food.[59] Twenty-five-year-old Private John Hennessy, hit by shrapnel in the groin and leg, was left untended for a full fortnight and, as the young prisoner was also suffering from a severe case of dysentery, he developed a fatal infection.[60] O'Connor had, in a significant understatement, a 'very rough time of it' at Tashkishla; his wounded leg was amputated and he was left with an infected stump that never fully healed during his time as a POW.[61]

Other prisoners suffered far less traumatic experiences of medical care and hospitalisation. Wounded Australians who passed through Damascus hospital were, in stark contrast to their 'fit' comrades detained in the city's barracks, full of praise for the medical staff at the 'well appointed' hospital where 'treatment was good all round' and the prisoners 'seemed to fare better than the Turks themselves'.[62] Both Private Ellis Gilman and Trooper Edgar Hobson reported expert treatment and good conditions in hospital at Jerusalem, while Vincent Parkinson was treated 'with nothing but kindness' at a hospital in Nazareth while receiving treatment for his broken skull.[63]

REFLECTION

Once the new prisoners stopped at their sites of temporary confinement, their initial reactions to capture settled as they processed what had happened. Many prisoners experienced a sense of melancholy torpor as they reached this final stage in the transition from combatant to captive. Doctors and psychologists who conducted studies of prisoners captured during the Second World War coined an evocative term for the sense of inertia that overcame men once they reached their first point of confinement: 'collection centre stupor', claiming that it is typically brought on by a combination of exhaustion, disappointment and fear.[64] Ex-army prison officer and sociologist Walter Lunden argued that this sense of stupor had several consequences, including the quashing of any thoughts of escape. Very few Australians taken prisoner by the Ottomans appear to have considered escape immediately after capture or during their journeys away from the battlefields. Wounded men were in no position to attempt escape, nor were those fit captured in the Dardanelles, where they were outnumbered by the enemy. It was equally impracticable for the men taken prisoner in Mesopotamia and Palestine, where the battlegrounds were usually surrounded by barren and inhospitable terrain. These physical constraints were compounded by the docility engendered by 'collection centre stupor'; Lunden wrote that prisoners tend to lie down alone or in small groups, and 'remain silent with no apparent interest in anything'.[65] This was certainly the case for John Halpin. 'Despondency … gripped many', he explained of his party of POWs at their first staging camp, adding that 'lassitude almost completely benumbed our faculties'.[66]

Time in temporary confinement also provided the men with the opportunity to reflect on their situation. Some prisoners were philosophical about their POW status. John Merson wrote that he spent much of his time recovering from his wounds in Nablus hospital reflecting on the 'strange whims of fate' that had delivered him into captivity.[67] Merson was instrumental in the capture of the first Ottoman prisoners taken by the 11th Light Horse Regiment in 1916, and felt it was 'poetic justice' that he was subsequently taken prisoner.[68] Lieutenant Stanley Jordan was frustrated but resigned. 'It was darned hard luck being captured within seven weeks of getting a commission as it did not give me a chance,' he wrote in a letter to a friend not long after his capture on Gallipoli, 'but I did my bit and now I am tied up till the end of the war.'[69] For Private Daniel Jones, captured at Gaza in 1917, 'things could have been worse'.[70]

For most new captives, however, this reflection brought with it uncomfortable feelings and emotions, including a strong sense of failure. Thomas White's realisation that he 'would be of no more use to our army for perhaps the duration of the war' plunged him into a deep despair that initially left him too miserable to eat.[71] Maurice Delpratt expressed similar feelings in a letter to his family in Queensland. Writing from a military barracks in Constantinople, Delpratt explained his position as 'having failed in my mission and [now] no longer able to serve my country'.[72] Some prisoners apportioned their sense of failure to others, such as members of other allied forces. Gallipoli POW Harry Brown considered his capture and subsequent imprisonment to be the fault of the British troops at Suvla Bay who failed to reach their objective during the August offensive, leaving the Australians stranded, while several of the cameleers taken at Gaza blamed their capture on the British officer who had surrendered without first asking their permission.[73] As historian Brian Feltman writes, moving from 'warriors to spectators with an obstructed view' was an extremely bitter pill for ex-combatants to swallow.[74]

Feelings of failure were often compounded by a sense of shame. Allowing oneself to fall into enemy hands was considered a far from honourable fate within the AIF, whose 'never give up' attitude was deeply entrenched from the beginning of the war. Historian Henry Gullett wrote of the expectations of the Australian Light Horse regarding their conduct on the battlefield: 'From the opening of the fight at Romani to the end of the campaign in 1918, the light horsemen observed a voluntary and unwritten law that no sound man should allow himself to be taken prisoner.'[75] Maurice Delpratt knew that 'with the Australians it is considered a disgrace to be captured'.[76] Reginald Lushington also felt the shame of his capture keenly. 'Our hearts were heavy as lead,' he wrote in his memoir of captivity, 'and we just stared at each other, feeling sure the one thought was shared by us all – what an ignoble ending to all our brilliant aspirations, death seemed almost preferable.'[77]

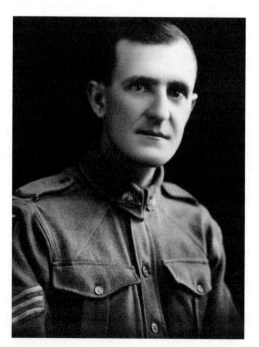

Maurice George Delpratt, c. 1919 (Courtesy Jan Delpratt)

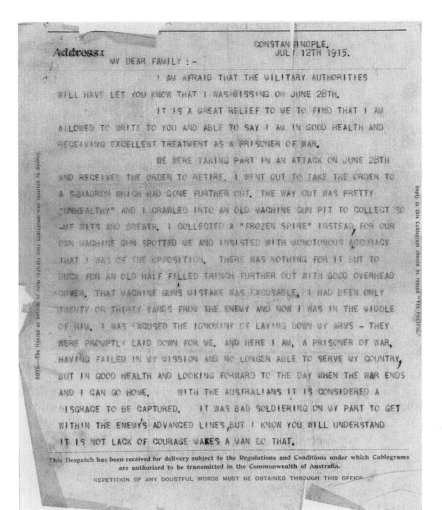

Address: CONSTANTINOPLE,
                                             JULY 12TH 1915.
           MY DEAR FAMILY : -

                    I AM AFRAID THAT THE MILITARY AUTHORITIES
    WILL HAVE LET YOU KNOW THAT I WAS MISSING ON JUNE 28TH.

                    IT IS A GREAT RELIEF TO ME TO FIND THAT I AM
    ALLOWED TO WRITE TO YOU AND ABLE TO SAY I AM IN GOOD HEALTH AND
    RECEIVING EXCELLENT TREATMENT AS A PRISONER OF WAR.

                    WE WERE TAKING PART IN AN ATTACK ON JUNE 28TH
    AND RECEIVED THE ORDER TO RETIRE. I WENT OUT TO TAKE THE ORDER TO
    A SQUADRON WHICH HAD GONE FURTHER OUT. THE WAY OUT WAS PRETTY
    "UNHEALTHY" AND I CRAWLED INTO AN OLD MACHINE GUN PIT TO COLLECT SO
    -ME WITS AND BREATH. I COLLECTED A "FROZEN SPINE" INSTEAD, FOR OUR
    OWN MACHINE GUN SPOTTED ME AND INSISTED WITH MONOTONOUS ACCURACY
    THAT I WAS OF THE OPPOSITION. THERE WAS NOTHING FOR IT BUT TO
    DUCK FOR AN OLD HALF FILLED TRENCH FURTHER OUT WITH GOOD OVERHEAD
    COVER. THAT MACHINE GUNS MISTAKE WAS EXCUSABLE, I HAD BEEN ONLY
    TWENTY OR THIRTY YARDS FROM THE ENEMY AND NOW I WAS IN THE MIDDLE
    OF HIM. I WAS EXCUSED THE IGNOMINY OF LAYING DOWN MY ARMS - THEY
    WERE PROMPTLY LAID DOWN FOR ME. AND HERE I AM, A PRISONER OF WAR,
    HAVING FAILED IN MY MISSION AND NO LONGER ABLE TO SERVE MY COUNTRY,
    BUT IN GOOD HEALTH AND LOOKING FORWARD TO THE DAY WHEN THE WAR ENDS
    AND I CAN GO HOME.   WITH THE AUSTRALIANS IT IS CONSIDERED A
    DISGRACE TO BE CAPTURED.   IT WAS BAD SOLDIERING ON MY PART TO GET
    WITHIN THE ENEMY'S ADVANCED LINES, BUT I KNOW YOU WILL UNDERSTAND
    IT IS NOT LACK OF COURAGE MAKES A MAN DO THAT.

This Despatch has been received for delivery subject to the Regulations and Conditions under which Cablegrams
          are authorised to be transmitted in the Commonwealth of Australia.
      REPETITION OF ANY DOUBTFUL WORDS MUST BE OBTAINED THROUGH THIS OFFICE

'And here I am, a Prisoner of War.' Typewritten copy of message sent by
Maurice Delpratt from Constantinople informing his family of his capture,
July 1915 (Maurice George Delpratt Correspondence, 1915–20, John Oxley
Library, State Library of Queensland ACC. 28115)

Those who responded to capture with feelings and expressions of
disappointment, failure, shame, anger and depression did so largely
because of the perception of passivity inherent in their new status as
prisoners of war. As captives, they moved from the hypermasculine
battlefront to occupy what historian Christina Twomey calls 'the more

culturally feminine site of containment'.[78] Capture threatened to tarnish a man's reputation as a brave soldier and a noble citizen – surrender carried with it the stigma of cowardice, treason or even desertion – and place him at the whim of an enemy he did not understand. With this in mind, it is understandable that so many Australians taken POW initially responded negatively to their altered position.

Becoming a prisoner of war, then, was a complicated, gradual and subjective process. The Australians taken captive by the Ottoman forces were subject to a range of conditions and treatment as they moved behind enemy lines and journeyed into imprisonment, before forced inactivity in temporary confinement allowed them time to realise the implications of their position and adjust to their new status as POWs. As they moved deeper into captivity, the circumstances of their confinement presented further tests of the prisoners' physical, emotional and psychological strength.

CHAPTER 2

THE CIRCUMSTANCES OF CONFINEMENT

At the outbreak of war the Hague Convention governed the conduct of belligerents. Chapter 2 of the 'Regulations Respecting the Laws and Customs of War on Land' in the Annex to the Convention focused on prisoners of war. The seventeen articles in chapter 2 explained (among other things) how prisoners were to be managed after capture, what they were eligible to receive, and how information about a prisoner's health and location was to be shared between the warring nations. Article 7 outlined the key principle directing the treatment of prisoners in captivity: 'Failing a special agreement between the belligerents, prisoners of war shall be treated as regards food, quarters, and clothing, on the same footing as the troops of the Government which has captured them.'[1] No prior arrangement between the British and Ottoman governments existed regarding POWs, so article 7 provided the basis on which Ottoman POWs would be treated in British captivity, and vice versa. But life in the wartime Ottoman Empire was markedly different from what Western prisoners, particularly those like the British and French who had benefited from the spoils of nineteenth-century imperialism, were used to. Pushed to the brink of bankruptcy, shrunk in territory after years of war in the Balkans, and divided politically and culturally, by the start of the First World War the once-mighty Ottoman Empire had been reduced to the 'Sick Man of Europe'. The exigencies of war exacted a severe toll on the Ottoman army and people which, combined with an intense sense of culture clash and the general restrictions of enforced extended imprisonment, would make the circumstances of their confinement particularly challenging for the Australian POWs.

IDEAS OF RACIAL AND CULTURAL SUPERIORITY

The men of the AIF came from a nation that placed much store on ideas of race. The relative ease with which the British colonised the country during the late eighteenth and nineteenth centuries had cemented social Darwinist notions of racial hierarchies or ladders, in which white people, or more precisely white men, occupied the top rung. Ensuring the purity of the white race in such an isolated outpost of the British Empire was a key priority for the colonists. Anxiety about the 'other', particularly the Asian other who, it was believed, could potentially invade the sparsely populated colonies, was one of the main driving forces behind Federation in 1901. One of the first acts undertaken by the newly formed government of Australia was the passing of the Immigration Restriction Act (1901) to control immigration on racial grounds. The pursuit of the white Australia ideal was not limited to restricting immigrants – the Indigenous inhabitants of the country were also affected. At the outbreak of war in 1914, Aboriginal Australians were denied basic citizenship rights. They were not permitted to vote and, for many, 'protection boards' controlled their ability to work, marry and even move. Such restrictive policies towards immigrants and the Indigenous population demonstrate, as Peter Stanley writes, that 'the Australia that raised and constituted the first Australian Imperial Force was a deeply racist society'.[2]

This sense of racial and cultural superiority was reinforced for the Australian troops through experiences in their different training camps. The majority of Australian servicemen spent some time in Egypt where, as historians Suzanne Brugger and Richard White explain, they were shocked and appalled by the 'native' way of life – particularly the poverty, squalor and inequality they witnessed in the cities.[3] In a letter to his father from a camp in Egypt, future POW Fred Hancock expressed his surprise at what he had seen in Cairo. '[S]ome of the Eastern customs are decidedly off,' he wrote. '[Y]ou have no idea of the way they live, to a person coming from Australia it is absolutely astounding.'[4] With their higher rates of pay, many Australians were able to hire Egyptian locals to perform cooking and cleaning work around the camps. They also regularly partook of the local goods and services on offer, going to Egyptian hairdressers and tailors, visiting local restaurants and, perhaps most infamously, frequenting bars and brothels. Such 'informal assertions of imperial authority' – to quote White – reinforced the Australians' place in what Brugger calls 'the top caste of the colonial hierarchy' and validated their belief that, as white men, they were true 'lords of the desert'.[5]

Such reactions to their exposure to Egypt and Egyptian people did not bode particularly well for the Australians held captive in the Ottoman Empire. Australians had little direct experience with ethnic Turkish people before the First World War. In the 1911 census, the last taken before the declaration of war in 1914, only 300 people identified as Turkish out of a population of nearly 4.5 million.[6] As such, Australian perceptions of their captors were based on contemporary British ideas – which had undergone several transformations during the nineteenth century. Historian Jeremy Salt argues that Western (particularly British) impressions of the ruling Turks in the 1800s varied depending on circumstances. During the first half of the nineteenth century, using them as a bulwark against Russian expansionism led to an alliance during the Crimean War. But in what Salt calls 'an age self-consciously and often aggressively Christian', the position of Christian minorities in the Ottoman Empire became a key British concern.[7] Drawing on Christian prejudices against Islam dating back to the time of the Crusades, perceptions of the Turks shifted to highlight their supposed innate brutality. According to Salt, their Islamic religion was 'held up as a sensual and depraved religion, a religion which destroyed all progress and happiness, a religion which ruled by the sword and which regarded the killing and plunder of infidels as being as much an act of worship as prayer'.[8]

Reports of the massacre of Bulgarians in the empire in the 1870s cemented these ideas and generated a wave of anti-Turkish sentiment throughout Britain. Perhaps the most strident proponent of such sentiment was former Prime Minister William Gladstone. In his 1876 treatise on the massacre, titled *Bulgarian Horrors and the Question of the East*, Gladstone denounced the Turks as 'the one great anti-human specimen of humanity'.[9] Lamenting 'the black day when they first entered Europe', Gladstone argued that the ruling Turks' supposed propensity for depravity and barbarism meant that 'wherever they went, a broad line of blood marked the track behind them and, as far as their dominion reached, civilisation disappeared from view'.[10] In the wake of Gladstone's publication, public enmity towards the Turks was so great that British politicians and diplomats initially refused to provide support or relief for their second war against Russia in 1877. Reports of attacks directed against another Christian group in the empire in the 1890s – the Armenians – further emphasised images of the Turks as barbarous and cruel, despite Turkish protests that they had also been victims of attacks from the Armenians.

Ideas of the ruling Turks' violent and warlike nature were used to partly explain the political, economic and social decline of the Ottoman

Empire. But the British – and others – also blamed the deterioration of the empire on other qualities perceived as innate to their religion and culture, including greed, corruption and 'intrigue'. Indeed, in his article 'Johnny Turk before Gallipoli', Salt quotes a British MP who stated that when the Turks were not fighting they reverted to a state of 'sloth, sensuality, and decay'.[11] As Edward Said, the first scholar to comprehensively analyse European discourses regarding 'the Orient', argues, such romanticised misrepresentations of places like the Ottoman Empire as sites of mystery and despotism bolstered ideas of the backwardness of their societies and, in contrast, the superiority of the Western European world.[12]

In Australia, such ideas were used to explain the Ottoman Empire's entrance into the war. Their alliance with the Central Powers was reported as having been brought about by German trickery, exploitation and manipulation of Ottoman naivety. This was evident in November 1914, when a Queensland newspaper labelled the Ottoman Empire 'Germany's catspaw' and a regional West Australian paper explained to its readers that it was 'Germany's evil influence' that had driven the Ottomans to war.[13] Australians were assured that the Ottomans did not pose a serious threat. The parlous state of the Ottoman forces was well known; nearly six years on a constant war footing and devastating casualties in the Balkans meant they were easily written off – indeed, the *Sydney Morning Herald* stated that their declaration of war would 'hardly affect the general situation ... [T]he creation of a new sphere of hostilities will not involve the detaching of a single army corps from either of the old fronts.'[14]

At the time of the outbreak of war in August 1914, then, Australian impressions of their Ottoman enemy were based on Orientalist ideas of savagery and backwardness and were far from favourable. Such impressions, as we have seen, shaped some of the Australians' reactions to being taken prisoner: a sense of surprise that they had survived the act of surrender at the hands of a supposedly brutal and uncivilised enemy. These ideas also affected the Australians' time in captivity. Indeed, one of the most significant implications of the 'same footing' principle embedded in article 7 was the sense of profound culture clash and inversion of the racial hierarchy that it engendered. For many of the men, the very fact that they had been taken prisoner was cause for resentment, but being held under the same conditions and receiving the same treatment as those they perceived to be inferior generated even greater anger and upset. This, together with their ignorance of their captors – William Carr, who studied American POWs in Vietnam, claims that such ignorance can be as confining for the prisoner as more tangible barriers like barbed wire and armed guards – coloured the Australians' attitudes towards the physical circumstances of their imprisonment.[15]

CONCERNS ABOUT CONDITIONS AND TREATMENT

Standards of accommodation, which varied according to a prisoner's rank, were of chief concern for the POWs. Prison camps in the Ottoman Empire were not the small collection of huts enclosed by metres of barbed wire and patrolled by sentries in watchtowers as presented in POW memoirs and popular culture after the Second World War. The Ottoman War Ministry's policy regarding prisoners of war stated that, in keeping with the Hague Convention, officer POWs were to be placed in hotels or private houses, while prisoners from the ranks were to be housed in garrison barracks or other 'available institutions', which ranged from school buildings and churches to wooden huts and tents.[16] Bigger camps, such as Afyonkarahissar, a town approximately 450 kilometres southeast of Constantinople, were not actually 'camps' at all, but rather sections of the town cordoned off for the prisoners. Similar situations prevailed across Anatolia; a POW camp was established when prisoners were housed in an existing building or in a collection of huts or tents raised on the outskirts of a town or village.

The majority of Australians spent some time at Afyonkarahissar (Afyon). The first arrived in early 1915, and it remained a site of confinement until the end of the war. Other rank POWs were accommodated in an old school building and in a church. Officers were quartered in two sections of the town in mud and timber houses that had previously belonged to local Armenians – victims of the mass deportations that occurred in the empire during the war.[17] The houses offered a place to sleep and eat and provided protection from the weather, and the officers' concerns related mainly to cramped conditions, spartan furnishings and lack of space to exercise. In keeping with article 17 of the Annex to the Hague Convention, POW officers received payments from their captors at the same rate as Ottoman officers (to be repaid by their own government), out of which their rent was deducted. The divide between officers and men first observed after capture continued in imprisonment, and Lieutenant William Elston grudgingly conceded in his report on his time in captivity that officer prisoners at Afyon had been 'fairly well treated according to Turkish ideas'.[18]

It was the prisoners from the ranks who really bore the brunt of the physical conditions of imprisonment, particularly with respect to accommodation, work, transportation and punishment. The majority of other rank POWs were accommodated in camps located in areas where building infrastructure, farming or other work was required. Some of these camps had favourable reputations. Belemedik, the base camp for those working on the Berlin–Baghdad Railway in the Taurus Mountains, was renowned as a model camp and, in one Ottoman Red Crescent report, was even likened to a Swiss village.[19] Prisoners at Belemedik lived in wooden huts, were provided with areas for exercise and entertainment, and were given relative freedom around the town. Keith Hudson believed that 'a man was lucky who went to Bilemedik [sic] and who could stay there'.[20] Yarbaschi in the Amanus Mountains, where prisoners lived in tents, was similarly remembered as quite comfortable. Later in the war, smaller camps were established closer to Constantinople. Their proximity to the capital meant that conditions were relatively favourable, and food, medical supplies and other assistance were more readily accessible.

Other camps, however, were notorious for being dirty, overcrowded, infested with lice and bugs, and poorly managed. At Gelebek, in the south Taurus region, POWs either slept in the open or lived in crowded, draughty barracks that offered little protection from the elements. 'Camp conditions very bad,' D'Arcy Armstrong wrote of Gelebek, 'a total lack of accommodation for the working parties, sanitation nil, fleas and lice abounded.'[21] In April 1918, Ottoman Red Crescent delegate Rifki Bey admitted that Gelebek was the worst of the railway camps.[22] Tasch Durmas, near Belemedik, was another camp known for its poor conditions. Prisoners at Tasch Durmas were accommodated in a windowless 'rotten room' that was perched on the edge of a large drop into a canyon. Australian, British, Russian and French POWs lived alongside local Turkish, Greek, Armenian and Arab workers, which caused conflict. The prisoners did not want to mix with the 'other' labourers, and fought to maintain a division between the groups. Solidarity in discomfort clearly did not extend to everyone. One POW recalled an occasion when a Turkish labourer attempted to eat with the prisoners – he was punched and his bread was thrown over the cliff.[23] The conditions in which the Australians at Gelebek and Tasch Durmas found themselves living reinforced their perceptions of the uncivilised nature of their captors.

Work itself was another significant issue for prisoners from the ranks as, in keeping with the Hague Convention, officers could not be made

'Like a Swiss village': Belemedik, the base camp of the Berlin–Baghdad Railway project (John H. Wheat Photographs, Mitchell Library, State Library of New South Wales)

to work in captivity. Most POW labour during the First World War related to the agricultural or industrial sectors of the captor nation – areas that typically suffered from a depleted workforce as mass mobilisation accounted for large numbers of available workers. Historian Heather Jones writes that the Central Powers, with limited access to colonial resources, quickly mobilised large numbers of their POWs as a workforce. By late 1915 between 60 and 70 per cent of prisoners in Austria–Hungary were organised into mobile *Kommando* work units. Similarly, in Germany, 90 per cent of POWs were involved in some form of work by August 1916.[24] The allies also made use of POW labour, with prisoners in France and Britain deployed to work on farms and in quarries, mines, and factories.[25] According to the Convention, POWs were not to be used for work directly related to the captor's war effort. Nevertheless, captives in France, Germany (including Australians) and other states were used in the manufacture of munitions or on work projects directly behind the lines, such as digging defences, moving artillery shells, burying the dead, and building huts and roads to facilitate troop movements.[26]

Australians in the Ottoman Empire were not employed directly behind their captor's lines. Rather, they were mobilised for agricultural labour at such places as Ada Bazar, for the loading and unloading of goods from barges and trains at the seaport of San Stefano near Constantinople, and for public infrastructure projects, such as road-making at Angora (Ankara) and Afyon. The project on which most Australian POWs were deployed was the Berlin–Baghdad Railway, an ambitious scheme that reflected German imperial designs on the Middle East. The railway, designed to provide a continuous rail line between the German capital and the city of Baghdad, was inaugurated in 1899 and construction started in 1903, but interruptions owing to various factors – including cholera epidemics among the local workers, the disruption of supplies during the Balkan Wars, and the mobilisation of the Ottoman Army in 1914 – meant that by the outbreak of the First World War, the line had only reached the Taurus Mountains (the approximate halfway point).[27] Engineers from Philipp Holzmann, the German construction company in charge of the project, estimated the need for three dozen tunnels through the mountainous section, and progress was slow.[28]

The prisoners were put to use on the railway project in various capacities. Some, like Corporal George Kerr, took on administrative positions. Kerr's previous experience as a clerk, his ability to speak French, and his injured leg as a result of wounds sustained before capture on Gallipoli meant that he was sent to work in the company's stores at Belemedik. His relatively comfortable position sorting out 'odds and ends' in the 'ragtime office' was created for him by the German engineers and did not prove particularly taxing. Indeed, Kerr confided to his diary, 'it strikes me that this is not a railway company running on commercial lines but a philanthropic society'.[29] Eventually Kerr rose to a senior administrative position at Belemedik. Other POWs were used as skilled labourers operating machinery and equipment necessary for the railway project, or as a manual workforce using pick and shovel to clear ground for rail lines, loading and unloading wagons with ballast, or blasting rock as part of the tunnelling effort. Maurice Delpratt was employed to clean and repair tunnelling machines at Hadjikiri, a railway satellite camp near Belemedik, while Arthur Tierney worked as a driller at Yarbaschi.[30] John Beattie moved between several jobs: he first worked in a tunnel a mile out of the main camp at Belemedik loading wagons with stone, before being moved to the power station, where he worked as a fireman on the boilers, and then later was sent to Gelebek to help repair engines.[31]

The prisoners were paid for their work and received rations, including black bread, peas, beans and boiled wheat, which they could, when the opportunity presented, supplement with food purchased at camp canteens or in local bazaars. As the 1918 British 'Report on the Treatment of

British Prisoners of War in Turkey' stated, POWs in the railway work camps lived 'the life of a labourer, though on short commons, rather than the restricted and supervised life of a prisoner'.[32] But the POWs were not always impressed by the conditions under which they were expected to work. The hours were long – twelve-hour shifts were common – and the work itself could be physically demanding and dangerous. Submariner Charles Suckling explained that the drilling machines in the tunnels sometimes struck unexploded charges set down to blast rock, while light horseman Richard Stripling died at Gelebek after being crushed by a landslide at the embankment where he was laying line.[33] Reginald Lushington explained his reaction to the working conditions at Belemedik in his memoir. Upon first arriving in the camp at night, Lushington and his fellow POWs saw a group of labourers working on the rail line by the light of flares. Their reaction – 'if the blankety Blanks think we are going to work like that they will be jolly well mistaken' – is indicative of the prisoners' view that conditions were not always believed to be of an appropriate standard for white men.[34]

Prisoners from the ranks were often transferred between different work camps, which presented yet another issue: transportation. Transport

Section of line at Hadjikiri. POW labour was used in the construction of the Berlin–Baghdad Railway line through the Taurus Mountains. (John H. Wheat Photographs, Mitchell Library, State Library of New South Wales)

infrastructure throughout the Ottoman Empire during the First World War was basic. Unpaved roads usually followed ancient caravan routes, and there were only 280 engines in use throughout the existing rail network, which comprised 5759 kilometres of mismatched gauges and lines covering an area of nearly 2.5 million square kilometres.[35] Ottoman troops were often transported in cattle trucks, where the cramped conditions took their toll. Charles Bean witnessed the transport of demobbed soldiers during his trip through the Taurus Mountains in 1919, and noted that they 'overflowed from every carriage, out of the windows, sometimes on the steps and even the roofs [sic]'.[36] Often the doors of the trucks were bolted shut to prevent attempts at desertion. The prisoners found this method of ensuring the arrival of troops on the battlefield particularly unsavoury. One English officer reflected that such measures would never be undertaken in the West: 'Imagine British troops being kept under lock and key on their way to the front!'[37] When rail travel was not available troops had to march. The lack of complete rail lines between Anatolia and Mesopotamia, for example, meant that Ottoman troops deployed to the Iraqi front marched for weeks to reach their destination. According to Turkish historian Hikmet Ozdemir, many troops became ill and fell out or deserted during these arduous marches, which resulted in depleted regiments upon arrival. One division of 10 000 Ottoman troops lost more than half its complement to disease and desertion en route from Istanbul to the Palestinian front.[38]

The prisoners, many of whom had already experienced travel via cattle trucks and forced marches on their journeys into imprisonment, were also subject to these transportation difficulties when moving between camps. Reginald Lushington described the general conditions under which POWs travelled between camps in what became known as the '40 Hommers':

> Our mode of transport when we moved from camp to camp for working parties was a closed goods wagon with two small carved windows ... This was generally a most painful and tiring mode of travelling, packed to suffocation with 40 men with their kit so that we sat on top of each other often for couple of days and nights. It was impossible to lie down, so you who read this can imagine what we were like and the language we used.[39]

Like their enemy counterparts, the prisoners were often crowded and locked into the trucks.

Perhaps the most infamous POW march was that undertaken by the British and Indian prisoners from the Kut-el-Amara garrison into Anatolia

Packed to the brim. Charles Bean witnessed the transportation of demobilised Ottoman Army troops away from the front while on his travels with the Australian Historical Mission in 1919. (AWM G02134)

in April 1916, as outlined in chapter 1. But other prisoners were forced to march on other occasions, such as in October 1915 when POWs captured in the Dardanelles were made to trek between Angora and Changri, a distance of approximately 130 kilometres over mountainous terrain. Daniel Creedon believed the march 'was a most inhuman thing'.[40] In rain and snow the poorly clothed prisoners, many still suffering from wounds received before capture, marched on basic rations of bread and olives. Many of the exhausted prisoners had to be helped or carried along the way. For Charles Suckling, the march was particularly traumatic. 'As long as I live I will not forget that four days of my life,' he wrote in a report of his time in captivity, 'the suffering and misery of that march would fill a book.'[41] Such marches – although a common method of troop movement within the Ottoman Empire – gave further credence to the POWs' impressions of the cruelty of their captors.

Another issue of significant contention was punishment. According to one historian of the Ottoman Army, Edward Erickson, training for new troops was 'particularly severe' and was based on 'draconian discipline'.[42] Daniel Creedon's observations reflect the tendency within the Ottoman Army for physical punishment. 'The way in Turkey to punish the soldiers is to strike them,' he wrote in his diary, 'then the soldier has to turn round and salute the one who had struck him.'[43] Physical punishment was not permitted in the AIF and such disciplinary action sat awkwardly with the Australians, but in keeping with the 'same footing' provision, POWs could be physically punished for alleged misdemeanours. Many Australians reported witnessing the physical punishment of other prisoners from the ranks, and several received beatings themselves. Edwin Rose stated that he had seen 'many of my friends flogged with the hide whips unmercifully by sentries' during his time in various work camps.[44] Maurice Delpratt received a flogging from the Hadjikiri camp doctor and guards after intervening on behalf of a British soldier, while William Mackay was struck with sticks by a camp guard for lagging behind in a work party and, after retaliating, was sentenced to three floggings and a stint in the cells. Similarly, Edgar Hobson was flogged after washing his shirt in a stream without asking permission, and John Romaro reportedly also received three floggings during his time as a captive.[45] The flogging of prisoners, and their own soldiers, reinforced the Australians' beliefs about Turkish savagery and backwardness.

Some of the physical circumstances of confinement cut across the rank divide. Food, for example, was the cause of much anger and angst for both officer prisoners and prisoners from the ranks. For men used to a largely meat-based diet, Ottoman food and its emphasis on vegetables and grains was seen to be totally inferior. The Australians loathed the unfamiliar black bread they were given, a regulation ration in the Ottoman Army, and repeatedly complained in their letters, diaries and post-war reports about its poor quality. They were also contemptuous of the common Ottoman meal of cracked wheat and olive oil – once they had determined what it actually was. Submariner Henry Kinder discussed his impressions of his captors' food in an account of his time in captivity. 'Can you imagine any Australian coming off good rations sitting down to a meal of fusty wheat which had rancid butter poured over it,' he wrote. 'It would make your stomach heave.'[46] For Kinder, 'it took ages to get used to the Turkish food'.[47] The American Ambassador to the Ottoman Empire reinforced these impressions of the inferiority of the food the POWs received in a report to the British Government, stating that it was 'not of the right kind for Englishmen'.[48] Some POWs initially believed that the food with which they had been provided was animal food served specifically to humiliate, an idea that was given further currency by their exposure to communal eating practices. The prisoners saw eating from a shared receptacle – a common practice in the Middle East – as unhygienic and uncivilised. John Wheat found communal eating particularly distasteful: 'There were three dishes brought into us and placed on the floor and we were given a wooden spoon each, and told to divide ourselves equally round the dishes. Just imagine Englishmen, with a dirty wooden spoon, squatting down on the floor, all eating from the same dish food not fit for a pig.'[49] Wheat's anger at being expected to eat in such a way, and his deep sense of culture clash, is clear.

Standards of health and medical care were another point of contention for all prisoners. Sanitation and public health infrastructure in the Ottoman Empire at the time of the First World War was rudimentary. The government attempted to reform the state of sanitation in the empire – first within the military and then among civilians – in the aftermath of the devastating Balkan Wars, when more troops died from disease than in battle.[50] But the practicalities of implementing these reforms in all areas of the empire proved problematic, and it became even more difficult once war had been declared and the mass movement of people added extra pressure. Many of the POWs were, as in Egypt, shocked by conditions in the towns and villages in which they were confined in Anatolia. George Handsley said of Angora that 'a walk through its streets soon convinces one that it still holds a reputation as the home of goats'.[51] John Merson claimed the standards of sanitation were 'a disgrace to civilisation and too abominable for words', an outlook echoed by POW doctor James Brown's assessment of their captors' attitudes towards hygiene. 'The Turks had no notions about sanitary measures,' he wrote in his memoir, 'except that they seemed to be utterly futile and unnecessary.'[52]

Despite reform attempts, epidemics of disease swept through the Ottoman Empire between 1914 and 1918, and infected thousands of people. Hikmet Ozdemir estimates that during the course of the war three-quarters of the population of the Ottoman Empire had malaria, and typhus and cholera were also endemic in many areas.[53] Disease did not discriminate between captives and captors or between ranks, and many POWs suffered. Several fell victims to an epidemic of malaria that devastated the Belemedik area in the summer of 1916. Others became sick with dysentery. Insect-borne diseases such as typhus also spread quickly as POWs, Ottoman troops and displaced civilians moved throughout the empire. For example, prisoners transported from a railway work camp to Angora contracted typhus when the crowded truck they were carried in picked up Russian prisoners suffering from the louse-borne illness. According to Sergeant Niven Neyland, only seventeen out of the party of forty-five were spared the disease.[54] A total of thirty-three Australian prisoners died in Turkey from diseases, including malaria, pneumonia, typhus and dysentery.

Prisoners requiring treatment for illness were generally shocked by the inadequacies of their captor's medical system. Many had already experienced the medical care available to Ottoman troops and civilians on their journeys to imprisonment. By 1914 the Ottoman Empire was suffering from a drastic shortage of trained medical staff – there were just over 2500 physicians to service more than a million soldiers in the Ottoman Army – and medical supplies were also in short supply. Quinine, used to treat malarial infections, was particularly hard to obtain, and the total stationary hospital capacity was estimated at only 37 000 beds.[55] Members of the German military mission assigned to assist the Ottoman forces were appalled by the primitive conditions of some of the hospitals they saw in the empire. 'One hospital had no doors and windows which would protect patients against cold,' wrote General Friedrich Kress von Kressenstein of the conditions at hospitals in Aleppo. '[I]n another one 3 patients were using the same glass to drink water. Another hospital accommodating 500 patients had only three body thermometers.'[56] In a letter sent to the British Government and later forwarded to the Australian Governor-General, a Swiss delegate from the Commission for the Inspection of POW Camps in Turkey reported that 'Turkish doctors are extremely inefficient, and when assistance is offered it is scarcely worth having'.[57] This perception could perhaps be explained by the practice of assigning dentists and veterinarians to the role of medical officer as Ottoman army doctors fell victim to disease.[58]

The Ottomans implemented various measures to provide health care to their POWs. An outbreak of cholera in mid-1917 around Bozanti, situated at the crossroads of routes leading from Palestine and Mesopotamia into Anatolia, was contained by the vaccination of army recruits. Prisoners were also inoculated.[59] A mobile bacteriology unit organised by the Germans was sent to Belemedik at the height of the malaria outbreak, and some prisoners received mosquito nets.[60] Camp hospitals were established at Afyon and at the more isolated work camps along the Berlin–Baghdad Railway in the Taurus Mountains, while prisoners held closer to Constantinople were often transferred to existing military or civilian hospitals in the city. Some prisoners were also sent to convalescent camps, such as the camp established in early 1917 at Bor, north of the Taurus Mountains. The POWs at Bor were accommodated in an old school building while they recovered.

But, as discussed in chapter 1, the prevailing concerns for the Australians were the cleanliness of military, civilian and camp hospitals, the lack of medicines and other supplies, and the quality of care provided by doctors and orderlies. Edgar Hobson was angered by his experiences of medical care in the Afyon hospital. He was placed on a mattress on the floor recently vacated after the death of the previous occupant, and was particularly contemptuous of the attention offered by the orderlies. 'Men were dying every day,' he wrote after the war. 'If a man was incapable of helping himself he invariably died as the Turkish orderlies would never help him.'[61] Although the prisoners recognised that their experiences of healthcare and medical attention were largely equivalent to that provided to any wounded or sick Ottoman troops (Ron McDonald claimed that 'Turkish medical arrangements are disgraceful, even for Turks themselves'), they attributed the poor conditions to the nature of their captors.[62] Non-Turkish medical care was praised – repatriated prisoners regularly expressed thanks to Armenian doctors and German medical staff – and parallels were drawn with the standards of care the prisoners would expect at home. One prisoner admitted in a post-war report that, although he had received medical care as a POW, 'it was of course not equivalent to English treatment.'[63]

PSYCHOLOGICAL PRESSURES

While the conditions of their captivity proved confronting, the particular nature of wartime imprisonment – its constraints and ambiguities – also presented other challenges for the prisoners. In 1919 Swiss doctor and International Red Cross representative Adolf Vischer published a book based on his observations as a POW camp inspector during the First World War. Vischer argued that POWs, like the inmates of civilian gaols, suffered from the general restrictions of imprisonment: lack of privacy, the monotony of routine existence, repetitive contact with the same people, and restricted communication with the outside world. He also believed the indefinite duration of wartime captivity exacted a severe psychological toll. 'In contrast with the criminal who knows to the day and hour the length of his imprisonment and can tick off each day,' Vischer wrote, 'the prisoner of war remains in complete uncertainty of the duration of his imprisonment.'[64] He claimed that these stresses deeply affected those living as captives and caused a recognisable psychological condition he termed 'barbed wire disease'.

One of the primary contributors to barbed wire disease, according to Vischer, was the *ennui* of camp life The routine existence of imprisonment engendered a monotony that sapped the will. It clearly affected George Kerr. By mid-1916 he was writing in his diary that 'the events of our daily life here are not of such importance that they would command any interest if they happened anywhere else'.[65] Monotony was a particular problem for officers in Turkey; although not being made to work had certain advantages – superior accommodation, less movement between camps, and no heavy manual labour – it also meant that the days melded into one long, continuous drag. Some officers were concerned that their time in captivity would adversely affect their careers and post-war employment opportunities, and the sense of stultification caused several prisoners to break down. One Australian witnessed the nervous collapse of a fellow officer at Afyon: 'One day I found Lieutenant LF ... walking up and down the promenade, cursing imprisonment ... and striking such an attitude as to suggest he was about to tear his hair and rend his clothes.'[66] British ex-POW Pat Reid, who successfully escaped from the notorious German prison camp at Colditz during the Second World War, believed 'inactivity could lead to idiocy' for prisoners of war, and it seemed that Lieutenant LF, at least, certainly felt the strain.[67]

Constant contact with the same people and general lack of privacy was another issue. Sharing sleeping, eating and leisure quarters meant that the POWs had no respite from each other. For Thomas White, the closely confined nature of the camp put pressure on relations among the prisoners. 'Prolonged and compulsory association in a confined space,' he wrote in his memoir, 'tends to enlarge the supposed weaknesses of one's fellows to iniquities of the first degree.'[68] Living in each other's pockets meant that otherwise overlooked eccentricities or undesirable personality traits were magnified and became a source of tension.[69] Such tensions sometimes bubbled over and, as one of George Kerr's diary entries for early January 1916 indicates, disagreements, petty fights and squabbles were commonplace:

> Last night, as is my custom, I went over the other side of the room after the beds were laid down to have a yarn with Cullen and Troy and during one of my tales ... Troy began joking about the amount of space I was taking up and told me several times to go to bed. Very soon the whole room was saying goodnight to me and when this had no effect, I was counted out ... Now ... instead of saying 'good day' to me, I am greeted with 'goodnight George' all the time.[70]

In the crowded, confined atmosphere of the prison camp, bored and irritated POWs targeted fellow captives to relieve some of their frustrations and modify seemingly undesirable behaviour.

Lack of contact with the outside world also caused psychological strain. The prisoners were isolated from news of the war. Edgar Green was particularly frustrated at not being able to assess any developments in the conflict and thus a likely end to his captivity. 'Terrible having no news,' he wrote in a 1916 letter to his sister. 'Cannot form any opinion as to the war finishing. Did we but know that, it would not seem so bad.'[71] A pro-German newspaper printed in French in Constantinople, the *Hilal*, was available, but it was only by reading between the lines that prisoners gained any idea as to what was happening on the different fronts. The arrival of new prisoners sometimes contributed to ideas of the conflict, but often these fresh captives had disappointingly little idea of the bigger picture regarding the war effort. Such lack of concrete information meant that snippets of news picked up from locals were overanalysed, resulting in rumours and speculation that were often damaging to morale. Maurice Delpratt explained the prisoners' cynicism regarding supposed news of the war in an August 1917 letter home: 'There is much excitement here over rumoured peace conferences and much speculation as to terms. Having been disappointed so often, we take these things quietly.'[72]

Restrictions regarding the arrival and dispatch of letters to family and friends compounded the POWs' sense of isolation. Historian Martyn Lyons notes in his work on reading and writing practices during the First World War the importance of regular communication between the battle-front and home to maintain the spirits of soldiers.[73] For servicemen in the trenches of the Western Front or the deserts of the Middle East, letters from home were comforting reminders of past lives and of lives they could look forward to in the future. The situation was the same for those in captivity, where letters from home informed prisoners about family happenings, reassured them that they had not been forgotten and, as one POW wrote, offered 'something to inspire one to keep fit for'.[74] During the early years of the war, the prisoners were permitted to write one four-line postcard per week and to receive one four-line message. This limited contact with loved ones was still received with gratitude; Maurice Delpratt told his sister that 'writers will never know how much joy their four lines brought'.[75]

Any interruptions to the arrival of post caused intense anxiety. Lyons writes that breaks in communication between French soldiers and their families led to panic and despair among troops at the front.[76] Prisoners also panicked and felt despondent without letters. Lack of communication implied abandonment and, as historian Annette Becker writes, the absence of letters from home in the all-masculine world of the prison camp also reinforced the lack of a feminine presence.[77] Light horseman

Lowes Skyring emphasised the importance of letters to his friend, Corporal Audie Grant. 'Now Audie don't forget to write it is a bit lonely, you can quite imagine that,' he explained. 'A man wants cheering up here if any where [sic] and letters and parcels are the only things that will have that effect.'[78] The case of Private Philip O'Hare also illustrates the prisoners' desire for contact with the world outside the camps. After not receiving any letters from his family or friends during the sixteen months he had been a prisoner, O'Hare wrote to the Red Cross asking them to find 'some benevolent person that would take a little interest in a lonely prisoner of war'.[79]

Regulations regarding length and frequency of letters were eventually relaxed, but the Ottoman postal system remained a cause of intense frustration for the POWs. The geographical spread of prison camps, lack of transport infrastructure, and movement of prisoners between camps meant that the arrival of letters from family and friends was erratic. Letters destined for prisoners were sorted via a convoluted process: they were first organised into districts in Constantinople, then sent to the military commander of each district who in turn passed them on to the British POW in charge of that district's distribution. If a prisoner was no longer held in that particular district, his mail was given back to the commander, who then sent it back to Constantinople, where the process began again.[80] This meant that, as one prisoner told AIF authorities upon his repatriation, 'no dependence could be placed on the arrival of mails' in the camps.[81] Other issues, such as backlogs in Britain and the closure of other nations' borders, also affected the arrival of post. Such difficulties affected outgoing mail as well. The prisoners recognised that their letters home were in all likelihood not always reaching their destinations, which increased their frustration and distress as they knew their friends and families were anxious to hear from them.

Aside from these particular constraints, other factors including lingering feelings of shame and failure, the advent of anniversaries and special occasions, or the death of a fellow POW also tested the prisoners. Several dwelt on the sense of failure engendered by their capture and subsequent imprisonment, which made them reconsider their public position and their private selves. In a letter to his sister in 1917, for example, Maurice Delpratt expressed particular concern regarding his personal contribution to the war effort and how others would perceive him. 'I've put in more years serving the enemy than I did for my own country,' he wrote.

I often think of that much advertised recruiting question: 'what did you do in the Great War?' I must think out some useful, evasive answer before peace terms are signed. There's such a tremendous lot of young relatives too, who will soon be inquisitive. When I visit their homes grown ups will have to warn the young folk not to ask Uncle Maurice anything about the war.[82]

Captivity also caused John Halpin to reassess his self-image and self-worth. 'I was an Australian Sergeant,' he wrote. 'I try to picture to myself and read the Regimental Orders wherein I was "Struck off Strength". Now I have lost all identity.'[83]

Special occasions or anniversaries also proved challenging. Birthdays, traditionally days of celebration with family and friends, emphasised a prisoner's distance from home, while anniversaries of capture were reminders of the passing of time and their impotence regarding the war effort. On his birthday in May 1918 William Randall wrote to his sister and brother-in-law stating he was well, but 'would like to be looking into the bottom of a glass today' while the anniversary of Claude Vautin's capture found him 'in sackcloth and ashes' feeling 'more than ordinarily fed up'.[84] Christmas could be a particularly hard time as it accentuated the cultural differences between the prisoners and their captors, although many camp commandants did permit POWs to observe the holiday. As Chris Gratien writes, Christmas accentuated the cultural differences between the prisoners and their captors, although many camp commandants did permit POWs to observe the holiday. Christmas also marked the close of the year – another reminder of the dragging of time – and brought back memories of happier times with family and friends before the war. British prisoner Leonard Woolley recalled in his memoir of captivity the special Christmas poem that had been composed by the prisoners in his camp:

> A Christmas in captivity,
>   Oh what a sorry travesty!
> A song to sing in a minor key,
>   Of things that are and should not be;
> Yet still I have to comfort me,
>   The Christmas of my memory.[85]

Christmas also served as a reminder of the loss of friends and fellow servicemen. For John Wheat, Christmas was a day of remembrance during which 'many a prisoner had an un-accustomed lump in his throat when he drank to the toast of "absent friends"'.[86]

'Absent friends' could include those who died in captivity. Indeed, the death of a fellow prisoner proved particularly distressing for the POWs. The industrialised warfare of the First World War resulted in carnage never before experienced on the battlefield. Hundreds, and sometimes thousands, of men died every day – buried alive, gassed, or torn to pieces by shrapnel and machine-gun fire. Historian Bill Gammage argues that such unprecedented casualties and regular exposure to wounds and suffering brutalised soldiers on the battlefront and left them inured to death.[87] For the Australians in Ottoman captivity, however, their distance from the battlefield and all it entailed meant that death was not such a regular occurrence. The prisoners had, according to George Kerr, 'practically reverted to their former impressionable state', so the intrusion of death and loss 'came home to them with all its force'.[88]

Although a death in the camp galvanised some prisoners into ensuring their survival – William Randall explained in a letter to his family in Victoria that 'I have made up my mind not to leave my bones in any of these Eastern countries, so I guess I shall pull through' – it also, for prisoners like William Cliffe, caused them to question their own mortality.[89] Cliffe told his brother in a 1916 letter that hearing about the deaths of fellow POWs and attending camp funerals 'makes you wonder how soon it will come your turn'.[90] That the majority of deaths in Ottoman captivity were attributed to disease was also difficult. For John Halpin, there was no glory associated with death in captivity. '"Killed in action",' he wrote in his memoir. 'There is a beauty in the utterance, an heroic halo round the memory of a mangled mass or stiffened limbs; but "died as a prisoner"... that sounds a condemnation of dishonour, an aimless and unnecessary sacrifice.'[91] A friend of Noel Sherrie, who died soon after his capture in Palestine in 1917, expressed similar concern for how the family would feel about their son's death in captivity. 'I do not know what Mrs Sherrie will do,' Miss Beatrice Butler wrote in a letter to Vera Deakin of the Australian Red Cross Wounded and Missing Bureau, 'what it will be for her thinking he died there – a prisoner.'[92] Foreshadowing issues regarding contribution to the war and commemoration, there was a sense that a POW who perished from disease in a prison camp far away from the action of the front was denied the valour of a soldierly death.

Clearly, life as a prisoner of war in the Ottoman Empire was challenging on several levels, and the Australians faced serious tests of their physical, emotional and psychological strength – some specific to their situation and some common to all wartime captives. Dealing with the constraints captivity imposed on freedom, privacy and communication, coupled with the uncertain duration of their confinement, caused great mental strain, while the hardships of life in the wartime Ottoman Empire, compounded by the Australians' belief in the barbarism and backwardness of their captors and intense cultural clash, led to concerns about the conditions of their imprisonment and their treatment. But the prisoners did not passively accept their situation. Rather, as we shall see in chapter 3, they determined effective ways and means of responding to these many challenges.

CHAPTER | 3

Shaping camp life

Several years after the war, Lieutenant Laurence Smith wrote a memoir of his time as a POW. In his account, the AFC pilot explained how he and his comrades had endured their captivity in the Ottoman Empire. The key to being 'a good Prisoner of War', according to Smith, was humour.[1] Maintaining a sense of humour was one method of dealing with imprisonment, but it was not the only approach employed by the POWs in response to the challenges of their situation. Cultural differences regarding food, accommodation, transportation, health care, work and punishment, coupled with the hardships of life in the wartime empire, emphasised for the Australians the supposed lack of civility of their captors and engendered concern over their ability to cope with the conditions of their confinement. Moreover, the constraints and ambiguities of captivity meant that many suffered from mental and emotional strain. To alleviate some of this strain and to bring a semblance of normality to their lives, the prisoners developed and implemented certain measures to manage their camp conditions and culture and thereby shape their experiences of imprisonment.

Modifying the physical environment

Exercising some control over their immediate physical environment was one way in which the Australian prisoners were able to mitigate some of the challenges of their captivity. The prisoners' dismay at the state of their accommodation sparked efforts to make their houses and barracks more comfortable and therefore more tolerable. At Angora, as Leslie Luscombe explained, officers captured on Gallipoli quickly set about improving their bathing facilities. 'Running water was connected to the house but no bath or shower was provided,' he wrote:

> We overcame this disadvantage by installing an overhead shower in the *g'haftis hana* ['secret house' – toilet]. Above the hole in the floor we mounted on a cross bar and pulleys an empty kerosene tin with holes in the bottom and a separate sheet of galvanized iron to cover the holes set inside the tin. When a shower was required the kerosene tin was lowered and filled with water. It was then hauled up into position. By releasing the water we were able to obtain a refreshing cold shower. Necessity is the mother of invention.[2]

Upon their arrival at Afyon some months later, the officers replicated these efforts, and also created household items and utensils with which to furnish their quarters. Beds were a priority, and were constructed with materials and tools bought from the local bazaar. Luscombe again offers the best explanation of how the POWs improved their level of comfort by making Western-style beds:

> The bedframe was of the usual dimensions, i.e. 3ft by 6ft 6in. The sides and ends of the frame were sawn from packing case timbers. They were then carefully planed and sand-papered and fitted together. When mounted on four (or sometimes six) stout legs, we derived much pleasure from our handiwork. Now for the mattress – this must also be a work of art. It was. With the rope we made a criss-cross pattern cradle. When suitably tightened and covered with a thick *yourgon* [feather-filled blanket] we had produced a bed that would be envied by many people in our so-called civilised countries.[3]

The construction of furniture became a business for some entrepreneurial prisoners who made desks, chairs and other items for their fellow POWs. Although the majority of this furniture was of necessity quite rough, Luscombe believed that some 'displayed really high-class workmanship that would have done credit to a cabinet-maker with all the appliances and means to boot'.[4] Less practical items such as picture frames, tobacco boxes and other trinkets were also popular. It was in their houses that POW officers spent the majority of their time; decorating their accommodation allowed the prisoners to create more of a homely, domesticated space.[5]

The prisoners also worked to overcome their concerns about sanitation. Fleas, lice and bugs were a pressing issue as they made life

POW officer houses at Afyonkarahissar. Despite complaints about cramped conditions, these houses afforded the officers a relatively comfortable home for the duration of their captivity. (AWM A02258)

uncomfortable and could also spread disease. James Brown recalled how the officers at Afyon rid themselves of infestations of bugs:

> Every day, we carried our beds to the vestibule and poured boiling water over the woodwork and particularly into the crevices.
> Later, we painted the woodwork with creosote and succeeded in maintaining an almost impassable gulf between the verminous denizens and ourselves. Stockholm tar, painted on the woodwork, was used by others and proved an effective barrier. Sleeping became possible.[6]

As a medical student, Brown was aware of the perils of inadequate sanitary practices and of the need to keep camp areas clean. He knew that flies were 'foes to be dreaded quite as much as the enemy', and was instrumental in establishing sanitation schemes at Afyon, including methods to dispose of rubbish effectively.[7]

Such altering of accommodation occurred mostly at the larger, permanent camps like Afyon and Belemedik. The smaller work camps were more temporary and more isolated, located further from marketplaces and bazaars, meaning that tools and supplies were harder to come by. Other rank POWs were also transferred between work camps regularly so the desire to create a 'home' was not as pressing. Nevertheless, in these camps the prisoners developed other ways to minimise their physical discomfort. The effects of fleas and lice were overcome by sleeping in the open, buckets were procured for the washing of clothes, wood was stolen to create sleeping platforms, wool blankets were re-spun to make underwear and other garments, and, in an effort to maintain general cleanliness and sanitation, prisoners bathed in local streams or negotiated with their guards to use their shower blocks.

Food was another key issue the prisoners endeavoured to manage. Australian officers at Afyon recreated the traditional military mess experience. The officers used their payments from the Ottomans to purchase their own food and were provided with an orderly – typically a prisoner from the ranks – to shop and cook for them. Funds were pooled to purchase items for the group, such as firewood to fuel cooking implements, while food and comforts parcels were shared. In this way, prisoners were able to blend traditional Ottoman food like *peckmez*, a grape extract, with more recognisable (and therefore acceptable) items such as eggs, cheese, tea, biscuits and meat. As the war dragged on and inflation rose within the empire, the prices of food and fuel increased, so the officers' ability to purchase locally what Thomas White called 'European groceries' diminished. Bread became 'an expensive commodity' and meat 'a rarity' as buffalo and donkey replaced beef and mutton.[8] But by pooling their limited supplies and resources, using a cook from a similar cultural background, eating in messes furnished in the Western fashion with tables and chairs, and dining at specific meal times, the officers were able to normalise their culinary experiences to some extent.

Prisoners from the ranks also worked to address the challenges of their food and dining conditions. These POWs received rations – chiefly bread, boiled wheat, and vegetables such as peas and beans. The arrival of comforts parcels, or money with which to purchase extra food from camp canteens or local markets, was celebrated as it meant that these lacklustre provisions could be supplemented. Prisoners at Changri in late 1915, for example, rejoiced that, after the arrival of money from the American ambassador, they were able to buy and cook 'English' food in the 'proper' fashion. John Beattie wrote that the POWs 'could buy eggs, flour, meat, potatoes, raisins, bread, butter, onions and almost anything else in the eating line we wanted':

> We bought plates, cups, basins, knives and forks, and no longer squatted round a food tin in the heathen Turkish fashion. We bought frying pans and cooking pots, wood and charcoal; on fine mornings there would be a lot of small fires scattered about the square, where men would be boiling a pot of tea and frying a couple of eggs for breakfast.[9]

Like their officer counterparts, prisoners at the work camps also divided into messes. Beattie explained that during the early years at Belemedik the prisoners 'used to have the same food as we would have at home'. But, as the war dragged on and supplies became more and more scarce, the prisoners 'had to eat what we could get' and were forced to improvise further.[10] At Tasch Durmas, Reginald Lushington and his fellow POWs cooked their meals of beans and bread in metal wheelbarrows, while at Hadjikiri Delpratt's mess-mates constructed a camp oven out of mud bricks and sheet iron, and kept chickens to ensure a supply of eggs.[11] George Kerr took on the role as caterer for his mess at Belemedik and experimented with the rations provided, creating dishes of macaroni and raisins when meat was unobtainable – although the others in his mess did not always appreciate his efforts.[12]

Altering and adjusting their accommodation and improvising with food rested upon skills traditionally associated with the feminine domestic sphere. The war caused something of an upheaval in gender roles, as soldiers on all fronts regularly assumed activities seen as the work of women (such as cooking, cleaning and sewing). According to Michael Roper, a large propor-tion of life in the trenches of the Western Front revolved around domestic duties to minimise discomfort and ensure both physical and mental health.[13] In the POW camp environment, such skills also gained a particular currency as they helped prisoners manage and cope with their captivity.

Although accommodation and food were the primary physical features of imprisonment that the POWs had the time, means and capacity to modify, they also worked to shape other aspects of their captivity. Work, particularly on construction projects, was tightly regimented and there-fore difficult to control. But in some instances work enabled the prisoners to alleviate other concerns. POWs with medical backgrounds, like James Brown or field ambulance man Deidrich Weidenhofer, worked at the hospitals of several permanent and work camps to assuage prisoners' worries about the medical care and treatment they received. Despite suffering from the same lack of supplies as their captors, POW doctors and medics administered to prisoners at Afyon, Belemedik, Tasch Durmas, Bor, Hadjikiri and Gelebek. With the shadow of the malarial outbreak of summer 1916 hanging over their heads, the Hadjikiri prisoners were especially grateful to their camp doctor – British officer and Kut POW Captain Jones – and his efforts to ensure the continued health of the men in the camp. Similarly, D'Arcy Armstrong explained to AIF authorities that the low death rate at Gelebek was due to the tireless work of Corporal Clifford of the Indian Medical Service. Clifford, also taken prisoner with the fall of the Kut garrison, 'worked night and day for the patients', Armstrong wrote after the war. 'Many prisoners have him to thank for their lives.'[14]

Modifying their physical conditions mitigated some of the immediate challenges of captivity, and also represented something of a moral victory for the POWs. By improving their accommodation through the construction of furniture and other household items, experimenting with food, and implementing schemes to maintain sanitation and treat the sick, the prisoners displayed an attitude of activity and positivity. Annette Becker writes, in reference to French prisoners holding on to tattered uniforms in captivity, that 'in the camp the soldier is prevented from physical fighting, but by maintaining his uniform he fights symbolically, and remains part of his nation's wider struggle against the enemy'.[15] In much the same manner, shaping – and to an extent controlling – their accommodation, food and medical care allowed the Australians in Ottoman captivity to feel as though they too continued to fight, symbolically at least.

REASSERTING A SENSE OF SUPERIORITY

The Australians also employed several tactics to alleviate the strain occasioned by the inversion of the racial hierarchy and to reinforce, or reassert, their shaken sense of superiority. One common, and obvious, method was to belittle their captors. Several camp commandants and guards were singled out for being friendly and fair – Ron Austin's first commandant had been taken captive himself during the Balkan Wars and was reportedly sympathetic to the plight of his prisoners – although others were, as we have seen, considered to be uncivilised and uneducated, and became the targets of the POWs' mockery. Camp guards, usually older men deemed unfit for the front, were nicknamed 'woolies' or 'greybeards' and their dress and equipment, 'tattered blue uniforms' and 'ancient blunderbusses', were a source of amusement to the prisoners.[16] Their obvious poverty also made them an object of ridicule. According to Reginald Lushington, the guards knew they could benefit from the prisoners. 'They soon found out it was better to keep in with us,' he explained. 'At times it was rather like a comic opera to see a British prisoner leading the way through a town in order to buy something, and the old grey beard of a guard trotting behind mildly remonstrating and being told to shut up.'[17] Care must be taken with Lushington's post-war evidence – remembering Robin Gerster's comments about ex-POW memoirs being a place for prisoners to exact 'belated revenge' on the former captor – yet other POWs report similar experiences. Guards were often coerced into escorting prisoners to marketplaces or to bring supplies to the camps, usually for a fee or some other form of reward, such as extra food.

Subtle belittlement masked as benevolence also gave way to open derision. Just as frustration and boredom among the POWs sometimes made them turn on each other, it also translated into the taunting and teasing of their captors. Such behaviour included the deliberate sabotage of roll calls and evening lock-downs, as well as the intentional misunderstanding of camp rules and restrictions. Playing tricks on their captors was also a common pastime. Maurice Delpratt told his sister that, on one occasion, the prisoners had changed the words to a Turkish song about the British. 'When we were tramping to Khiangeri [Changri],' he explained in a 1917 letter home, 'the escort sang a song which we picked up. The only line I can remember is this one: *"Inglis asken salmon kaffa was"* – English soldiers are straw-headed. We sang it too but made a simple and obvious alteration.'[18] Although it is doubtful that the guards comprehended the change Delpratt and his comrades made to their song, this retaliatory measure allowed the prisoners to feel a few moments of superiority over their captors.

One of the most blatant incidents of belittlement involved a British and an Australian officer of the Royal Flying Corps at the officers' camp at Yozgad. In a fit of boredom, Elias Jones and Cedric Hill assumed the role of spiritualists who could direct the camp commandant to buried Armenian treasure. The two men arranged a series of 'treasure hunts' designed to convince the commandant and guards of their powers. Hill planted items for one hunt in specific locations to ensure that his fellow prisoners could witness the event from one of the camp houses, believing 'it might be fun to allow some of the others to watch us'.[19] On the day of the treasure hunt Hill, and presumably his fellow prisoners, enjoyed watching the guards fall for their ruse:

When the piece of paper containing the first clue was found wrapped round a gold lira ... the three Turks talked excitedly to and across each other. The Commandant shook hands with every one several times, Moise [camp interpreter] almost exploded with enthusiasm and to cap everything the bloodthirsty-looking little Cook tried to kiss Jones. Only with a tremendous effort of self-control did I manage not to laugh.[20]

Although Hill and Jones were trying to 'get one over' and humiliate their captors, they soon also realised the implications of their con for being released from captivity. The prospect of escape from the Ottoman Empire was slim. The obviously different ethnic background of the prisoners made blending in with the local population difficult, while the isolation of most prison camps meant that escape would involve surviving long journeys across harsh terrain exposed to the elements. Several Australians attempted escape, some after careful planning and some more spontaneously, yet success was rare. Several British prisoners made it to allied territory during the war, but only two Australians achieved a similar feat. Thomas White persuaded medical staff at Afyon that he required hospital treatment in Constantinople: while there, he was caught up in a train crash and seized the opportunity to evade his guards. With the help of some sympathetic Greek locals, White and a British POW were smuggled onto a ship bound for Odessa, from where they travelled to Salonika. For all his efforts, White made it back to British territory less than two weeks before the Armistice.[21] Cedric Hill also made it out of the Ottoman Empire: along with Jones, he escalated the spiritualism ruse, feigned insanity and eventually was medically repatriated to England. Despite the popularity of escape stories in the post-war period, the reality was that very few Australian prisoners successfully escaped from captivity in the First World War.[22]

Cultural and racial superiority was also emphasised by playing up Britishness. Unlike in the many Japanese or German prison camps of the Second World War, where the thousands of Australians captured in the Pacific and in North Africa, Greece, Crete and Germany went to great lengths to ensure the maintenance of their national identity and culture, the Australians in Ottoman captivity were too small in number and too diffuse among the disparate camps to express any marked Australian identity. Although some cultural peculiarities were noted, and at Afyon several Australian officers banded together and nicknamed their residence 'Australia House', the Australian prisoners were effectively seen as British by their captors, by their fellow POWs and significantly, by themselves. Even in sporting competitions, an aspect of prison camp life in which Australian POWs of the Second World War were determined to prove their national prowess, the Australians in the Ottoman Empire competed as British.[23] After beating a French prisoner in a race held at an Easter sports carnival at Belemedik in 1918, for example, Maurice Delpratt was proud to be called 'the Wallaby who upheld the British prestige'.[24]

Such affinity with the British runs counter to the dominant narrative of Australian–British relations during the First World War. At the turn of the twentieth century when men from the Australian colonies had gone to fight the Boers in South Africa, fuelled by heroic tales of cavalry charges and the like from the Napoleonic Wars, they had initially been in awe of their British counterparts. But this soon collapsed into disillusion and disappointment, not least because of the brutal and incompetent methods used by the British to handle their Boer enemy. Disenchantment with the British was reinforced during the First World War when being in close contact with British troops in the field and in training camps threw into stark relief the perceived physical and cultural differences between the Australians and their counterparts from the 'mother country'.[25] These differences were instrumental in sharpening the Australian troops' grow-ing sense of national identity; as historian Alistair Thomson notes, 'for most Australian soldiers the war was undoubtedly a potent experience of national self-recognition'.[26] For the Australians in Ottoman captivity, however, asserting Britishness was closely linked with asserting racial superiority, and it minimised the sense of inversion that their confinement wrought.

The Australians also asserted their Britishness in their relations with captives from other national groups. The Ottoman Army had captured troops from France, Russia and India, many of whom lived alongside the Australians in the bigger work and convalescent camps as well as at officers' camps and in hospitals. The Australians' opinions of their fellow captives were often couched in terms that emphasised their belief in the superiority and civility of the British. The French, for example, although noted for their ability to put on a decent party, were often scorned for their attitudes towards imprisonment. One Australian gave the French a backhanded compliment regarding their prowess at manipulating their captors: 'I think the French are better at getting what they want than we are ... Like us they can be firm but they are quicker at knowing the time for meekness, and the assumption of it doesn't seem to go so much against the grain as it does with us.'[27] Nevertheless, the Australians mingled relatively easily with the French, often forming messes with them to combine rations. Although this sometimes caused tension – Maurice Delpratt claimed that ideas about food 'sometimes run pretty wide of each other' in the combined British and French mess at his camp in the Taurus Mountains, joking that the French POWs 'love a pot of snails' – there were enough similarities between the French and the Australians to sustain relative harmony.

Russian prisoners, particularly those from the ranks, were often viewed more negatively. By the time of the First World War, the Russians were seen as a firm ally of the British, but a sense of 'Russophobia' dating back to the Crimean War lingered. Russian prisoners received little in the way of external assistance; some 2.8 million Russians were taken prisoner during the war, but political turmoil in their homeland, particularly the 1917 revolutions, meant that they received limited financial or practical aid, which affected their physical and emotional condition in captivity. The long-held animosity between the Russians and the ethnic Turks – historian Yucel Yanikdag explains that 'most Ottomans of all ranks viewed the Russians as the principal enemy' during the war while for the Russians, 'Ottomans ranked third on their traditional enemies list' – also negatively influenced their treatment and condition.[28] The Australians generally appreciated that the Russians were suffering as a result of circumstances beyond their control, but this did not stop several from commenting on what they believed to be the uncivilised nature of their counterparts. When George Handsley arrived at his work camp in Angora, he was dismayed to find himself having to sleep near a group of Russians who, he claimed, 'smelt worse than pigs', 'were in a filthy condition' and 'appeared to be of low moral type'.[29] Russian POWs were often blamed for carrying and spreading typhus in the prison camps – an accusation that was also levelled at Russian prisoners in Germany.[30] John Halpin wrote that the Russians' constrained condition left many reliant on the charity of their captive comrades and emphasised the civilised hand of kindness the British (and therefore the Australians) often extended. 'They come to us that they might live,' he wrote, 'because the Britisher . . . is the refuge of the helpless.'

Australians also exerted superiority by reproducing colonial power relations. Thousands of Indian troops had fallen into Ottoman hands at Gallipoli and in Mesopotamia, particularly after the capitulation of the Kut-el-Amara garrison in April 1916. Heather Jones has explored the experiences of the Indian prisoners during the march from Kut into Anatolia, and notes that, despite popular ideas that fellow Muslims received preferential treatment from their captors, Muslim Indians among the group were subject to harsh treatment.[31] In keeping with the hierarchy of the Indian Army, Indian troops were separated from their British superiors in the camps but often remained under their administrative control regarding the division of money and comforts. At one railway work camp in the Taurus Mountains, an Australian assumed the role of quasi-administrator of an Indian camp. As one of the highest-ranking troops at Hadjikiri, Maurice Delpratt was responsible for the distribution of letters and comforts among the prisoners at his camp and the Indian POWs at a nearby camp. Delpratt approached his job with a sense of superiority over his counterparts from the subcontinent. 'The Indians live all together,' he explained in a letter to his sister. 'They are, very unwisely, a mixed lot of Hindoos [sic], Mahommedans and Ghurkas, and row continually. I am afraid I don't know much about handling Indians, but I have more authority and get more respect now that they know they must come to me for all clothing.'[32] At another work camp, Edgar Hobson was assigned a similar quartermaster-like position, which included being in charge of the distribution of rations among a contingent of 500 Kurdish workers.[33] The authority that Delpratt and Hobson maintained over those they perceived to be lower on the colonial and cultural orders seemingly went some way to reaffirm their shaken sense of racial pride.

Along with emphasising Britishness, many Australians also aligned themselves with the Germans in the prison camps to reinforce their place at the top of the racial and cultural hierarchy. As part of the alliance between the Central Powers, German military officers, healthcare professionals and civilian engineers were scattered throughout the Ottoman Empire, and played a significant role in many of the prisoners' experiences of captivity. Historian Sean McMeekin explains in his study of the German–Ottoman alliance that relations were often fraught, and several Australian prisoners commented on tensions between the two groups.[34] Many Ottoman troops seem to have resented the presence of their Teutonic allies – one ex-prisoner claimed that 'the Turks used to state that Germans got all the medals and food and did not fight, while they received nothing and had to do the lot' – and the Germans, like the Australians, appear to have viewed the Ottoman Empire as something of a backward place that offered only a 'veneer of civilization'.[35]

Conversely, the Germans generally accepted the British and Australians as racial and cultural equals. A shared sense of whiteness transcended enemy boundaries and, according to one British officer, the Germans 'seemed to think it their duty to protect us, as fellow Europeans'.[36] Laurence Smith believed the Germans who brought down his plane deliberately hid him for as long as possible before he was finally collected by Ottoman troops. Fellow Flying Corps officer Douglas Rutherford expressed similar sentiments, claiming the Germans told him 'they were sorry to see me a prisoner in the hands of the Turks'.[37] With few notable exceptions – such as the reportedly tyrannical rule of the German commandant in charge of San Stefano camp in early 1918 – the prisoners were grateful for the treatment they received from the Germans, particularly those affiliated with the construction of the Berlin–Baghdad Railway, and praised their efforts to assist the captives. Harry Foxcroft wrote that the Germans at his railway camp gave prisoners absolute freedom, while Private Bernard Dunne claimed that 'the Germans that I met were gentlemen and if they could do you a kindness they were not long in doing it'.[38] In some cases, relationships between the prisoners and their German counterparts carried on outside the prison camps. After the war, for example, British doctor Captain Jones remained in contact with the German nurse who had helped him in the Hadjkiri camp hospital.[39]

DEALING WITH MENTAL AND EMOTIONAL STRAIN

Reaffirming a sense of superiority went some way towards mitigating the psychological strain of captivity, but the implementation of varied strategies was required to manage other mental and emotional pressures. These ranged from light-hearted ways of bringing men out of a 'funk', to private means of escapism to combat loneliness and depression, to more formal, structured programs designed to minimise monotony, allay fears for the future, and deal with death.

As the quote from Laurence Smith at the beginning of the chapter suggests, consciously making light of their situation was one of the ways the POWs tried to alleviate depression. Both George Kerr and Reginald Lushington noted that fellow prisoners often ridiculed captives who openly admitted to feelings of misery and hopelessness. In his diary entry for the first day of 1916, Kerr explained that 'whenever anyone expresses an opinion here that does not sound happy, someone cries, "all is lost" and raises a laugh at the expense of the speaker'.[40] Similarly, Lushington recalled that 'a certain grim humour prevailed' among the prisoners. Upon arrival at new lodgings in the agricultural town of Ada Bazar – a barn that 'an English farmer would never have put his cattle into' – a particularly glum-looking man was called out in front of the party and told 'laugh, damn you!' by a fellow captive.[41] On another occasion Lushington observed a prisoner pull a large worm out of his ration of bread, to which another responded by laughing and telling him to 'make a ham sandwich of it'.[42] Irreverent humour was used as both a denial strategy and a tool to prescribe behaviour – gentle ribbing informed others how to act in order to cope and conform to the expectations of the group.

Letter-writing was another method used by the prisoners in response to the psychological strain of captivity. Writing letters offered servicemen during the First World War the ability to maintain a connection with home, as well as a break from monotony and a means of temporary escapism.[43] Composing letters home was also, as historian Clare Makepeace writes with specific relation to POWs, one of the ways that prisoners 'imagined themselves living in their civilian worlds even while in captivity'.[44] We have already seen how, at first, the prisoners' ability to correspond with home was restricted to official postcards of four lines, but that later in the war they were permitted to write longer letters. Many prisoners kept meticulous records of correspondence received and sent. For some, letter-writing was a ritual and letters were composed on the same day at the same time, while others preferred to add to letters every day to provide a diary-like account of their week. For others, however, the writing of letters could be a source of anxiety. Content and style had to be carefully gauged – prisoners were concerned that their letters were boring or would make their family worry – while the process of putting one's thoughts down for loved ones to read at home could bring about a sense of despondency. One POW reported feeling a 'very pronounced fit of the blues' after completing a letter to a friend; perhaps he felt unable to express himself properly, or the act of writing brought back memories, or he wrote of plans for the future that seemed far removed from the reality of the prison camp.[45]

Mess parties were another common means of escapism. Parties and get-togethers between houses, huts and barracks allowed prisoners to let off steam and boosted morale, if only temporarily. Alcohol was a key ingredient in these celebrations, and the ready availability and accessibility of homemade spirits in the local markets and town bazaars led to some colourful gatherings. Thomas White wrote that all prisoners in Anatolia knew the aniseed-flavoured spirit *raki* as 'a cheap and useful aid to forgetfulness', and many Australians appear to have used it as such.[46] George Kerr wrote evocative accounts of bouts of heavy drinking in the diary he maintained during the first years of his captivity. An entry from mid-December 1915 explains how his mess-mates at Belemedik smuggled in liquor and then overindulged to the point of illness. 'Two of them were very sick outside our building,' he noted, 'while others were strolling about their rooms in various stages of intoxication.'[47] Indeed, at Belemedik a party scene appears to have developed with Kerr himself being a regular contributor. On the night of 3 March 1916 he reportedly 'made enough row for a dozen' after drinking twenty small glasses of *raki* and the next day suffered from a terrible hangover. 'Felt very bad all day,' he confided to his diary, 'and, I believe, looked it.'[48]

Parties were also held to mark special events or occasions. Where possible, prisoners' birthdays were celebrated. Writing after the war, George Paltridge stated that one of his happiest moments at Afyon was his birthday in 1918. In a stroke of good luck and fortunate timing, he received an allotment of money and a Red Cross parcel three days before his birthday, which allowed him the funds and supplies to create a 'dinkum Aussie feed' for himself and five others.[49] Several Australians also marked the first anniversary of the Gallipoli landings – at Belemedik the day was celebrated with wine and 'yarns' and at Afyon a 'sing-song' was organised, but sadness seems to have dominated much of these proceedings. According to George Kerr, the men at Belemedik 'became sentimental over the thought of the lads killed on the peninsula' while celebrations at Afyon were subdued owing to the less than positive news about the besieged garrison at Kut.[50]

The multinational nature of the camps also saw the Australians participate in such cultural events as St Patrick's Day and Bastille Day. On 14 July 1916 the French organised a Bastille Day party that turned into another boozy night, as evidenced by the bill. 'The drink cost the party 50 piastres per head,' George Kerr wrote, 'the food amounted to 6 or 7.'[51] The comments of a high-ranking Ottoman official at a St Patrick's Day celebration in Belemedik indicate that the guards were aware of the prisoners' penchant for alcohol. 'During the concert we had a visit from Osman Effendi,' Kerr noted in his diary, 'and later ... from the Imperial Commissioner whose first remark was that this was the proper manner in which to enjoy ourselves – not by fighting and drinking.'[52] Considerable efforts were also made to observe markers of British culture and customs. The prisoners celebrated Christmas Day in as traditional a fashion as possible, usually by saving supplies in order to put on a special meal and playing sport or putting on some form of concert. After a dinner of boiled turkey and plum duff on Christmas Day 1915, for example, Daniel Creedon played in a football match between the army and the navy (the army won 4–1) and later in the evening attended a musical performance.[53] New Year's Eve was also celebrated. A letter from Maurice Delpratt to his sister explains how the prisoners at Hadjikiri welcomed 1918:

> We saw the old year out and the new one in with the Frenchmen, in the good old tin-can noisy way ... After the Frenchmen had kissed each other (some of us were kissed too – I got one on each cheek from the French Sergeant) they made a decent brew of coffee and *koniak* and we soon forgot we were 'but poor prisoners'.[54]

Although alcohol and celebratory events might have helped the captives forget they were 'but poor prisoners', their effects were only temporary. The highs brought on by parties often gave way to further feelings of despondency and despair. 'It's jolly while it lasts,' Delpratt went on to explain in his New Year letter, 'but there's a rather flat, listless feeling comes after.'[55]

More structured ways to combat the mental and emotional strain of captivity were also implemented. Officers were the chief instigators, and usually the chief beneficiaries, of these more organised programs. Their greater amount of free time allowed them the opportunity to organise and run debating clubs, lectures and classes, concerts and theatrical productions, and sporting events. At Kedos, an officers' camp established later in the war and at which several Australians were held, instructional classes covering topics as diverse as art history, astronomy, shorthand and car maintenance were popular, as were lessons in languages including German, Spanish, French, Arabic and, naturally, Turkish. The prisoners staged theatrical productions and in one, George Handsley, there as an officer's orderly, dressed up as an 'Aussie' bushwoman.[56] The Kedos group also established a butterfly collection club, a group of prisoners who made their own musical instruments developed an orchestral society, and such sports as rugby, soccer and badminton were played with improvised equipment. Kedos prisoners could even join a painting club. Officers purchased paints and brushes in the markets and were assigned a guard to watch over them as they wandered the local area. 'The scenery at Kedos is lovely,' British POW officer Leonard Woolley wrote. 'A veritable paradise for the landscape artist, so all through the summer months there were fellows with drawing boards, paint boxes etc and a few of those less sensitive to ridicule with chairs and even easels to be seen wandering far and wide.'[57] The image of a POW carrying easel and brush wandering off to paint a landscape scene of the Anatolian countryside is striking, particularly when compared with the conditions their counterparts still active in combat were experiencing on the various fronts.

Kedos was known as a particularly relaxed camp where officers were given a significant degree of freedom in return for their parole (their agreement to not attempt escape), although similar programs were also developed at other camps. Officers at Afyon also appreciated the need to keep occupied. Leslie Luscombe and Thomas White formed their own debating club and took it in turns to read texts sent to the prisoners by the protecting powers or other welfare committees, including such stalwarts as Gibbon's *Rise and Fall of the Roman Empire*.[58] Languages and other skills were also studied. 'The combined subjects being read,' James Brown explained, 'covered almost the whole range of human knowledge.'[59] Elements of these programs were also established at various work camps, but to a lesser extent. Work took up most of the men's time and

Australian officers at Afyonkarahissar. Standing from left: Leslie Luscombe, Stanley Jordan, William Elston, James Brown. Seated, from left: Claude Vautin, Thomas White and William Harold Treloar (AWM A02265)

energy, and those who pursued languages or educational classes usually did so informally. George Kerr, for example, taught English lessons to French submariners at Belemedik in exchange for French lessons, and trained other POWs in shorthand. Such sports as boxing and football, card games and mess parties were the chief recreational outlets for prisoners from the ranks.

One significant cause of emotional strain in the camps, as we have seen, was the death of a fellow POW. In some camps, the burial of the dead was organised by the guards or other staff. Some prisoners reported that their captors took great care over the deceased; however, others believed that their treatment of dead POWs was cruel. Several prisoners reported seeing prisoners placed in shallow graves with no markings.[60] At Angora in 1917, light horseman George Roberts stated that prisoners were not permitted to attend the burials of fellow captives. 'They are taken to a room in the Hospital,' he wrote in a letter to the Red Cross, 'and washed and then conveyed on a stretcher to the Hospital's graveyard and buried by Turks (shrouds are unnecessary luxury according to these people) there are no marks to show where buried in certain places we know they are English that's all.'[61] Cameleer Arthur Tierney reported a similar method of disposing of the dead at Nigde, where four of the men he was captured with died from disease and were buried in unmarked graves without the presence of any other prisoners.[62] Accusations of callousness might have seemed justified at the time, but cultural differences between the captives and the captors must be taken into account. Traditionally Muslim burials are conducted soon after death, typically within twenty-four hours, with the body usually being buried in a simple white cotton shroud. The practicalities of sanitation and disease management might also have necessitated speedy burials. The funerals Roberts referred to were of prisoners who had died from typhus and other contagious diseases: the quick removal of the dead might have been brought on by the need to make room in hospitals or as a way of minimising the potential spread of illness.

In other camps, including those in established towns such as Angora and Afyon, and at the bigger work camps, fellow POWs could exercise some control over the ways in which the dead were buried. In much the same way as their comrades on the battlefield who buried those killed as best they could, prisoners often became what historian Bart Ziino calls 'guardians of the dead' by conducting funeral services, protecting personal possessions, contacting relatives and other authorities, and constructing and maintaining graves and cemeteries.[63] Most prisoners were buried in the closest Christian cemetery. When Lowes Skyring died of pneumonia at

POW graves in the Christian cemetery at Belemedik. The grave in the middle is that of Private William Allen, captured on Gallipoli. Allen died at Belemedik in December 1916 from malaria and dysentery. (AWM P01645.002)

Afyon in 1918, he was buried in the town's Armenian cemetery, as was George King. Their graves were marked with wooden crosses erected by their camp mates.[64] At Belemedik, prisoners were buried in a cemetery that was also used by the Germans working on the railway project. After Len New's death following an accident in a work camp, the prisoners made him a wooden coffin and conducted their own funeral. A large party of prisoners attended the service at Belemedik and sang hymns and recited prayers.[65] New's grave was marked with a cross, although George Kerr reported that the cross was later vandalised.[66] Brendan Calcutt was buried in a similar fashion by his fellow prisoners at Hadjikiri (his grave was photographed by Charles Bean on his travels through the region as part of the Australian Historical Mission in 1919).[67] Similar funeral services were conducted in other work camps; in August 1918 at Gelebek, Cecil Spencer attended the funeral of a fellow prisoner and read a portion of the funeral service, while Reginald Lushington reported that the eighteen prisoners who died of disease at Ismidt were buried in the town's Armenian cemetery, 'laid to rest by our men and the burial service read over them'.[68] Enacting these traditional cultural funeral practices provided the prisoners with a way to cope with the loss of another captive.

Prisoners also played a key role in ensuring that relatives of the dead, as well as government and aid officials, were aware of the loss. Bart Ziino, Joy Damousi and Pat Jalland have each written about soldiers at the front taking on the role of agents for the bereaved during the First World War.[69] The prisoners acted in a similar manner. George Roberts became an unofficial liaison between the Australians in Ottoman captivity and the Red Cross regarding POW deaths. On several occasions he provided the Red Cross POW Department with lists of deceased Australian prisoners and, in doing so, was able to confirm the deaths of different men. In one instance a list of New Zealanders who had died in captivity, compiled by Roberts, was duly passed on to an appreciative New Zealand High Commission in London.[70] Aware of the poor communications between the camps and those at home, several POWs also took it upon themselves to inform family members directly of the death of a loved one. Lowes Skyring felt the loss of his friend Richard Stripling keenly, and wrote several letters to Stripling's family before his own death in late 1918.[71] Maurice Delpratt also wrote several letters to Brendan Calcutt's father after Calcutt's death in January 1917 to explain how Brendan had died, and to assure the family that Delpratt had kept his personal possessions.[72] Ensuring that family members knew the particulars of their loved one's death helped to assuage the impact of death for those in the camps.

In actively responding to the challenges of their captivity – by modifying their physical environments, reaffirming their sense of racial and cultural superiority, and implementing formal and unofficial ways of overcoming mental and emotional stress – the POWs were able to shape their camp life to make it as tolerable, and therefore acceptable, as possible. But the prisoners were not the only ones who had to negotiate the difficulties of captivity. How the official agencies charged with helping Australian POWs navigated the constraints of wartime imprisonment that they encountered is the focus of chapter 4.

CHAPTER 4

OUTSIDE CONNECTIONS

Much of what the prisoners were able to achieve in shaping their lives in the POW camps was made possible through important connections with a network of external agencies – government departments, neutral powers, and aid organisations – that worked to ensure their protection and support. The notion that prisoners of war were deserving of assistance from their home state was relatively recent at the time of the First World War. It was only from the latter half of the nineteenth century, as post-Enlightenment ideas about the rights of the individual challenged existing beliefs about wartime captives, that POWs moved from being seen as the possessions of their captor to persons worthy of protection.[1] The struggling financial state of the Ottoman Empire during the war, and the Ottoman Government's ability to provide for and maintain POWs, was a key concern for British, Australian and other international authorities and the provision of money, food and other supplies to the prisoners was a chief priority. Each part of this network adjusted to the role of supporting and upholding these new ideas about prisoners of war, in spite of multiple challenges and difficulties, to best ensure the welfare of those in the Ottoman prison camps.

GOVERNMENT RESPONSES

As we have seen, the Hague Convention regarding POWs stipulated that prisoners were to receive the same treatment as troops from the captor's military. The majority of key world powers had ratified the Convention but even those states that had not formally signed up understood that the humane treatment of any prisoners taken in battle was the responsibility of the captor government.[2] These understandings were designed to promote comity between warring nations.[3] But the unprecedented – and unexpected – number of POWs taken by the belligerents during the First World War tested the feasibility of the Hague Convention. Between 1.3 and 1.4 million prisoners were captured in Europe within the first six months of the war. Numbers rose as hostilities continued until more than 6.5 million servicemen were in captivity at war's end. The flaws of the Convention were exposed as the war dragged on. There was, as Heather Jones writes, 'a disjunction between the universal aspirations set out in international law and the reality on the ground'; some detaining powers, struggling to ensure the welfare of their own population, relegated the care of prisoners to the sidelines, while the 'same footing' provision effectively permitted inequality of treatment.[4] Such inequality, particularly regarding food, clothing and accommodation, was a significant concern for the belligerent governments. According to historian Richard Speed, 'Virtually everything that was subject to divergent interpretation or practice became the focus of controversy. Article 7 had, in effect, papered over the inherent contradiction between the implicit assumption of equal treatment and the reality of divergent practice and custom.'[5] Such divergences meant that there was room for disagreement and controversy even if the Convention had not technically been breached.

The Ottoman War Ministry's official policy concerning POWs indicated that they intended to operate within the Hague framework. Their *Manual Concerning Prisoners of War* (1914) outlined provisions for the administration of prison camps, accommodation and supervision of prisoners, financial support and work, and made it clear that any POWs taken by the Ottoman Army would receive the same treatment as Ottoman troops of equivalent rank.[6] But the allied governments were well aware of the parlous state of the Ottoman Army and the Ottoman Empire more broadly. Although Ottoman leaders were adamant that prisoners of war in the Ottoman Empire were not mistreated, they did acknowledge that lower standards of living caused many Western captives to suffer.[7]

Political efforts were therefore focused on ensuring that the POWs were treated on par with British standards. A complex machinery of government departments was established early in the war to obtain information about and minister to captive British servicemen in enemy hands. The Directorate of Prisoners of War, led by Lieutenant-General Sir Herbert Belfield, was formed within the War Office, and the Foreign

Office also created a Prisoner of War Department. A Prisoner of War Information Bureau was established to keep records of prisoners in British hands for transmission to the enemy, and in 1915 the Government Committee on the Treatment by the Enemy of British Prisoners of War was convened to document any instances of abuse of POWs.[8] The unprecedented nature of the work of these different departments and committees, coupled with uncertainty over which department was ultimately responsible for POWs, led to inevitable tensions. The refusal of the Foreign Office to continue work on prisoner of war matters in October 1916 meant that the British War Cabinet was forced to create an independent POW Department under Lord Newton, Assistant Under-Secretary of State for Foreign Affairs.[9]

The chief issue for the British Government was the provision of money to POWs. In line with the Hague Convention, the Ottoman Government paid captive officers at a rate commensurate with their rank; four shillings per day for lieutenants and 4/6d per day for captains and above (equivalent to approximately A$20–22 in 2016).[10] These amounts were agreed upon after some diplomatic to-ing and fro-ing among the British, the Germans and the Ottomans.[11] The pay of a prisoner of war did not stop during his time in captivity, nor did any allotments or separation allowances he had arranged to be deducted from his pay, so payments received by officers from the enemy were deducted from their accounts.[12] However, as we have seen, officers in Ottoman captivity purchased their own food and fuel, and had to pay rent. The British Government thus permitted a ration allowance of 1/9d per day to cover the cost of these expenses. As NCOs and other rank POWs were supposed to have their food, clothing and accommodation requirements met by their captors, they did not receive a similar allowance.

But as the war dragged on, the price of food and fuel in the Ottoman Empire increased dramatically. This made the payments to captive officers inadequate, while the rations received by other ranks decreased in quantity and quality and required supplementing with food available from local markets. The prisoners needed more money. The challenge for the British was to discern exactly how much they needed. In early 1915 a relief payment of three shillings per week to each British prisoner of war was approved. This amount was deemed enough to cover captives' immediate wants and, as these payments were regarded as 'in aid of maintenance', the funds were not deducted from the prisoner's pay.[13] Further application from the prisoners themselves to the British Government in late 1917 led to an increase in monthly relief payments to a maximum of £7 Turkish for officers and £3 Turkish for the other ranks ('£ Turkish' refers to Ottoman lira – in 1914 one British pound equalled 1.1 Ottoman lira; seven Ottoman lira therefore equated to £6/7/-. By 1918 this amount had risen to the equivalent of a maximum monthly payment of £18 Turkish for officers and £10 Turkish for men.[14] These higher relief payments reflect the drastic rate of inflation in the Ottoman Empire and the ever-escalating expenses of life for the POWs.

In keeping with the political and diplomatic arrangement between Britain and Australia at the time, the Australian Government did not establish any official departments to deal with POW affairs. Despite the formation of a federated Australia in 1901, the official view remained that Australia was part of a larger British nation encompassing the United Kingdom, Canada, and parts of Africa and the Pacific. The British monitored Australian and British issues and interests in Australia through the Governor-General. As the chief representative of the monarch, the Governor-General of Australia acted as liaison between the two governments. Indeed, it was only through the Governor-General that Australian federal ministers could contact their British counterparts.[15] British control over Australian foreign affairs and interests continued during the First World War. At the outbreak of the conflict Australian military personnel were placed at the full disposal of the British and, while the Australian Government committed to equip, pay and feed its servicemen, and insisted that they be retained as national units rather than, as the British initially suggested, be subsumed into existing British regiments, they had little to do with how or even where their troops were used.[16] Although Australian forces had taken a lead role in organising the occupation of German New Guinea in late 1914, the Australian Government did not take an active interest in strategic decisions relating to the main theatres of war.[17] Prime Minister Andrew Fisher did not know Australian units were to take part in the Gallipoli campaign until they were already en route for the peninsula, and it was not until mid-1918 that an Australian general, John Monash, took tactical command of Australian forces on the Western Front.

Australian authorities used, and aligned with, the British system of POW welfare to provide relief to Australian prisoners of the Ottomans. The British expected such alignment. In mid-1915, the Australian High Commissioner was informed of the War Office's decision to provide money to British prisoners in the Ottoman Empire. Although staff at the Colonial Office explained that the Australian Government was free to make independent arrangements regarding their prisoners, they also warned that it would be wise to maintain parity among the POW population. Keen to ensure that previous tensions over the issue of pay were not replicated in the prison camps – British soldiers had not reacted well to the discovery that their Australian counterparts were paid at a much higher rate – the Colonial Office went to great pains to point out that separation allowances and other allotments to dependants of British soldiers were minimal, meaning that family members of British POWs, unlike many Australian families, would not be in a position to send extra money to their captive loved one.[18] In the face of such warning, the Australian Government requested that existing British arrangements be extended to Australian prisoners, and relief payments for the Australians were set at the same rate as those provided to British prisoners.

However, not all official relief payments for Australians in the Ottoman Empire went through the British system. Care of the Australians from HMAS *AE2* initially fell to the Naval Adviser to the High Commissioner for Australia in London, Royal Navy Captain (later Rear Admiral) Francis Haworth-Booth. Certain allowances and special considerations for the nature of their work meant that submariners were highly paid men but, unlike their army counterparts, their dependants could not draw separation allowances, meaning that the ability of submariners' families to purchase and send extra comforts was limited. The Australian High Commissioner therefore stated that the submariners would require a higher amount of financial relief.[19] Upon receiving official confirmation of their capture, Haworth-Booth approved an advance of thirty shillings of pay per rating per month, and arranged a clever way of ensuring that the prisoners received the money.[20] He organised for a British bank with a branch in Constantinople to send 'dead money' – money that could not be transferred out of the empire owing to the war – to the senior Australian rating, Chief Petty Officer Harry Abbott, for him to distribute among the *AE2* men. The British bank was then reimbursed with a cheque from Haworth-Booth.[21] The submariners' higher rates of pay ruffled feathers in Britain. In July 1915, after an objection from the Army Council that it was 'considered undesirable that one class of prisoners should be placed by Government action in a better financial position than the general mass', Haworth-Booth was forced to hold off on further advances until the end of September, at which point payments at a reduced scale were to be arranged.[22]

Advances of pay were also given to the submariners in kind. In January 1916, each RAN rating in the Ottoman Empire received two pairs of drawers, two pairs of thick socks, two flannel vests, one jersey or cardigan, one pair of boots and one serge suit. All captive British Navy ratings received the same clothing allowance.[23] Towards the end of that same year, other articles of clothing were supplied to the *AE2* prisoners in accordance with their specifications. Food parcels were also sent at the express request of the captive submariners. The total cost of the clothing and food was to be charged against the men's accounts.[24] However, this money was later refunded by the Naval Secretary, who stated: '[I]t is not desired that any charge for food parcels should be made against Australian Naval Ratings who are held prisoner by the enemy.'[25] In November 1916 Haworth-Booth ceased relief work for the men of the *AE2* after the submariners were added to the lists of the official Australian aid agency, the Australian Red Cross POW Department.

Simultaneously with arrangements for financial assistance, the Foreign Office, and later Lord Newton's Prisoners of War Department, were involved in continued negotiations with the Ottoman Government regarding camp inspections, the privileges afforded officer prisoners, reprisal actions and POW exchanges. Such negotiations were often frustrating and drawn-out; one issue could take many months to resolve, and even then it was usually on an *ad hoc* basis.[26] The Australian Government was not directly involved with these negotiations. It was, however, informed of the essence of correspondence between the British and the Ottomans through a convoluted bureaucratic channel including the Foreign Office, the POW Department, the Colonial Office and the Australian Governor-General. This meant considerable delays in the transmission of information; in one instance, Prime Minister William 'Billy' Hughes, who had taken over as leader after Fisher's resignation in October 1915, did not receive a copy of an April 1918 report into the conditions at various prison camps until some six months later when the war was nearly over.

One of the most significant agreements between the British and Ottoman governments regarding POWs was finalised in late December 1917. After a Swiss inspector's report highlighted the declining conditions in many prison camps throughout the Ottoman Empire, the British pushed for a face-to-face meeting to discuss their concerns. Delegates from both governments met in Berne, Switzerland, to negotiate a reciprocal treaty of improved conditions and prisoner exchange. This treaty, known as the Berne Agreement, codified each belligerent's administration of prisoners of war. It outlined the establishment of camp help committees to be chaired by the POW of senior rank in each camp, the process for censorship of incoming and outgoing mail and other printed material, the provision of religious services in the camps, and the ways in which prisoners could be punished.[27] It also detailed the responsibilities of the captor government regarding the maintenance of nominal rolls of prisoners and the issuing of death certificates.[28]

Importantly, the Berne Agreement also established a program of medical repatriation. Under this scheme, sick or incapacitated prisoners could present themselves before a medical commission consisting of three doctors (two from the captor nation and one from the captive) to be assessed for repatriation.[29] It was through this avenue that Privates Patrick O'Connor and John Davern, both suffering from complications from wounds received before capture, were repatriated early. Medically repatriated POWs, once recovered, were prohibited from serving on the battlefront or in lines of communication.[30] The Berne Agreement was translated into different languages and made available in both British and Ottoman prison camps. By mid-1918 the British Government, still concerned about what it now believed to be the 'deplorable condition' of prisoners in the Ottoman Empire, pushed for a revision to the Berne Agreement.[31] Instead of making prisoners go before a commission to determine their suitability for medical repatriation, the British wanted all prisoners who had been in captivity for longer than eighteen months to be exchanged.[32] By the time this policy could be agreed on, however, the war had ended.

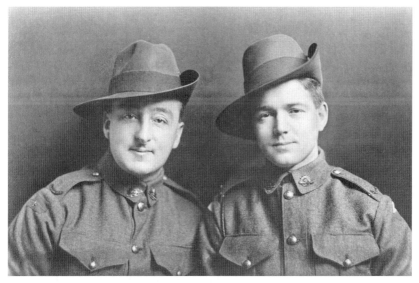

Medically repatriated POW Patrick O'Connor (left) with an Australian prisoner of the Germans, Philip Warburton Symonds. O'Connor's leg was amputated in Constantinople soon after his capture on Gallipoli; he was repatriated from captivity in the Ottoman Empire under the provisions of the Berne Agreement. (AWM P03236.020)

THE ROLE OF THE PROTECTING POWERS

While British politicians organised welfare efforts for the POWs, there was little they could do to ensure that these measures were implemented. Representatives of the protecting powers in the Ottoman Empire were charged with distributing official relief and executing any diplomatic arrangements. Protecting powers – neutral states that assume responsibility for the interests of belligerents during times of war – have been a figure of wars and conflicts throughout the world for years. During the Franco-Prussian War (1870–71) the United Kingdom took on the role of protecting power for the French; in the Sino-Japanese War (1894–95) the United States acted as protecting power for both parties; and during the Spanish/American conflict of 1898, France and Austria–Hungary assumed a joint protecting power role for the Spanish.[33] As ideas regarding the humane treatment of prisoners of war shifted, so came the understanding that prisoners of war were one of the interests of belligerents and therefore part of any protecting power's remit.

Several neutral states took on protecting power roles during the First World War. Between the outbreak of war in July 1914 and its own declaration of war in April 1917, the United States accepted responsibility for allied interests in Germany and the Ottoman Empire, and German and Ottoman interests in allied nations. In Constantinople, American Ambassador Henry Morgenthau was responsible for the interests of British (and therefore Australian) prisoners of war, including negotiations with the Ottoman Government on behalf of the British and vice versa. But the stalemate of the Gallipoli campaign meant that few prisoners were taken during 1915, and instead Morgenthau was busy compiling reports on his – and other diplomats' and missionaries' – observations of the deportations and massacres of Armenians throughout the empire. The stressful situation took its toll on Morgenthau's health, and he returned to the United States in January 1916.[34]

Abram Elkus arrived in Constantinople in April 1916 to replace Morgenthau. His arrival coincided with the fall of the Kut garrison, and Elkus was immediately thrust into negotiations between the British and Ottoman governments regarding the supply of food and comforts to the increased number of prisoners in Ottoman hands. With the funds sent by the British Government, he built on the preliminary work of the American YMCA regarding POW relief and set up a Constantinople-based committee dedicated to assisting the men in the camps. Two US Embassy staff members were seconded to the committee, and two British civilians and a

Dutch YMCA worker resident in the city – Dirk Johannes Van Bommel – were also involved.[35] The committee took over the YMCA building located next to the embassy and used it as their headquarters, where they met once every fortnight to discuss POW issues, and as a storeroom for supplies and to pack and inspect parcels. They arranged for the distribution of money and food parcels to the prisoners and stockpiled blankets, overcoats, and wool and cotton fabric for distribution around the camps. Clearly the Americans had not anticipated an early end to the war.[36]

The purchase, organisation and delivery of these goods proved challenging. The cost of basic items increased, the market for ready-made clothes was exhausted, and the price of cloth ballooned to more than seven times its pre-war price, from three piastres per square metre to twenty-two piastres (according to captive officer Ron McDonald, at this time five piastres equalled one shilling).[37] Elkus and his team also lamented the inefficiency of Ottoman authorities regarding notification of new prisoners of war or when prisoners were moved between camps. Such lack of communication made keeping track of new arrivals, and who had received what, extremely difficult, with the inevitable consequence that some prisoners missed out.

All supplies were sent through the Ottoman Red Crescent, the Ottoman counterpart to the British Red Cross, for distribution to different locations. The Americans sent itemised lists of the goods in each parcel to the prisoners for their acknowledgement, and confusion as to the origin of the supplies – prisoners believed they had come directly from the Red Crescent – meant they also added a US Embassy label. Before December 1916 the volume of goods that could be sent was restricted to twenty bales of forty kilos per day, but after some negotiation the Americans persuaded the Ottomans to double this allocation. An extra carriage on trains leaving one of Constantinople's main stations was also put at the Americans' disposal.[38]

As the war progressed and more prisoners were sent to scattered, isolated work camps, the American consuls at Smyrna, Mersina and Aleppo also became involved in POW welfare work. The number of prisoners needing assistance and the desperate condition of many of the men in these camps taxed the smaller consulates. Prisoners in the Taurus Mountains, for example, were supposed to be supplied by the Americans at Mersina, but the quantity of goods required overwhelmed the consulate staff. This explains, to some extent, why POWs who worked on the railway felt they often missed out on relief supplies. Nevertheless, by late January 1917 the US Embassy had equipped each

British prisoner of war with a suit of clothes suitable for the winter and could report the successful arrival of goods as diverse as quilts, socks, toothpaste, raincoats and Christmas puddings at various camps including Afyon, Belemedik, Ismidt and Angora.[39] The prisoners appreciated the efforts of the Americans; after the war David Boyle reported to AIF authorities that 'we were well clothed and looked after by the American Ambassador'.[40]

The success of US relief efforts can be attributed to the tireless efforts of Elkus' team, including Hoffman Philip, Chargé d'Affaires, in Constantinople. Elkus' negotiating skills in the face of divided Ottoman authorities were of significant benefit to the British Government and the prisoners.[41] He persuaded the Ottoman Government and military officials to increase the number of parcels provided and, when the postal authorities refused to accept embassy parcels in early 1917, he persuaded the Ottoman Minister for War Enver Pasha to permit the use of military transport to ensure the delivery of goods to the camps. Moreover, along with other American diplomats, he brokered an agreement with Austro-Hungarian authorities ensuring that relief supplies for prisoners in Ottoman captivity had free passage through their territories.[42]

As their official representative in the Ottoman Empire, the British Government relied on Elkus for advice on how to best support the prisoners. Often this meant following his recommendations regarding financial payments. For example, in early 1917, after discussions with Enver Pasha and reports from prisoners that the rations they received were insufficient, Elkus wrote a letter to the American Ambassador in London, which was forwarded to the Foreign Office, explaining that British POWs needed more money – a request that, as we have seen, was approved.[43] Elkus also drew attention to the fact that Indian officers received no welfare payments from the British and advised that a monthly allowance for these prisoners was necessary.[44] The American was also quick to protest against what he perceived to be unproductive diplomatic practices, specifically the threat of reprisals. As Heather Jones notes, the disconnect between international law and reality meant that reprisal actions were employed by belligerents to influence the enemy regarding POWs.[45] In January 1917, after the Foreign Office threatened to stop the passage of parcels to Ottoman prisoners in allied hands as an act of reprisal against the Ottoman Government's refusal to permit a neutral medical mission to visit British POWs, Elkus strongly suggested another course of action. 'I beg leave to state that this threat would in my opinion be ineffective and unwise,' he wrote.

> According to our information very few parcels are thus forwarded
> and the Government here appears to be indifferent as to how the
> ordinary Turkish prisoner is treated. Should such a threat be made the
> Turkish government would probably retaliate by forbidding the
> sending by this Embassy of food and clothing to the British
> prisoners ... which would result in more loss of life and greater
> suffering ... I will of course transmit this threat if you so instruct me
> but I believe that in the present case threatening is now of no value.[46]

The delicate nature of Elkus' role as intermediary is clear. On the basis of
his advice, the British abandoned their plans for reprisal action.[47]

Elkus' diplomatic skills were also used to arrange for the inspection of
prison camps. Rumours of poor treatment, especially after the capitulation of Kut, had been a point of contention for the British Government
since mid-1916. By December of that year they believed the conditions in
Ottoman prison camps to be 'a disgrace to humanity', and frustrations
rose over the seeming reluctance of the Ottoman authorities to allow
objective reports of camp conditions.[48] Elkus continually encouraged
the Ottomans to permit inspections; he stressed the need for reciprocity,
arguing that American inspectors were able to visit Ottoman POWs in
camps in Malta and Egypt, and that Ottoman reluctance to allow similar
inspections fuelled ideas of mistreatment: 'The continued refusal of the
Imperial Government to allow this Embassy to send representatives to
visit the prisoners of war will doubtless create the impression that the
conditions existing in the prisoner internment camps in Turkey are so bad
that the Ottoman Government is unwilling to have them inspected and
made known.'[49] This approach worked, and in early 1917 two Swiss
representatives from the International Committee of the Red Cross,
M. Boissier and Dr Adolf Vischer, were invited to inspect the Ottoman
camps.[50] However, their visit was not without restrictions. Boissier and
Vischer were only permitted to visit certain camps and were not allowed
to mix freely with the prisoners, which Elkus argued affected the reliability
of their report. He emphasised the importance of comprehensive inspections of the camps in order to ascertain the prisoners' needs, stressing in a
March letter to the Ottoman Government that 'it is absolutely essential
that the Embassy obtain first-hand knowledge of those needs through its
own representatives'.[51]

The Americans continued to act on behalf of the British Government
until their own declaration of war against Germany in April 1917, when
responsibility for British interests in the Ottoman Empire passed to the

Netherlands Legation in Constantinople. The Dutch POW efforts were led by Van Bommel, the YMCA worker previously seconded to the US relief committee. Like their predecessor, however, the Dutch were also hampered by restricted access to supplies and by high rates of inflation. Many prisoners commented on the poor quality of clothing sent by the Dutch to the camps and the seemingly sporadic ways in which parcels were distributed. David Boyle, who was full of praise for the Americans, felt 'the Netherlands Ambassador did not trouble about us at all as he should have done' and believed his work for the prisoners 'should be inquired into'. Other Australians were similarly scathing. Harry Brown wrote: 'The American embassy clothing was good, but that issued by the Dutch Embassy was very poor stuff and the winter clothing came at the end of the winter too late for cold weather. Owing to working conditions this clothing and boots only used to last 3 months.'[52] Inferences of neglect and poor administration were, however, unfair. By the time the Dutch took over POW relief, the number of allied prisoners scattered throughout the Ottoman Empire was estimated at around 15 000. The Dutch staff entrusted to ensure the welfare of this group numbered only twenty-five.[53] Indeed, the British Government recognised the enormous size of the task before the Dutch, and explained that it would cover the costs of any additional staff required.[54]

The Dutch also faced other challenges, including one case of misappropriation of funds. In an effort to ensure the arrival of relief to southern railway camps, the Dutch had established a connection with the Spanish Consul at Aleppo. They were sent significant funds every month from the British money forwarded to the Dutch in Constantinople on the understanding that they would supply extra money, food, clothing and supplies to the prisoners in the railway camps. However, during an inspection tour of the camps in early 1918, an Ottoman Red Crescent delegate observed that the staff at the Spanish Consul appeared to be more concerned with their own well-being than that of the prisoners:

> One of the Consul's principal assistants is a certain Mr Prince, who was pennyless [sic] before the war and is now worth LT15,000. He spends each night several hundred of pounds in gambling ... All these men are supplying for the prisoners is bad: boots bad, clothing bad, felt [for bedding] useless ... Not only Prince but the whole staff should be dismissed. They are all personally interested in the buying and selling of prisoners [sic] supplies. They buy things not because the prisoners need them but because they want to buy them.[55]

It is little wonder that, in the prisoners' eyes, the Dutch did not seem to have the same success as the Americans regarding the despatch and delivery of relief parcels and payments.

Just as they had done with Elkus, the British relied on Dutch discretion to distribute payments and supplies. They entrusted them to make use of the revised amount of funds after increased payments were approved, requesting that they 'may be good enough to treat them as confidential ... or make it clear that they are maxim rates and not to be issued universally nor irrespective of actual needs'.[56] The British also depended on the Dutch to improve the Aleppo connection, and expressed 'their best thanks' for intervening.[57]

Like the Americans before them, the Dutch also worked to secure inspections of the camps. In keeping with the arrangements set out in the Berne Agreement, three Dutch delegates were permitted to visit certain prison camps between May and August 1918 and report their findings. Dr E. Menten, J. Van Spengler and Van Bommel provided a comprehensive report regarding the condition of the prisoners in various camps, the accommodation in which they were housed, the temperament of the different camp commandants, and the type and amount of work in which prisoners were engaged.[58] Their report was duly forwarded to the British in late August 1918, who expressed their gratitude for the important insight into the lives of the prisoners and suggested avenues for the Dutch to pursue regarding improvements.[59] The cessation of hostilities meant such improvements were never implemented.

Aid agency efforts

Charitable organisations and aid agencies formed the third branch of the POWs' external network of support. In the early stages of the war independent organisations provided captives with food, clothes, money and comforts. One of the first schemes established to provide assistance to British prisoners was Lady Victoria Herbert's 'Scheme for British Prisoners of War'. Lady Victoria, a goddaughter of Queen Victoria, started her London-based scheme as an act of *noblesse oblige* just after the declaration of war, and sent parcels of food and tobacco to British prisoners in Germany. She encouraged other benevolent supporters to 'adopt' prisoners of war in both Germany and the Ottoman Empire; Lady Victoria herself adopted Australians Martin Troy and William Elston, both captured on Gallipoli, and sent them monthly care parcels.[60] Many British prisoners also received comforts from Regimental Care Committees. British regiments were often raised according to locale, and these care committees operated on the premise that men and women from the particular region would look after 'their' sick, wounded and POWs. In the first years of the war a staggering number of care committees and other charitable organisations aimed at POW relief – more than a thousand, according to the War Office – were operating in Britain.[61]

Initially, there were no restrictions on the size, form or number of parcels sent to captives in enemy countries. But by December 1916 the numbers of British and Dominion prisoners in enemy hands had increased, and the amount and type of parcels that could be sent to POWs was regulated. This intervention was explained as necessary to stop what was perceived to be a confused and uneven system of unofficial aid, and to prevent food and other goods being used by the enemy. The War Office claimed that lack of restrictions on the sending of parcels resulted in an unfair distribution of comforts among prisoners; some prisoners in Germany were reported to receive very little while others received far more than necessary.[62] Those in the fortunate position of being in receipt of excess parcels were known to have sold food to the Germans. This meant, according to the War Office, that 'charitable organisations and persons who send parcels without due inquiry as to the need for them … run the risk of depleting the food supplies in this country in favour of the enemy'.[63] Clothing restrictions also applied: just as the War Office did not want British food falling into enemy hands, neither did it want to be providing the enemy with uniforms or other clothes.[64]

To ensure more centralised control and that War Office regulations were complied with, the British Government designated responsibility for charitable relief for POWs to one London-based agency, the Central Prisoners of War Committee (CPWC). In its official role, the CPWC coordinated and controlled existing relief efforts, although not without some initial problems. As John Yarnall notes, the CPWC's rush to control all POW relief caused significant tensions between it and the existing care committees and other associations. A British Parliamentary Joint Committee Report of July 1917 into the efficacy of the CPWC argued that representatives of local committees should be incorporated into CPWC administration and work. The new, enlarged CPWC proved more successful.[65]

The CPWC authorised other committees and associations to take on aspects of POW welfare. This included the care of certain groups of prisoners, like the Indian Soldiers Fund's remit over all Indian POWs, the provision of specialised items, such as the Invalid Comforts Fund, which sent medicines and medical supplies to prison camps, and the British Prisoners of War Book Scheme, which, in association with the Department of Education, sent POWs scholarly books and other reading material. In December 1916, the CPWC authorised the Australian Red Cross Prisoners of War Department to assume formal responsibility for the relief of Australian POWs in Germany and the Ottoman Empire. This organisation had operated in London since July, after the capture of approximately 470 Australians at Fromelles. The daughter of a Victorian judge, Mary Elizabeth Chomley, who was living in London and working in a hospital, became the department's Honorary Secretary.[66]

The Australian POW Department was divided into subunits staffed by volunteers, primarily other Australian women living in London. These different sections organised food parcels, clothing (a prisoner's measurements were taken from his attestation papers), correspondence, finances and general administration. As soon as an Australian was officially confirmed as a prisoner, the POW Department added his name to a central register for inclusion on separate section indexes and sent him a letter outlining their work.[67] All correspondence with the POWs was meticulously recorded, which helped workers keep track of the location and condition of individual men.

Chomley and her team appreciated that the prisoners in the Ottoman Empire were in a 'very serious' position.[68] The department's food section sent each prisoner three 10lb food parcels per fortnight (War Office regulations stipulated a rank-based system of supplying POWs with food – privates were to receive 60lb per month and officers 100lb – but Chomley adopted a more egalitarian approach).[69] Concerns about the quality of foodstuffs available in England at the time, and the desire to 'maintain a standard of excellence', meant that the department's parcels always included Australian goods. The arrival of such items as IXL jam impressed the prisoners, who 'expressed themselves very much delighted' to receive such reminders of home.[70] Packages of cigarettes and tobacco were also sent regularly, along with parcels containing items specifically requested by POWs that were purchased using either money allotted to the department by the prisoner, or funds authorised to be deducted from his pay.[71]

Like the government departments and the protecting powers, the POW Department faced several challenges in its work for the prisoners. Although parcels were sent regularly, their actual arrival could not be guaranteed. By March 1917, for example, Chomley had still not received

The staff of the Australian Red Cross Prisoner of War Department in London. Honorary Secretary Mary Elizabeth Chomley (seated fifth from left, front row) and her team provided vital assistance to Australian POWs in enemy hands during the First World War. (H2013.234/7, State Library of Victoria)

any acknowledgements of parcels sent some five months earlier, while parcels of underclothes and boots sent to each prisoner in January 1917 took, in some cases, nearly a year to reach the intended recipients.[72] Such low rates of acknowledgement and delays were frustrating, as it indicated that the hard work of the department staff did not always benefit the POWs. War Office and CPWC regulations and restrictions also proved trying, while the day-to-day work of the department was hampered by the location and condition of its offices. Their initial premises were badly ventilated, dirty and poorly lit. The limited size of the office restricted the number of staff, which meant that those who could work worked long hours. Chomley vented her frustration in a post-war report: 'We lost many good workers who did not feel inclined to face the discomforts, and possible injury to their health, which might have been caused working under these circumstances. Those who remained often looked shockingly ill, and it was only their interest in their work and their realisation of its vital importance that made them remain at their post.'[73] Matters were also complicated by the fact that the department's administrative premises were in a different part of the city from the parcel packing rooms. Wartime transportation restrictions made travelling around London difficult, and there was a sense of disconnect between the two sections.

Chomley and the POW Department improvised to meet these challenges. Plans for the provision of parcels, money and other comforts were continually revised and refined. In an effort to overcome some of the limitations regarding the number of food parcels that could be sent, ten shillings was included in the fortnightly packages to enable the prisoners to purchase extras. When the parcel post was stopped altogether because of the closing of Austrian borders or the British Post Office's refusal to accept parcels owing to blockages, the POW Department sent remittances of cash instead.[74] In December 1917, the department moved to new, bigger premises. Staff numbers increased and morale improved, although the separation of administration and packing rooms – and the attendant difficulties of coordinating the two sections – remained. In her final report on the work of the department Chomley even admitted, in at least one instance, to breaking War Office and CPWC regulations. In January 1918, contrary to restrictions, she authorised the despatch of clothing parcels to all Australian prisoners, which were successfully delivered.[75]

The work of the POW Department and the support and succour they provided was gratefully recognised by the prisoners. By the end of the war Chomley and her team had organised the despatch of 395 595 food and 36 339 clothing parcels to Australians in enemy hands.[76] Chomley often received correspondence from the Australians thanking the department for its efforts, even from those who did not regularly receive such parcels. In one such letter, submariner Benjamin Talbot's pleasure at receiving Red Cross comforts is clear:

> You must excuse me writing these few lines to you but I think it my duty to write and thank you for parcels I have received through the Australian Red Cross. My first parcel I received was on my return from hospital to prisoners camp, just think of my surprise to be able to make a cup of tea, especially with milk and sugar [sic] a thing that had left my life as I thought, bacon and jam at my service. Oh, imagine my surprise when I received the other two, I must thank you again and again.[77]

Alongside other benefits, the department's food parcels offered the prisoners the ability to supplement rations and include familiar items in their diet. Indeed, after the war, as Robert McColl explained to AIF authorities, 'it was mainly by our Red Cross parcels that we existed'.[78]

Other aid agencies also worked for the benefit of the POWs. The International Committee of the Red Cross (ICRC), based in Geneva, Switzerland, established a POW agency almost immediately after the declaration of war.[79] As a neutral organisation, the ICRC's mandate was to monitor the belligerents' treatment of prisoners in accordance with the Hague Convention and to facilitate the transfer of information about all prisoners of war between enemy states. The committee also operated as a channel through which correspondence and money could be sent to those in enemy hands – indeed, the POW Department forwarded cash remittances to Australians in Turkey through the ICRC.[80] Inspections of prison camps were often conducted by ICRC representatives, as were negotiations regarding early repatriation of POWs and agreements for the internment of the sick, wounded and maimed in neutral territories.

The Ottoman Red Crescent also played a key role in the dissemination of aid and welfare to the POWs. Despite allegations of inefficiency by the frustrated Americans, and accusations of corruption and deceit by at least one prisoner, several Australians commented favourably on the work of Red Crescent officials.[81] Leslie Luscombe remembered a positive experience with Red Crescent representatives at Angora in December 1915. Luscombe believed the officials were anxious to impress the British prisoners, and he permitted them to take supplies of linen, cutlery and other household items from an Armenian warehouse in the town to furnish their accommodation.[82] Other prisoners also stated how an Ottoman official responded to grievances against the Afyon commandant by having the commandant removed from his post and tried for misconduct.[83]

A comprehensive account of Red Crescent activity is documented in the 1918 report of Hussein Rifki Bey, an official of the organisation who spent nearly four months touring prison camps throughout the empire. Rifki Bey distributed supplies on behalf of the protecting powers and compiled a summary of the different camps, explaining how he had improved conditions by impressing upon Ottoman authorities in Constantinople the need to make the censorship of reading material for prisoners more efficient, arranging for prisoners to be given wood and charcoal for heating and cooking free of charge, and improving the prisoners' access to medicines and medical facilities at Afyon and camps along the railway line.[84] Rifki Bey was also instrumental in highlighting the abuse of British funds by Spanish Consul staff at Aleppo. The Dutch delegate who received Rifki Bey's report stated: 'It is quite evident that

Rifki Bey has done a fine piece of work and has everywhere acted in the interest of and done his best for the prisoners.'[85]

In the latter stages of the war another influential committee dedicated to prisoners in the Ottoman Empire was established in Britain. The Prisoners in Turkey Committee (PITC) was formed at the insistence of Captain (later Sir) Edward Keeling, a British officer captured at Kut who later escaped. Keeling believed that British POWs suffered from the inefficiency of a government obsessed with victory rather than their maintenance. Reflecting in his 1924 memoir on the restrictive regulations regarding POW aid, Keeling railed that the prisoners 'fell between two stools during the war', and stated that the War Office 'cared as little for them as butchers for meatless days'.[86] The PITC included representatives of existing care committees, relatives of officer prisoners and other interested and influential people. They pushed for better awareness of the captives' conditions and the lessening of War Office restrictions in light of their specific situation. The PITC also prioritised the communication of rules and regulations regarding POW relief work to the families of those in Ottoman captivity.[87] The PITC was becoming a formidable and, for the War Office, somewhat frustrating force when the Armistice was signed and the war ended.

Providing aid and support to POWs in the Ottoman Empire was clearly no easy task. Concerns about the extent to which the Ottoman Government would – or indeed could – provide for POWs, particularly in light of the 'same footing' principle embedded in the Hague Convention, meant that relief efforts for the prisoners focused primarily on improving conditions and treatment, and the British Government, the protecting powers and the Red Cross POW Department worked within their respective mandates – negotiating multiple challenges of their own along the way – to mitigate the discomfort and distress of the men in the camps. This official welfare work was organised mainly from London and within the Ottoman Empire but, as chapter 5 reveals, the resonances of captivity were felt in Australia too.

CHAPTER 5

REACTIONS AT HOME

Captivity in the Ottoman Empire posed certain challenges for the men in the camps and those involved in the provision of official welfare and support to the prisoners. But Australians at home also felt the effects of imprisonment – both in the public and private spheres – as they became aware of, and subsequently engaged with, the plight of the POWs, and as they too absorbed and adjusted to this new wartime reality.

PRESS COVERAGE OF CAPTIVITY

Australians learned about the POWs chiefly through the press. The first mention in Australian newspapers of allied forces taken prisoner by the Ottomans came with the report of the sinking of the British submarine HMS *E15*, which, in an attempt to break through the Dardanelles, had run aground on the morning of 17 April 1915. Several members of the crew, including the captain, were killed, and the remainder were taken prisoner. The loss of the submarine was lamented and, in a reflection of ideas about the potential brutality of the Ottoman enemy, it was reported that the rescue of the stricken survivors was 'a matter for congratulations'. As historian John Williams writes, there was initially 'a fog over the Dardanelles', and further information about the Gallipoli campaign trickled in slowly.[1] In the meantime, however, a communiqué received from Constantinople reporting the defeat of the allies and the capture of hundreds of Australian troops was published in several Australian newspapers. The message was reprinted under such headlines as 'Turks claim victory and to have imprisoned Australians' and sensationally detailed the repulse of the Australian landing parties back to their boats, the supposed defection of French Muslim soldiers to the Ottoman ranks, and the capture of more than 200 prisoners, including a captain and a lieutenant.[2] The bulk of this message was eventually reported as fake (the last statement was in fact correct, as Captain Ron McDonald and Lieutenant William Elston were both taken prisoner on the first day of the landings), but for readers, the prospect of Australian troops being captured by the enemy was brought to the fore.

The loss of the submarine HMAS *AE2* provided the first confirmed report of Australians taken prisoner by the Ottomans. On 12 May 1915, several Australian newspapers published a British Press Bureau statement outlining the fate of the submarine and the capture of its crew. The next day, the Melbourne *Argus* printed a full crew list, with the disclaimer that it was not yet known which ratings were actually on board the submarine at the time of capture. As news of the ill-fated August offensive reached home, reports that more Australians had fallen into enemy hands were published. But any information about their condition or the treatment they received from their captors, or exact numbers of POWs, remained rather vague. In the House of Representatives in June, July and August, government ministers reported that they, and other officials, were unsure as to exactly how many Australians were in Ottoman hands and that they could not envisage when such details would be available.[3]

The absence of information about the prisoners, coupled with what media scholars Kerry McCallum and Peter Putnis claim was a reliance on purposefully 'glorified reporting' in the first half of the war to meet stringent censorship requirements and maintain morale at home, meant that early portrayals by the press of captivity in the Ottoman Empire were generally reassuring.[4] In June 1915 it was reported that the American Ambassador in Constantinople would act as intermediary between the Ottomans and the British on all matters regarding British and Dominion POWs. In the same month, an article in the *Argus* stated that those in captivity were, according to the Americans, 'being treated well' and were 'in good health'.[5]

Many of these early reports echoed the style and content of the press coverage of the most recent British experience of wartime captivity: that of the prisoners of the Boers during the South African War of 1899–1902. With some exceptions, Boer military POW camps were portrayed as well equipped and relatively comfortable, and it was reported that prisoners of the Boers enjoyed a fair degree of liberty, including the ability to purchase beer and newspapers.[6] A feature article in a May 1900 edition of the *Queenslander* stated that prisoners at Pretoria, the site of a main Boer prison camp, were treated well and provided with adequate rations and medical care. One POW even told the article's author that the prisoners at Pretoria were treated like gentlemen, stating: '[T]here has not been a hard word spoken to us since we were taken prisoner.'[7] Fifteen years later, the *Queenslander* published an article based on an extract from a letter written by an Australian captured on Gallipoli that portrayed captivity in the Ottoman Empire in a similar vein: 'I am living real well but it is a darned lazy life. I study most of the day and play bridge or chess at night ... the Turkish officials are exceedingly kind and courteous. Most of the time I was at their headquarters and in Constantinople I was treated more like a guest than a prisoner.'[8] Other reports reinforced this idea of a comfortable captivity. Another *Argus* piece, headlined 'As comfortable as possible', drew upon a letter from a British captive who explained that 'we receive very kind and considerate treatment'.[9]

Newspaper coverage of the prisoners remained limited throughout 1916. While some of the major papers of the capital cities – including the *Brisbane Courier*, Melbourne *Argus*, *Sydney Morning Herald* and Adelaide *Register* – printed articles related to the POWs, these reports focused on lists of names of prisoners, instructions on how to send letters to the prison camps, or the work performed by the protecting powers and aid agencies to provide POWs with money and provisions. Very little was reported about the actual conditions of captivity or the treatment the prisoners received. Although it was noted that information about the captives was limited and communication with the camps was difficult, articles entitled 'Anzacs in Turkey have no immediate wants' or 'Turks kind to prisoners' continued to portray the prisoners as living quite comfortable lives.[10] Published around the same time as Australians went into action on the Western Front, these articles offered an idea of captivity that stood in stark contrast to the growing lists of dead and wounded from France. Moreover, they indicate that public concerns for the POWs – who were reportedly treated more like guests than prisoners – were not particularly great.

In mid-1917, however, as enlistment numbers continued to decline and support for the war among the increasingly divided Australian population faltered, ideas and impressions of captivity in the Ottoman Empire under-went a drastic change. The numbers of Australian POWs increased after the Battle of Romani in August 1916 and the second attack on Gaza in April 1917, while the numbers of Australians in German hands had similarly risen after the fighting at Fromelles and Bullecourt. The Australian Government exploited this heightened awareness of Australians in captivity, and used the treatment of prisoners of war by the enemy as a strategy both to encourage eligible men to enlist and to boost support for the war effort. The publication of an impassioned speech calling for new recruits given by the Minister for Defence, Senator George Pearce, outside Melbourne Town Hall in July 1917, marked a significant shift in rhetoric regarding POWs in the Ottoman Empire and their experiences of captivity. Pearce told his audience about 'the callous brutality and the inhuman treatment of the unfortunate soldiers who have had the awful fate of falling into the hands of the Turks' and stated that the stories coming from the Ottoman prison camps 'are such that would make your blood run cold'.[11] In keeping with historian Bill Gammage's claim that shame replaced patriotic fervour in Australia as the major inducement for recruitment from 1917 on, Pearce argued that it was only more eligible men enlisting that could save the prisoners and bring those responsible for the mistreatment of Australian servicemen to justice: 'Is it conceivable that there are men in this country whose souls are so dead that they will stand by and take no part in a war in which victory for the Allies means that vengeance shall be executed upon that Ottoman Government for its cruelties perpetrated upon our soldiers?'[12]

Australia was not the only belligerent nation to use POWs for recruitment purposes and to encourage continued support for the war. In Britain, posters depicting wounded British POWs being deliberately mistreated and humiliated by their German captors were in circulation. One of the most famous was titled 'Red Cross or Iron Cross'. It portrayed a visibly wounded British prisoner watching a German nurse pour a glass of water onto the ground in front of him, above the caption: 'There is no woman in Britain who would do it. There is no woman in Britain who will forget it.'[13]

Pearce drew on long-standing Orientalist discourses to frame the prisoners' experiences of captivity in such a way that would resonate with the Australian public. His comments about 'callous brutality' and 'inhuman treatment' echoed pre-war ideas about the treatment of Bulgarians and Armenians in the Ottoman Empire. But in a notable departure from these ideas, Pearce emphasised that the Ottoman soldiers themselves were not to blame for the mistreatment of POWs. Instead, he encouraged Australians to blame the Ottoman Government and, above all, the German military who, as we have seen, were portrayed as having 'tricked' the Ottomans into the war.[14] By emphasising the suffering of

Australian POWs in the Ottoman Empire, Pearce hoped to shame eligible men into joining the fight to beat the real enemy: the Germans.

From this point, media coverage of the prisoners of war in the Ottoman Empire became increasingly alarming. Reports detailing the suspension of the parcel post between Britain and Turkey and the fact that the prisoners were not acknowledging receipt of comforts packages sent by the Red Cross POW Department reinforced Pearce's rather grim image of captivity. Public anxieties were compounded by reports from prisoners' relatives that some men had not been heard of for nearly six months. In November 1917, the *Sydney Morning Herald* printed a letter to the editor written by a prominent rural journalist, William Sherrie, in which he hinted at the possibility of a high casualty rate among the POWs. Sherrie, who was also the father of captive cameleer Noel Sherrie, stated: '[O]ur boys who have made the great sacrifice for their country and for humanity might be perishing of starvation or dying from pestilence.'[15] Comparisons between conditions in German and Ottoman POW camps were in Germany's favour, with newspaper reports stating that prisoners of the Ottomans were 'generally worse off than in Germany'.[16]

In early 1918 stories of the poor condition of those in Ottoman captivity became more prevalent as reports from escaped British prisoners and those repatriated on medical grounds gave further credence to ideas of mistreatment of POWs. Ex-prisoners arriving in England spoke to government and aid agency officials of the life of a captive in the Ottoman Empire being one of bad food, hard work and regular bouts of debilitating sickness. The first two Australians to reach England from captivity in Anatolia – Patrick O'Connor and John Davern, both medically repatriated in early 1918 – gave interviews to Colonel Murdoch of the Red Cross, which were then printed in Australian newspapers. According to O'Connor and Davern, the prisoners had received 'passable treatment at first' but then suffered from worsening conditions. In their interview, the two men stated that they 'unanimously condemn the unfailing inhuman treatment they received'.[17] Despite the somewhat questionable nature of this evidence, O'Connor and Davern's stories added weight to the idea that captivity in the Ottoman Empire was not the easy existence portrayed earlier in the war. The Australian Government again looked to the POWs for recruitment purposes; a representative of the Prime Minister's Department requested that the Governor-General ask the British for permission to publish in the press an official report into the conditions of the Ottoman POW camps, as they 'considered it would probably improve recruiting'.[18]

Updated information regarding the fate of British troops taken after the capitulation of Kut-al-Amara further shook the image of a relatively comfortable captivity. The arduous march from Kut was reported under such headlines as 'Sufferings of British prisoners: Men captured at Kut', 'The brutal Turk: Fate of Kut prisoners' and 'Shocking Turkish revelations: Intense sufferings of the Kut garrison', which accused the enemy of deliberate mistreatment. Such allegations led to discussion of the true nature of POW casualties; in June 1918, the Sydney periodical *Triad* highlighted 'rumours ... that many of the Australians who have died in Turkey from one stated cause and another have really died from exposure and slow starvation'.[19] Articles relating to developing military policies regarding the repatriation of POWs gave further currency to the idea that poor conditions had taken a toll on the captives. The *Brisbane Courier* explained to readers in early 1918 that, at the end of hostilities, repatriated prisoners were to be treated as invalids and would return to Australia only 'when their health and other conditions permit'.[20]

Although it is impossible to tell how – or even whether – these shifting representations influenced enlistment rates, the sensationalised accusations of brutality and mistreatment did foster a change in public engagement with captivity. One of the results of this change was criticism of perceived government inaction to ameliorate the prisoners' lot, particularly claims that the captives had been abandoned by the government that called upon them to volunteer to fight. In May 1918, William Sherrie again wrote to the editor of the *Sydney Morning Herald*. Strident in his criticism of the Australian Government's response to the POW situation, Sherrie was also far more direct with his concerns for the prisoners. 'It has been mentioned', he wrote, that 'Australian prisoners are succumbing to attacks of "fever and dysentery":

In other words, they are perishing of starvation, resulting from bad and insufficient food, aggravated by unhygienic conditions. And while this heartbreaking tragedy is slowly working itself out, while our lads (who gave their all that Australia might remain safe and free from enslavement by a ferocious alien Power) are being slowly done to death under circumstances of unimaginable cruelty and misery, their bodily sufferings [are] no doubt accentuated by the inexpressibly bitter reflection that they have been practically abandoned by their own country.[21]

Sherrie asked Pearce how long relatives of the POWs would have to put up with the 'seeming indifference' of the government regarding those who had 'the misfortune' to fall into enemy hands.[22] Sherrie had seemingly internalised the stigma of surrender – evidenced by his reminder that the prisoners 'gave their all' before they were captured – and felt what he termed the 'let-someone-else-look-after-our-men doctrine' of the government in relation to prisoners of war was a 'cowardly attitude' that belittled the sacrifices of the prisoners.[23]

Some newspapers also professed outrage at the perceived passivity of Pearce and the government. An article in an October edition of the Adelaide *Advertiser* relating the formation of the Prisoners in Turkey Committee in London argued that Australia should form a similar organisation. 'The question is', the newspaper asked, 'what is Australia going to do about it?'

> Does she know how many of her prisoners in Turkey are living or dead? Does she care? She has paid and equipped her men in a way that had made them the envy of their soldier comrades. By their magnificent gallantry they have won for themselves and her the admiration of the world. Are her care of and pride in them to fail when they have the misfortune to fall into captivity? The fate of the British prisoners there is also at last – thanks to the Prisoners in Turkey Committee – rousing widespread anxiety and attention. Is Australia alone to say nothing in defence of her sons who have suffered so much?[24]

But accusations of government inaction were misguided. As we have seen, the diplomatic circumstances of the time meant that the Australian Government was reliant on Britain and the protecting powers to communicate with the Ottoman Government and implement aid to the prisoners. Pearce was not in a position to publicly proclaim Australian government assistance to the POWs.

PATRIOTIC ENDEAVOURS AND FUNDRAISING

Australian awareness of, and engagement with, the POWs also occurred through the medium of patriotic work. One of the first attempts at home to connect with the prisoners in the Ottoman Empire was the work of Rita Duffy. As a young woman with relatives of her own away at the war, Duffy was anxious to contribute to the supply of comforts destined for the men at the front. But her self-professed inability to sew pyjamas or knit socks meant that she developed a different method of providing solace to Australians overseas. Having heard of the capture of several Australians on Gallipoli, Duffy took it upon herself to write to the prisoners. 'Down

I sat – pen in hand – with a double sheet of foolscap in front of me,' she explained. 'I began to write to the Australian Prisoners of War in Turkey ... I addressed them as "my dear unknown brothers" and tried to convey to them, by mentioning "blue skies" and "good crops" etc that things were going fairly well in Australia, and that they were not forgotten.'[25] Her letter, dated 6 September 1915, reached the Australians at Angora later that year and was then circulated among other Australian prisoners at Afyon. It was the first letter from Australia delivered to those men captured in the Dardanelles and was received warmly. Duffy's correspondence with the Australians continued until the Armistice, and she struck up strong connections with the POWs. Indeed, when Duffy married in 1917, several prisoners wrote to send their congratulations.[26]

Other efforts for the prisoners rested on the more organised work of patriotic associations. Historian Melanie Oppenheimer has written extensively about the vast array of patriotic organisations and charitable funds established in Australia from 1914 onwards. These organisations aimed to provide assistance to Australian servicemen and their dependants as well as other international victims of war, and were based on the same principles as those established during the Boer War: public subscription, fundraising and private donations. During the First World War participation in, or donation to, these organisations and myriad funds were a way for those at home to express their patriotism and show support for Australian troops and their families. The significance of public desire to contribute to the war effort is reflected in the strong response to the work of these organisations, with approximately £14 000 000 being raised during the four years of the war.[27]

During the early years of the war there was little government control over patriotic work. If an individual or a group possessed the necessary networks and finances to send money or comforts overseas, they were free to do so. One such organisation established early in the war by a group of women in Melbourne identified the POWs as worthy recipients of their work. In April 1916 the Victoria League of Victoria, together with the Lady Mayoress' Patriotic League, organised the shipment of three cases of books to Australian captives in the Ottoman Empire. The Melbourne ladies' efforts reflect early Australian understandings of captivity – as it had been reported the men were 'kindly treated', the Victoria League claimed that they had sent the books to help alleviate the prisoners' 'extremely dull' lives.[28]

The Australian Red Cross was one of the largest and most extensive patriotic associations in operation during the war. Lady Helen Munro

Ferguson, wife of Governor-General Sir Ronald Munro Ferguson, established the Australian Branch of the British Red Cross Society in Melbourne soon after the declaration of hostilities, and encouraged the wives of each state's governor to inaugurate their own branches. The Red Cross had a strong presence in wartime Australia. The national headquarters, presided over by Lady Helen, was situated in Government House, Melbourne, and divisions were founded in every Australian state. A multitude of town, suburb and country branches were also established; according to Ernest Scott, official historian of the Australian home effort during the war, there was 'no hamlet or township ... too small for the formation of a red cross [sic] branch'.[29] With its vice-regal patronage and appeal to Australians from all social classes, the Australian Red Cross was a chief supporter of various war causes. Under its auspices clothing, medical aids and other goods were sent to Australian troops at the front; rehabilitation and convalescent programs were organised for sick and wounded returned soldiers; female volunteers were trained to work as nurses in both civilian and military hospitals and convalescent homes; food depots and kitchens were established for the benefit of soldiers' dependants; and funds were raised for victims of war overseas.

The founder of the Australian Branch of the British Red Cross Society, Lady Helen Munro Ferguson, wife of Governor-General Sir Ronald Munro Ferguson (B3862, State Library of South Australia)

The Red Cross was also a key provider of support to Australian prisoners of war. As we have seen, when the provision of food and comforts to POWs became, at the British Government's insistence, more centralised and regulated, the Australian Red Cross POW Department in London assumed responsibility for all relief work relating to Australian prisoners of war in Germany and the Ottoman Empire. The Red Cross in Australia bolstered its efforts through the formation of the Red Cross POW Fund (RCPF). Its goal was to provide financial assistance to the POW Department to help with the expense of relief parcels, which, as the numbers of prisoners grew, became increasingly costly.

The desire to supply aid to Australian POWs increased from mid-1917 as public awareness of captivity grew. The increasingly stark impressions of captivity portrayed in the Australian press were mirrored in the work and rhetoric of the Red Cross as it also used a narrative of suffering to press for donations. Articles and advertisements in newspapers reported the work of the POW Department in London, and tapped into impressions of Australian prisoners of war as brave but unfortunate men. Such representation of POWs by patriotic associations was also common in other nations. Historian Brian Feltman claims that humanitarian organisations from belligerent nations often portrayed prisoners 'in less than flattering terms'.[30] Such images were not always easy for the captives themselves to accept – as Feltman writes, 'prisoners took little comfort in being portrayed as disarmed soldiers begging for the enemy's mercy' – yet reliance on Red Cross parcels and funds to supplement rations left those in enemy hands with little choice other than to accept charity.[31] Maurice Delpratt understood how POWs were represented in Australia, explaining to his sister that 'we are humble in knowing what useless nuisances we are'. He stressed in a letter home that the prisoners appreciated the work that was performed in their name, explaining that 'we are proud that we are of those same people who make such sacrifices for us'. Indeed, at his camp at Hadjikiri, the prisoners drank a special toast to those who helped ameliorate their lot – at meal times the men would raise their mugs and say, '[W]e think of those who thought of us.'[32]

Donations to the RCPF came from various sources and in different amounts. Many Australians gave their time and money to the POWs' cause. An October 1916 edition of the *Argus*, for example, indicates that several Melbourne citizens donated amounts varying from ten shillings to £1 to the fund throughout the month, while the New South Wales division of the Red Cross received £2147 in donations to the RCPF during the

1916–17 financial year.[33] Although donations and contributions to the RCPF were usually for the benefit of all Australian POWs, occasionally money was donated for a specific prisoner. Once these monies reached London, they were held against the prisoner's name and could be used to supplement basic food parcels, or to purchase specific items requested by the captive.[34] Family members were naturally the chief contributors for particular men, but others also donated on behalf of certain individuals. Sometimes a Red Cross branch associated with a locality from which a prisoner came made a donation in his name: the Coolamon Branch in the Riverina region of New South Wales regularly donated £1 for Wagga Wagga local John Kerin of the *AE2*, while Stanley Jordan received a monthly donation from the Soldier's Aid Society in his hometown of Lismore, New South Wales.[35]

The RCPF also relied on the fundraising efforts of various small groups. In Queensland in late December 1917, the Western Women War Workers' Association, an organisation of women in the isolated western rural districts of the state, paid £5 to the RCPF.[36] Other funds also donated some of their earnings. The Victorian Education Department's War Relief Fund, inaugurated in the same month that war broke out, was one such patriotic endeavour that gave to the prisoners' cause. This fund was based on the efforts and work of teachers, administrators and children from state schools across Victoria. They were generous with the money they raised and goods they produced; by October 1916, the fund had already donated more than £1256 to the Victorian branch of the Red Cross, £3250 to the French Red Cross, materials worth more than £11 000 for Australian troops overseas, £10 000 to Caulfield Repatriation Hospital, £400 to the Anzac Buffet in London, and nearly £20 000 to benefit Belgian, Serbian, Montenegrin and Polish civilian casualties.[37] The RCPF was also given £1500.[38] As historian Rosalie Triolo writes, the Victorian Education Department was a large organisation with access to a vast number of volunteers and support staff for its war relief work, which helps explain its many donations to various causes.[39]

Donations also came to the RCPF after special events were held that were dedicated to the prisoners' cause. These ranged from performances of theatrical companies or musical groups to specific fundraising days. Designated days for the benefit of particular war causes were a common means of encouraging donations and raising money for patriotic associations during the war. They also allowed the general public the chance to relieve some tension and anxiety. 'Button days', in which small decorative buttons, much like badges, were sold and the proceeds then forwarded to the relevant fund, were a typical approach. The sale of these buttons served two purposes: they helped raise money for war-related causes, and they allowed the purchaser physically to display their patriotism and loyalty to the troops and the war effort in general. In late November 1917, the editor of the Melbourne *Argus* was urged to spread the word about a possible 'button day' specifically aimed at prisoner-of-war relief: 'As an ardent supporter of the Button Fund collections I should like to urge the organisers ... to arrange for a Prisoners' Day and that without delay ... Can we not have a button day 'for all prisoners and captives'? These touching words from the beautiful Litany might be inscribed in white letters on a grey button.'[40] The proposed button day was welcomed by one respondent – the mother of a prisoner in Germany, who wrote that 'we must try and help by swelling the funds of our good Australian Prisoners of War Committee'.[41] Although it appears that this button day never eventuated in Melbourne, others did occur. In Adelaide in September 1917, for example, a group of patriotic 'circles' came together to sell buttons for POW relief at stalls during the annual Adelaide show.[42]

As the war dragged on, the plight of Australians in enemy hands became of even greater concern to the Red Cross. The Queensland branch estimated that it sent approximately £2100 per month to London for the purposes of providing relief to Australians held captive in Germany and the Ottoman Empire, but that to continue this work it needed 'money – always more money'. An article from a July 1918 edition of the *Queenslander* reinforced the narrative of POW suffering and plucked at the emotions of readers, asking them to 'picture the life of these unfortunate men' and 'think of the misery should parcels fail to come'.[43] Readers of the *Daily News* in Perth were similarly entreated to imagine 'the pangs of hunger of the unfortunate prisoners of war'.[44] Those who did not donate were accused of negligence equal to that of the prisoners' captors. 'If you do not do your share in support of the Red Cross movement,' the July *Queenslander* article stated, 'you place yourself among the culprits who have contributed to the delay of the parcels or, worse still, to the non-materialisation of the parcels.'[45] The act of contributing to patriotic funds during the war was positioned in terms of the performance of civic responsibility, placing considerable pressure on those at home to respond. Donations to patriotic funds were often published in local and state newspapers, and the fear of being accused of being unpatriotic or indifferent was one of the factors that motivated Australians to continue to give.[46] As with recruitment and enlistment, shame became a persuasive factor in ensuring continued support for war relief work.

Appealing to the Australian public through images of the captives as victims and ideas of patriotism based on a combination of loyalty and shame worked. Individuals and families continued to donate money for the prisoners' cause throughout 1918. Mr W.T. Robertson of Brisbane donated £8/6/8 in the latter half of 1918, while the Sparsholt family, also of Brisbane, gave £2/2. In late 1918 Mr Sam Crouch donated £5 after taking advantage of crowds waiting to welcome returned soldiers at his local railway station in western Sydney to collect on behalf of the RCPF.[47] Donations were also received from groups or associations such as sporting teams or theatrical companies that held special events for the benefit of the fund. The Women's Hockey Association of New South Wales, for example, held a sports meeting at the Sydney University Oval in August 1918 in aid of the prisoners' cause while, in the same month in Tamworth, New South Wales, a local revue company staged a carnival night, with all ticket monies going to the RCPF.[48] The Victorian Education Department's War Relief Fund continued their support too: in July 1918 they donated another £6300 after schoolchildren across the state participated in a week of 'self-denial' specifically to raise funds for food and comforts parcels for Australian POWs.[49]

Red Cross branches across the country also organised their own fundraisers. Town and country branches arranged appeals for donations from their locale, which they would then forward to the RCPF. In June 1918 in Tasmania, the Launceston Red Cross branch bottled and sold preserves at a local market in aid of POW relief, while an annual meeting of the Port Adelaide Red Cross Circle in November 1918 recorded that they had raised £365 throughout the year for the fund.[50] State branches also contributed. The Queensland branch of the Red Cross employed a novel approach to bolster donations by opening a 'Prisoner of War Gift House' in the Colonial Mutual Society rooms in Brisbane city in mid-1918. Instead of appealing for direct financial contributions, the Gift House Committee called for the donation of premium items they could then sell, with all proceeds to go towards POW relief. In several newspaper articles the committee asked citizens for 'plate and silver, lace and linen, vases and jewelry [sic] – things of real value – that may be sold for good figures'.[51] This appeal for assistance continued to play on the emotions and sense of duty of Australians at home through impressions of the prisoners as desperate and helpless. 'There are thousands of people in Queensland,' claimed the *Queenslander* in September 1918, 'who would be glad to give some piece of plate or china to help the lonely, heart-weary Australian boys who stand in such need of succour.'[52] The

Gift House's inventory upon its closure at the end of the war indicates that the call for goods was obviously well received; still in stock were 'a number of solid silver table appointments, sapphire, pearl and diamond rings, gold bangles, a beautiful cameo brooch and other jewellery'.[53]

The RCPF closed as news of the Armistice and the release of the prisoners from Germany and the Ottoman Empire reached Australia. The POW Department in London used leftover funds to provide entertainment for ex-prisoners while they awaited repatriation, while the Red Cross at home diverted all remaining monies and goods to provide for the influx of servicemen returning from the war. In the aftermath of the war, the upkeep of convalescent homes and hospitals for the maimed, blinded, gassed and shell-shocked, and the care of physically and emotionally fragile returned soldiers, became the focus of charitable organisations and patriotic funds. With their captivity at an end, it seemed that the prisoners would no longer have need for the funds specifically raised on their behalf.

FAMILIES AND EMOTIONAL STRAIN

Newspaper coverage and patriotic work demonstrates the broader, ripple effects of captivity on Australians at home, but it also had a much more intimate impact. The particular ambiguities of wartime imprisonment and the many restrictions it imposed caused certain challenges for the families of POWs in the Ottoman Empire, including intense feelings of physical, communicative and emotional separation. Psychologist Edna Hunter, in her work on American families affected by captivity in Vietnam and later conflicts, argues that POW families are thrust into a particular world of prolonged indefinite stress, and suffer from 'feelings of helplessness, hopelessness, powerlessness, anger, guilt and rage'.[54] The majority of those taken prisoner by the Ottomans were, in keeping with the general demographic of the AIF, bachelors with either a parent or sibling listed as next-of-kin. These relatives' thoughts and feelings about captivity indicates that they suffered significant emotional strain as they endured the peculiar absence of their loved ones.

One key problem for many POW families was their ignorance of the Ottoman Empire. As we have seen, at the time of the First World War most Australians knew very little about 'the Turks', and for most of the families of prisoners, the interior of Asia Minor and the Ottoman way of life was a mystery. This gulf of understanding proved difficult, particularly as the ability to determine the location of a captive loved one is an important means by which families maintain a sense of connection with their POW sons, husbands, brothers and fathers.[55] The prisoners' families had been desperate to identify where their menfolk actually were. In January 1917 Mr F. Adams wrote to AIF Base Records in Melbourne, anxious to pinpoint the location of his captive son. He had received a postcard from Francis, an air mechanic captured at Kut and imprisoned at Bagtchi, but had no clue as to where his camp was. Mr Adams begged the office staff to 'please inform me of the locality of Batche [*sic*] as I am unable to find it on any maps'.[56]

Communication was another issue. During the war, the increased volume of mail sent between Australia and servicemen overseas, coupled with delays imposed by shipping restrictions, meant that it took considerably longer for windows into home life to reach the troops, and for a glimpse of battlefront life to reach families at home. The prisoners' families had to contend with this general lag in communication and the added delay of getting any letters into and out of the Ottoman Empire. In keeping with the Hague Convention, the postal fee for sending letters between the prison camps and home had been waived, but the Ottoman postal system was inefficient – a problem exacerbated by the movement of POWs between camps – and letters often took an excruciatingly long time to reach the prisoners, and vice versa. Many POW families experienced long silences between communications. It was not unusual for relatives to wait four or five months between letters from the camps, with some families reporting delays of nearly ten months. Despite the families following specific instructions from the Department of Defence and the Red Cross POW Department about addressing their messages, the return of undelivered letters was common.

Even direct communication could cause great uncertainty. Censorship affected what the families could know of the prisoners' lives in captivity, and what the POWs could know about what was happening outside the camps. As part of their policy regarding POWs, Ottoman military authorities imposed censorship checks on the letters leaving and entering their prison camps, and several original letters from Australian prisoners bear evidence of the censor's scissors. Edgar Green's sister Maude explained to Chomley how such censorship caused anxiety. 'Only 6 lines came through, the rest being cut out by the censor,' she wrote. 'The first sentence cut out started "must ask" which is rather worrying, as it probably means he wants something badly.'[57] The prisoners and their correspondents understood that censors read their letters. Maurice Delpratt's sister, Elinor (Nell) White, appreciated that their letters were not private and complained of being unable to write freely. 'I rattle off pages to Bert [brother on active service],' she wrote, 'but to you I always feel the fear of the censor upon me!'[58] In return, Delpratt wrote of potentially censorable events in a family-friendly code. He explained his 1917 flogging, for example, as 'having just received from a nice person with a sense of justice quite his own something I've seen Mr Dixon [family neighbour] give his boys'.[59]

There was also an element of self-imposed censorship at work in communications between the prisoners and their families. In much the same way as soldiers on the front lines often censored their own descriptions of life in the trenches or in the desert, prisoners self-censored their accounts of captivity, particularly regarding their health and well-being, to protect their families. Many existing letters to relatives contain cheery messages about the man's health and his life in the camps; such phrases as 'I am doing A1' were particularly common. Historian Marina Larsson refers to such self-censorship in communications home as 'epistolary silences'.[60] As was the case in Larsson's work on wounded servicemen writing to their families from hospitals and convalescent homes, messages professing health and happiness were also far from the truth for many of the prisoners. After responding to a Red Cross enquiry into the state of his health by writing 'malaria fever has taken hold of me and I cannot get rid of it . . . dysentery I have had four attacks and it has left me in a weak state', POW Ernest Ingram also wrote to his mother imploring her not to worry as he was 'quite well'.[61] Similarly, Private Robert Peters, who contracted smallpox in captivity, begged the Red Cross not to inform his family of his potentially deadly infection. 'I hope you will keep this from my people,' he wrote in 1918, 'as it could have left me much worse. I have not written home without giving them to understand I was quite well.'[62]

The desire to protect family members at home – particularly mothers – was seen as a manly act of duty during the First World War.[63] It is impossible to tell how many families believed accounts of good health and enjoyment of camp life; however, it is clear that some recognised their loved one was putting on a brave face. Nell White was appreciative of Maurice Delpratt writing in such a way. 'We are always grateful for your brave efforts to keep us comparatively free from anxiety about you,' she wrote in a letter to her captive brother. 'I think it is a great help for Father that you write as you do. Of course, we know that you are making the best of things for our sakes.' Nell analysed her brother's letters for deeper meanings: 'You said "at work again", which points to your having been ill.'[64] The performative nature of correspondence between the prisoners and their families often masked real feelings and worries. It was only by reading between the lines – finding cracks in the mask – that those at home could discern the more realistic condition of their captive loved one.

The sporadic nature of the Ottoman postal system also affected the arrival of food and comforts parcels in the camps, which added to family anxieties. They also read the newspaper articles that painted a grim picture of the conditions of the Ottoman prison camps – William Elston's sister Violet wrote to Elizabeth Chomley in early 1918 of the 'horrible accounts of the Prisoners in Turkey in today's *Argus*' – and were naturally concerned and desperate to help.[65] During the early years of the war, private parcels could be sent to all captives but, as we have seen, this practice was stopped in mid-1916 when the British Government deemed it necessary to control the amount of food and clothing sent to their POWs. Regulations were changed and, although private parcels could still be sent to officers as long as a special coupon was used, for most of 1917 only official aid agencies were able to pack and send parcels to other ranks in captivity.[66] Several prisoners' families expressed profound sadness at their inability personally to pack and send items of comfort and memories of home. In his discussion of families of British soldiers in France during the First World War, Michael Roper stresses the significance of the comforts parcel in providing solace to both parties. Those at the front received special treats and extras while, through the inclusion of items deemed necessary for protection from illness – food, clothes and home remedies – families were able to exercise some agency over the health and welfare of their sons, brothers, husbands and fathers.[67] Restricting the sending of parcels to an external agency meant that the prisoners' families were less able to select and send specific items to minimise their loved ones' discomfort, so their sense of powerlessness and separation was intensified. Maud Gilbert, for example, the mother of cameleer George Gilbert, found it 'very hard' that she was not able to send her captive son the scarf and soap she had specifically picked out for him.[68] Indeed, John Yarnall writes that the reintroduction of private parcels in December 1917 – albeit at a restricted rate of one per quarter and limited to next-of-kin – was a measure designed to minimise the strain felt by relatives of the POWs rather than provide for the captives.[69]

But families continued to worry about the actual arrival of parcels in the camps. To reach the men parcels had to take a convoluted route – from London they travelled to Geneva, then through Austria before arriving in Constantinople, where they would have to be despatched throughout the camps – and were subject to long delays, often of eight months to a year.[70] Adding to the concern of those at home was the fragile nature of the transport agreement; the parcel post between London and the Ottoman Empire was completely shut down in 1917 and for another six months in 1918 as a result of Austrian border closures. Frustrated relatives expressed concern over the amount of supplies the men received. Private Charles Flatt's mother was deeply worried about her son, claiming that the men at his camp were surely 'nearly starving', while John Merson's cousin was similarly concerned about clothes for the captives, particularly as the War Office forbade the sending of replacement uniforms.[71] Such concern over the health and comfort of the prisoners was centred on fears for their capacity to cope. Edna Hunter notes that parents of POWs, in particular, tend to infantilise their captive child and typically express doubts about his or her ability to withstand the rigours of enforced imprisonment, particularly strange food, isolation and lack of exercise.[72] Frederick Ashton's mother, Frances, was clearly worried that her son was struggling with the restrictions of camp life. 'He has been a prisoner since the famous landing at the Dardanelles,' she wrote in a letter to the Red Cross POW Department in early 1917, 'and he has had a very rough time indeed, being without bread, meat, tea or sugar for 4 months, and months and months without boots or a change of clothing.'[73]

Concerns regarding the physical condition of the prisoners were compounded by anxieties about their emotional well-being. Another reason friends and relatives worried about whether the men were receiving parcels and letters was their fear that the men would think they had been left to languish. One concerned relative of Trooper Colin Spencer Campbell felt sure 'it must make them feel they are quite forgotten if nothing ever reaches them', while cameleer Allan Kimber's sister was desperate to ensure that reminders of the outside world reached her brother, explaining to the Red Cross that she 'would not like him to think for one moment that he had been forgotten'.[74]

Faced with a seemingly interminable period of misery and worry, the families of the POWs responded by developing an informal, private network to help alleviate the burden of their collective concerns. Historian Jay Winter describes such networks as a form of 'fictive kinship'; the coming together of people not necessarily related by blood or marriage but connected instead by shared understandings of, or interests in, a certain event or experience.[75] Several scholars have written about the role of groups of fictive kin to provide support for, and commemoration of, the maimed, the disfigured and the bereaved during and after the First World War.[76] The forming of such groups or networks were a reaction to the distressing situations in which many people found themselves, and demonstrate what Winter sees as 'the powerful, perhaps essential, tendency of ordinary people ... to face together the emptiness, the nothingness, of loss in war'.[77]

The prisoners' families' network of fictive kin comprised three branches. As the only formal organisation that dealt specifically with Australian prisoners of war, the Australian Red Cross POW Department in London was the main point of contact for those with loved ones imprisoned in either the Ottoman Empire or Germany, and formed the cornerstone of the network. The Red Cross POW Department acted as a conduit between the prisoners and their families. They gently offered advice and guidance to relatives and informed them of official policies and regulations, and Chomley and her team became well known to the family and friends of the captive men. Alongside the Red Cross there were other, more private, aspects to the network. Families also very much depended on each other, and the comrades of the POWs, for information and support. Although there were other associations and organisations designed to assist the relatives of those involved in the war, such as Dr Mary Booth's Centre for Soldiers' Wives and Mothers, these organisations were targeted at the families of those killed and maimed, or of men still fighting, not at the relatives of those taken prisoner, whose anxieties and concerns were different. Extended family, particularly those in Britain, formed the third part of the network. These kin in the traditional sense of the word were enlisted by Australian families to communicate with the POW Department or the local relatives of other prisoners, and pass on money and letters sent from Australia. The Sydney-based Gilman family, for example, recruited a relative in London to help with the search for news of their captive son, Ellis. Christina Gilman, Ellis's aunt, wrote to Chomley:

> I know how difficult it is to get any information about our poor fellows in Turkish hands, but I should be so grateful if you could get me any news or in all events tell me the correct way in which to address letters to him. His father and mother in Australia have asked me to make enquiries for them.[78]

The inclusion of these extended family members, as well as the families of prisoners who enlisted in Australia from other locations, such as New Zealand, Ireland and South Africa, made this a global network.

This unofficial network worked to alleviate families' angst. Through it, they were able to learn more about their POW relative and his life in captivity. Relatives and friends sent letters to their loved ones via the

POW Department as, like the prisoners themselves, they believed mail would have more chance reaching its destination this way than through private post. Indeed, Chomley actively encouraged family members to send any letters through the department, reasoning that they had the most up-to-date addresses for the men and could despatch any mail most effectively. In their covering letters family members expressed their desire for information, and if the department had any news a worker would duly reply. For those they could not immediately assist, Chomley and her representatives wrote carefully worded letters explaining that opportunities for prisoners to write were limited, and that letters and postcards would quite often go missing in the post. Such letters helped calm the concerns of relatives like Noel Sherrie's mother. After receiving a message from the POW Department's sister branch, the Wounded and Missing Bureau, she explained that while the family was longing for a message from Noel, they appreciated that no news was essentially good news. 'After reading your letter,' Bessie Sherrie wrote, 'that the mail from Turkey was so irregular … I knew I just had to expect not to hear so you see what your letter did for me.'[79] They also implored relatives to remain positive: in a letter to Reginald Lushington's mother, Chomley stated, 'I know it must be a terribly anxious time for you, but your boy is young and it is wonderful how they get over things.'[80]

Families who did receive letters from their POW also wrote to the department, informing them of any relevant information gleaned from their communication. Occasionally a prisoner's family sent in the original letter or postcard they had received for Chomley and her representatives to scrutinise. This must have been difficult for letters received during the war were considered extremely precious.[81] They represented cherished, tangible connections with loved ones – they had written it, touched the paper and sealed the envelope – and relatives usually asked that letters be returned, a request with which Chomley readily complied. Other families sent copies to Chomley, as well as to extended family and friends. Copying out letters, usually by hand, was a time-consuming process and indicates the strength of the desire for information and the sense of mutual obligation families felt to the POW Department and those similarly affected by captivity.

Many families received updates about their captive loved one because of this sharing of information. After enquiring at the Red Cross about his brother William for example, Chomley was able to tell Staff Sergeant George Rayment that a recent letter from an Australian POW officer had mentioned that William was in the Taurus Mountains and was well.[82]

Similarly, submariner William Falconer's sister was informed of his move from a work camp to a convalescent camp after a letter from George King, another Australian prisoner, was received by the department.[83] The Red Cross also facilitated the spread of information by putting relatives of the prisoners in contact with each other. Many department case files contain requests from a prisoner's family for contact details of the relatives of another prisoner whom their POW had mentioned. For example, the brother of Keith Hudson asked Chomley for the contact details of Edgar Hobson's family, as Keith had mentioned Hobson in a letter.[84] The multinational nature of the Ottoman prison camps meant that Chomley occasionally received similar requests from the families of men from other nations, particularly the British. In one case, the mother of a Royal Flying Corps POW wrote to the department asking for contact information for the next-of-kin of Ronald Austin and Oliver Lee, the two Australian pilots who had tried to assist her son before the three men were captured together in March 1918.[85]

Such information also allowed the families of prisoners to feel more of a connection with their captive loved one. The families of those in Ottoman captivity strove to discover as much as possible about their POW's location in an effort to imagine his life as a captive. In discovering the daily life of their prisoner – what he did for work, how he spent his leisure hours, what kind of food he ate and who he associated with – relatives were able to foster connections between prison camp and home, and keep his presence in the family alive. A clearer understanding and appreciation of Maurice's captivity was obviously important for the Delpratts; Nell explained to her captive brother that she was eager to learn all she could about his day-to-day experiences so that 'bit by bit we are able to picture your life a little better'.[86] Relatives turned to the network for assistance in creating these connections. A friend of Delpratt's aunt enquired about the location of his camp, Hadjikiri, asking the Red Cross POW Department whether it was close to a railway, and whether this would enable the men to receive letters.[87] The Red Cross's reply – 'as far as we know [it is] a working camp. We understand it is not far from the Railway, in fact we believe the men to be working at the construction of the Railway line' – soothed Delpratt's aunt's anxiety about his ability to receive comforts parcels and helped her construct an idea of her nephew's daily activities.[88] Similarly, the Red Cross described Harry Foxcroft's camp at Ada Bazar to a friend – 'one of our workers is a lady who has spent a great deal of her time in the East and knows the district in Asia Minor in which Ada Pazar is situated ... She tells us it is a large town on the Baghdad Railway in a fertile agricultural district' – and helped give some indication of Foxcroft's living and working conditions.[89] Frederick Ashton's father, a corporal in the AIF kit stores in London and a regular visitor to the POW Department offices, was also told of 're-assuring [sic]' news about the conditions his son was living in after Chomley spoke to a British officer who had escaped from Ottoman captivity. After interviewing the escapee, Chomley felt 'very much happier about the condition of our men' and told Ashton's father she 'thought you might like to know what I was told'.[90]

The network also helped alleviate family concerns that they were not doing more to help and that their POW would feel forgotten. In their role as organiser of the food and comforts parcels sent from London, the POW Department was able to ensure, within reason, the inclusion of certain extras in the prisoners' parcels or the forwarding of sums of money at the request of relatives and friends. In this way, Edgar Green received the extra surprises of a chess set and chocolate thanks to his sister Maude, who sent money to Chomley with covering letters emphasising the fact that her brother was 'very fond' of the sweet treat.[91] Chomley was not afraid to veto some requests, however. After a relative of Corporal Clyde Currie asked the department to send him some cream, Chomley replied: '[D]o you think that cream would keep for the 8 or 10 months it sometimes takes to get parcels delivered in Turkey?'[92] Of course, the ability to include these extras depended on the family's financial situation. While Colin Campbell's father was 'most willing to send any money which can help at all', not all relatives were in a position to forward sums of cash.[93] Chomley assured these anxious families that the Red Cross would continue to send the maximum amount of comforts possible to the POWs.

One of the most important ways in which the network assisted POW families was in the case of death. Quite often a POW died many months before any official confirmation of his death reached AIF Headquarters or the POW Department. If the Red Cross did discover that a prisoner had died, usually via an official death list compiled by their Ottoman counterparts or through correspondence with a fellow POW, Chomley wrote to the family to break the sad news. Occasionally, however, families would learn of the death of their loved one through more brutal means. Noel Sherrie's family discovered he had died after a postcard written by a family friend working as a nurse in France was returned marked 'mort' (dead). Similarly, Sergeant George Drysdale's family only learned of his death when his mother had one of her own letters returned marked 'decede' (deceased). Too distraught to write herself, Edith Drysdale enlisted her married daughter in London, Mary, to ask the POW Department for confirmation of George's death. An upset and frustrated Mary wrote to Chomley, stating that 'it does seem hard that one gets such bad news in that way, with no further information'.[94] Some families did not learn that their prisoner had died until after the Armistice. Trooper Claude Redman's family had no idea that their much-loved son and brother had perished in a Damascus hospital soon after his capture in March 1918. Redman's father and sister made persistent enquiries of the Red Cross and AIF Base Records to no avail; it was not until February 1919 that the family received an unofficial report of his death from disease, a finding made official at a court of enquiry later that year.[95]

Bereaved families turned to the network for help discovering 'particulars'. In some cases, as we have seen, fellow prisoners were able to initiate communication with the relatives of the deceased to provide some details. Maurice Delpratt wrote to Brendan Calcutt's father after Calcutt's death in early January 1917, partly to soothe his own grief and partly to provide Calcutt's father with an account of his son's last days and burial. Aware of the unreliability of the Ottoman postal system, Delpratt also reported Brendan's death to his sister and asked her to communicate with Mr Calcutt. In a clear example of a fictive-kin-style relationship between the Delpratts and the Calcutts and of the network in action, Nell assured her brother that she had been in contact with his dead friend's father. 'I told Mr Calcutt those official photos had been taken [of Brendan's grave],' she wrote. 'I quoted all your letters in which there was any mention of his son.'[96] In a similar case, the mother of Private Alfred Nelson, who died in November 1916, was provided with information about her son's death from one of his captive comrades, Alfred Carpenter. Mrs Nelson was so grateful for the details she obtained from Carpenter that she sent him ten shillings for him 'to share with his chums as he wishes'.[97]

The bereaved also wrote to the Red Cross or directly to other prisoners to learn more. One of the most distressing pleas for assistance came from the family of Irish-born Air Mechanic David Curran. In August 1917 Samuel and Esther Curran were informed of their son's death on the basis of news the POW Department had received from another prisoner. With no further information available, Curran's family tried different branches of the network to obtain details. They first wrote to Chomley to enquire whether she could communicate with the prisoner who had notified them of David's death:

We hope the sad news is not true and are anxiously waiting for further news from you if it is true we want you to get all information you can from the Prisoner of War who communicated the news to you concerning his death ... I wonder was he wounded or what was the cause of his death? ... Please try and find out all you can about him.[98]

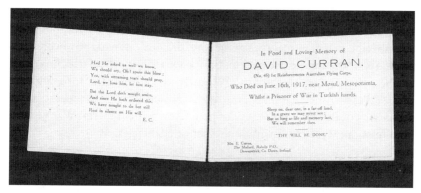

'Sleep on, dear one.' Memorial card produced by Esther Curran to commemorate the death of her son David as a POW of the Ottomans (AWM RC00932)

The Currans also approached the prisoner who had informed the Red Cross directly, stating 'we should like to keep in touch with someone who knew him', and wrote numerous letters enquiring how their son had died and where he was buried.[99] This correspondence continued until the end of the war, when Esther again sent a heartfelt plea to Chomley, asking for the names of any ex-prisoners who might pass through Belfast and who could visit her and her daughter.[100] Recently widowed – the blow of their son's death reportedly bringing on Samuel's own passing – Esther was desperate to talk with anyone who had been with her son in captivity.[101]

It is difficult to determine whether Esther ever did discover the full details of her son's death, as the end of the war brought about not only the closing of the prison camps but also the end of the POW Department. For families like the Currans, the Drysdales, the Sherries, the Redmans and the Calcutts, any unofficial investigations into the deaths of their loved ones came to a stop. The best Chomley could do for Esther Curran was promise that she would leave a note requesting information about David from any repatriated prisoner passing through London.[102] For the families of those prisoners who did return from captivity, the closure of the POW Department, and the subsequent end of the network, was met with gratitude. In the many messages Chomley received, the importance of the network is made resoundingly clear. Perhaps the simplest but most poignant vote of thanks came from the sister of light horseman Leslie Lambert: 'Very many thanks, for all you have done for us.'[103]

It is clear, then, that wartime imprisonment had consequences that extended far out from the confines of the POW camps. The prisoners of the Ottomans, and captivity more broadly, had a significant impact at home, and both publicly and privately Australians actively responded to this specific wartime reality. As the war drew to an end, however, concerns about the immediate aftermath of captivity – particularly the return of the prisoners and locating POW graves – came to the fore, and the former POWs, their families and those responsible for commemorating the deaths of British Empire servicemen, namely the Imperial War Graves Commission, were faced with a new set of challenges.

CHAPTER | 6

AFTER THE ARMISTICE

As 1918 drew to a close, the prisoners sensed that the Ottomans were losing the fight. Town bazaars and work camps became hotbeds of rumour as locals spoke of the imminent defeat of the Ottoman Army. Such speculation had clearly proven untrue before, and many of the prisoners initially dismissed reports of the allied advance through Palestine. However, visibly increased tension between Ottoman and German soldiers in and around the prison camps was also attributed to the breakdown of defences in the Middle East, and the sighting of allied warplanes in the skies over Constantinople provided more fuel for the fire. After the strain of prolonged imprisonment – more than three years for some POWs – the end of the war was not only a relief but also exciting. As the prisoners made the reverse transition out of captivity and efforts turned to locating camp graves, however, the resonances of wartime imprisonment and the changing political landscape in the Ottoman Empire in the aftermath of the Armistice presented new challenges for the former prisoners, their families and official attempts to commemorate the dead.

FIRST TASTES OF FREEDOM

In late October 1918, the Ottomans sent Major-General Charles Townshend, captive leader of the British imperial forces at Kut, to begin negotiations for an armistice to conclude hostilities in the Middle Eastern theatre. The British battleship HMS *Agamemnon* arrived in Mudros harbour, off the coast of Lemnos, on 27 October, and the British Com-mander-in-Chief of the Mediterranean Fleet, Sir Somerset Gough-Calthorpe, met Rauf Bey, Ottoman Minister for Marine Affairs, on board. The two men spent several days negotiating terms before an agreement was reached on 30 October. At noon the next day, an armistice between Ottoman and allied forces came into effect.

The Mudros agreement included provisions for the demobilisation of the Ottoman Army, the surrender of all Ottoman garrisons in Mesopota-mia and Syria, the opening of the Dardanelles and the allied takeover of rail and telegraph networks. It also outlined instructions for the uncondi-tional handover of all prisoners of war.[1] At the time of the Armistice, allied POWs were spread throughout Anatolia – some were working around the capital, others were at Afyon, Angora and Kedos, while many more were still labouring on the Berlin–Baghdad Railway in the Taurus Mountains. News of the Armistice reached the prison camps through different means. Edgar Hobson was told by his commandant at Nisibin that the prisoners were now 'his guests', while an interpreter informed Leslie Luscombe and the rest of the POW officers at Afyon.[2] Representa-tives of the protecting powers told others, and some found out from newspapers or local residents. In several camps, celebrations were the order of the day. Maurice Delpratt told his sister that the British and Australian prisoners at Afyon 'all went mad' upon receiving confirmation that the war with the Ottomans was over and they were no longer POWs. After the town crier announced the news, the prisoners hoisted a Union Jack (produced by Scottish prisoners) over the Armenian Church and marched into the town bazaar.[3] Closer to the capital, Reginald Lushing-ton and his fellow prisoners rushed out of their billet 'like foxhounds suddenly let out' and took a train to Constantinople.[4] When they arrived, the excited prisoners bought drinks for everyone, including the sentries who had travelled with them.

But celebrations came in different forms. Luscombe, anxious to do his bit for the ongoing war against the Germans, was desperate to find a way to rejoin his battalion on the Western Front, while for Captain Ron Austin exacting some small measure of revenge on the people he held responsible for his hardships as a POW was important. Austin and his roommate organised an auction to dispose of the belongings they had accrued in captivity, but low bidding prices from the local townspeople frustrated the two men and, with a lack of compassion for those who had also suffered the difficulties of war in the Ottoman Empire, they decided to destroy the items. 'A crowd formed outside,' Austin wrote in his memoir of captivity, 'chiefly women and children, and we would hold these things up and ask them how much they would give':

> They only made low bids and if the bid was not enough Pettit used to chop the thing up with an axe and we made the people pretty wild. They were crying, shouting, and yelling, asking us not to smash these things up; but we said unless they paid a fair price we were going to break everything. We sold an odd thing just to keep them going, but we chopped up almost everything we had there.[5]

There were no heroic stunts to liberate the various prison camps, and in some instances prisoners were effectively left to make their own way to the main collection point at Constantinople. Those close to the capital, like Frederick Ashton at San Stefano, simply walked out of their camps and into the offices of the Dutch Legation, where they were welcomed with money and food, or gravitated towards a hotel that had been turned into reception rooms for incoming POWs. The prisoners received a hearty welcome at the Hotel Crocker. 'What a blessing it was!' Ashton wrote in a post-war memoir:

> We tried, inadequately I fear, to convey our thanks to these wonderful people, who almost seemed to us like inhabitants from another world! To be handed a cup of freshly made tea, in a fine china cup, in a well-furnished lounge, by a charming well-dressed lady who added a few well-chosen words of welcome, sympathy and encouragement, was something to which we had been strangers for so long that it was no wonder a lump came into our throats.[6]

The men were free to roam the city, visiting significant cultural sites such as Hagia Sophia and taking boat trips down the Bosphorus and into the Black Sea. After boarding a troopship in late November, these POWs sailed for Salonika, then the port town of Taranto in southern Italy. After a short period in Taranto, the former prisoners entrained for Calais and then were shipped to Dover, eventually reaching London in early December.

But for some prisoners, particularly those in camps deeper in the Anatolian countryside, getting to Constantinople was more difficult. Escaped British officer Edward Keeling argued in his 1924 memoir that the idea of establishing one central collection point for POWs in the Ottoman Empire reflected the lack of appreciation the military authorities had for the prisoners' situation.[7] Keeling went back into the Taurus Mountains region in late 1918 to facilitate the return of these POWs.

He arranged for prisoners in the Nisibin area to be transported via the newly occupied rail network to Aleppo and then to Tripoli and Port Said, while prisoners at work camps in the mountains were sent on trains to Afyon, where officers arranged passage by train to Smyrna (modern-day Izmir).[8] The newly released prisoners were welcomed at Smyrna in much the same manner as those who had arrived in Constantinople. According to British officer Leonard Woolley, 'the Turks had washed their hands' of the POWs. The ex-prisoners were accommodated in buildings requisitioned by the American Red Cross, were taken in by local French and English families or stayed in hotels. They too were able to wander the town, visit the theatre and the bazaar, and dine in local restaurants.[9]

Eventually the ex-prisoners were collected from Smyrna by the hospital ship *Kanowna* and sailed for Alexandria. The trip on board the *Kanowna* was particularly exciting for submariner John Wheat as it marked the first time he had seen an 'English' woman (a nurse) in more than three years.[10] Landing at Alexandria was also a particularly poignant moment for Maurice Delpratt, who had embarked for Gallipoli from the same wharf over three years earlier.[11] From Alexandria the ex-POWs travelled to Port Said and were concentrated at No. 14 Australian General Hospital, where they received medical treatment from Australian doctors and nurses. These signs of familiarity offered the former POWs reminders of places and people associated with home and normality, and marked significant moments in their transition out of captivity. For Edgar Hobson, the realisation that he was free from life as a captive of such a foreign culture was overwhelming. He completed a report to the AIF by stating that he '[thanked] God that I am now once more amongst my own people'.[12]

Prisoners no longer

The British Government had specific interests in the repatriated prisoners. Eager to 'counteract any Bolshevik propaganda' that threatened British claims to the moral high ground regarding their conduct during the war, they wanted to create a comparison study between the treatment of British POWs in enemy hands and the treatment of enemy prisoners in British hands.[13] At Taranto, British journalists talked to the ex-POWs about their experiences of captivity. But, according to one ex-prisoner, the press received little for their efforts. Frederick Ashton explained that 'we didn't want to think or talk about the past. The future was all important to us now.'[14]

Australian officials followed the British lead. Major John Treloar, officer-in-charge of the Australian War Records Section and the brother of captive pilot William Harold Treloar, despatched a photographer to Calais to take pictures of the recently liberated prisoners. To Treloar's consternation, the photographer arrived too late to take pictures of the worst cases. An AIF representative at Calais stated that 'so many of our British prisoners have been receiving such excellent treatment from British and Allied authorities that by the time they reach here, the prisoners have regained their bodily strength'.[15] Photographs that were obtained were too cheerful, seemingly 'taken with a view of showing the lighter side'.[16] According to the secretary of the British Photographic Section, 'in nearly all the cases the men are smiling with pleasure at the thought that they are free once more'.[17] Ideas about the usefulness of prisoners for propaganda purposes, first realised during the war to boost recruitment, were clearly still in circulation.

Ex-prisoners arriving in Egypt were also of interest to the military authorities, and an AIF memorandum was issued instructing all officers, NCOs and other ranks returning from Ottoman captivity to submit a full report of their experiences. It compelled the men to 'give a faithful comprehensive picture of the circumstances attending the capture and life in enemy country'.[18] Items to be addressed in the post-war report included 'treatment while being conveyed to place of internment', 'nature of employment and scale and nature of rations' and 'when and how news received of great British advance'. A separate section asked for information about missing men or those who died as prisoners.[19] Like the photographs, these reports were collated for the benefit of the Australian War Records Section (the same request was issued to ex-prisoners arriving in London). Such interest in the POWs' experiences of imprisonment marked a different approach towards British prisoners of war from early 1918, when the first medically unfit repatriates were brought back from enemy countries. These prisoners were asked to complete a similar report with far less importance being placed on their time in captivity: '[T]he circumstances of a man's capture,' Treloar explained in a February 1918 letter to AIF Headquarters in London, 'are of greater historical value than the details of his treatment as a prisoner.'[20] During the war significance was placed on any information former prisoners could provide about the strength of enemy forces or ways to avoid potential capture. The cessation of hostilities meant that the emphasis shifted to the experiences of

Australians at the hands of the enemy and the stories they could provide for post-war propaganda purposes.

Although the authorities wanted to use the ex-prisoners, they also acknowledged the difficult nature of their experiences. A high-quality lithographic reproduction of a handwritten note from King George V, in which the King expressed his and the Queen's pleasure that the prisoners had been released 'from the miseries and hardships' and the 'cruelties' of captivity, was issued to British and Dominion former POWs and, in a move that suggests the AIF and the Department of Defence felt ex-POWs deserved some measure of special treatment, repatriated prisoners were offered the choice between priority return to Australia or two months leave in England.[21] For many men the desire to be reunited with anxious relatives, or to restart civilian life after years away, was strong, and they opted to return home as soon as possible. There were other motivations as well. George Handsley rather boldly told AIF authorities he wanted to get home as soon as possible as he had realised that he was 'not in love with the army', while Keith Cahir admitted that he was 'rather afraid of the English winter'.[22] Forty-five of the former POWs left for Australia before the end of 1918.

Others chose England. Although some men were concerned they would be deemed selfish by anxious families for not returning to Australia straight away, the excitement of finally being able to visit the 'motherland' was hard to resist. Travel, as historian Richard White notes, was a keen motivator for enlistment in the First World War.[23] The ex-prisoners were eager to tour sites of historic and cultural significance that, from their prison camps, many had assumed they would never have the opportunity to see. Spotting the iconic white cliffs of Dover was a particularly special moment for those travelling from Calais, like Leslie Luscombe. 'Ever since the Declaration of War,' he wrote in his memoir, 'I had looked forward to the possibility of catching site [sic] of these White Cliffs.'[24] Once in London they joined other Australian servicemen to explore such places as Westminster Abbey, Tower Bridge, Buckingham Palace, St Paul's Cathedral and the Houses of Parliament. Maurice Delpratt conveyed his excitement at being at the centre of the British Empire in a letter to his sister in Queensland. 'Here I am in London,' he wrote, 'with my mouth wide open at its wonders.'[25]

The ex-prisoners received a welcome reception in England. Officers could partake of the British Empire Hospitality Scheme's many facilities for accommodation in stately homes throughout the country or take a room at a hotel. Repatriated prisoners were not charged for lodging at soldiers' hostels (at which a certain number of beds had been reserved specifically for their use), and they were able to join sightseeing tours, attend the theatre and meet friends.[26] British civilians, keen to entertain an Australian soldier, accommodated some. Colin Campbell told Elizabeth Chomley of his appreciation of the family who put him up during his period of leave: 'I am having a lovely holiday so far and hope it continues. The people where I am staying are very kind to me they cannot do enough for me. I feel absolutely at home one cannot help it.'[27] The POW Department had set aside funds to provide entertainment for Australians returned from captivity in Germany and the Ottoman Empire, and many men were treated to afternoon teas and other social events at the department's offices. Some were also able to visit family in Scotland, Ireland and Wales while others, including George Kerr, took the opportunity to travel further abroad to France.[28]

While the initial transition out of captivity proved straightforward for many of the repatriated POWs, there is evidence to suggest that others struggled. Ill health was a significant concern for the ex-POW population, and many men were hospitalised for extended periods. Joseph O'Neill was one of several ex-prisoners to be transferred between different hospitals in England. Suffering from recurrent attacks of acute malaria, he spent time in various hospitals and rest homes between December 1918 and his embarkation for Australia in May 1919.[29] Chomley and others from the POW Department visited those in hospital, where they found the health of the repatriated prisoners 'better than we had expected', but presciently noted that 'a very large number of cases ... will need care and consideration for a long time to come'.[30]

The stigma of surrender continued to prey on the minds of others. At Chomley's afternoon teas, ex-POWs were introduced to royalty and dignitaries, as well as notable men of the military interested in their experiences.[31] Maurice Delpratt told his family about meeting the previous Governor of Victoria, Lord Carmichael, and his wife. 'I think we managed to interest the old man though a lot of his questions were a long way out of our depth,' he wrote. 'Certainly he looked down our noses when Lady C held matches to light the cigarettes of the "splendid defenders of the Empire"– both of us with 3½ years service ... in Turkey!'[32] Delpratt's obvious excitement at meeting such prestigious individuals and being in what he termed 'exalted presences' could not quite quash his lingering doubts about how capture and imprisonment affected peoples' perceptions of him.

Some men also appear to have indulged in questionable behaviour. In an article outlining some problems of the repatriation process faced by ex-POWs from the Vietnam War, US Army psychologists Robert Ursano and

James Rundell argue that for men moving from a period of prolonged imprisonment to freedom, 'the brief period of euphoria upon release is often replaced by a period of overstimulation'.[33] Many ex-POWs compensate for things they had been denied, or missed out on, during their confinement. Overeating, for example, was a common problem.[34] Several of the Australians repatriated from Ottoman captivity appear to have tried to reclaim lost time or experiences. Cases of going Absent Without Leave (AWL) were common, and a few were admitted to hospitals with venereal disease. The excitement of release seemingly got the better of Ernest Ingram in Egypt – he went AWL twice in January 1919, was admitted to hospital with VD once in February and again in April, and was charged with resisting arrest and using threatening language to superior officers while they attempted to return him from another AWL episode in April.[35]

One of the ways the AIF authorities quashed opportunities for such behaviour – among all servicemen – was through the establishment of educational and vocational schemes. Prime Minister Hughes and Lieutenant-General Sir John Monash, who was in charge of repatriation and demobilisation, developed these schemes for two key reasons: to maintain morale – Monash argued that the 'violent extinction' of the common purpose holding together the AIF could lead to loss of *esprit de corps* among the troops – and to instil ideas of 'useful and efficient future citizenship' in the men as they made the transition to civilian life.[36] Hughes and Monash wanted the troops to explore ways they could be of benefit to themselves, their families and the post-war Australian state, sentiments that were echoed by Edward Millen, Minister for Repatriation, in the booklet *What Australia is Doing for Her Returned Soldiers*. The schemes outlined by Monash and in Millen's booklet encompassed educational work and industrial employment, and many Australian servicemen availed themselves of these opportunities in fields as diverse as engineering, architecture, accountancy, farming, dentistry and textile production. Some requested extra training in their previous field, while others recognised that the effects of war rendered them unable to resume their pre-war occupation and were placed in retraining programs.[37] William Mackay, for example, who was left with extensive scarring after being shot in the back and buttocks before his capture on Gallipoli, received training as a wool classer as his reduced mobility meant it was unlikely he would be able to return to his pre-war position as a miner. Other ex-prisoners deemed fit enough were able to participate in these educational and vocational classes, which kept several of the men in England until late 1919.[38]

(RE)LOCATING THE DEAD

Fifty-five Australian prisoners of the Ottomans never returned home. These POWs, as we have seen, died from disease, accidents in work camps or wounds received before capture, and were generally buried in the Christian cemeteries of the various towns or work camps in which they were confined. Where possible, their graves were marked by fellow prisoners and information about the death and burial was forwarded to military authorities, the Red Cross POW Department and, occasionally, bereaved families. Upon the cessation of war, political instability in the Ottoman Empire and worries over the continued maintenance of existing burial sites made locating and identifying POW graves an important job.

Indeed, the unprecedented number of dead, and the enormous grief experienced by families, communities and nations, meant that locating the graves of all British Empire servicemen was a key priority for the British and Dominion governments in the aftermath of the First World War. The Australian Graves Detachment (AGD) and later the Australian Graves Service (AGS), often working in tandem with the British Graves Registration Unit, oversaw the identification and exhumation of the remains of Australian soldiers from various battlefronts and maintained records for relatives. In 1920, after recognising the desperate need of families to obtain information about the graves of their loved ones, the AGS, together with the government, published a booklet titled *Where the Australians Rest*. Historian Bart Ziino notes that the sketches of cemeteries and memorials to the missing in the booklet offered the relatives of the deceased a sense of connection with the distant graves, and reassured them that their lost husbands, fathers, sons and brothers were being cared for.[39] The many cemeteries on the Gallipoli peninsula and in France and Belgium dominated the booklet, although the graves of prisoners of war were also mentioned:

> Even in far Turkey, in the wild passes of the Taurus Mountains, there are the graves of Australian soldiers who were captured . . . High up on the summit of the railway line in the Amanus Mountains . . . near Hadschikiri [*sic*], are the graves of perhaps a score of British or Dominion soldiers . . . Steps are being taken to trace all such outlying graves in Turkey.[40]

Although this circumspect statement offered little in the way of comfort for bereaved POW families, especially when contrasted with the beautiful sketches and descriptions of cemeteries in Europe, steps had indeed been taken to trace the graves of prisoners in the Ottoman Empire. After touring various cemeteries purported to hold the remains of British POWs in 1919, Graves Registration officials concluded that maintaining these existing sites was not feasible. In a statement to the Director-General of Graves Registration and Enquiries at the War Office in London, officials wrote that the sites they had been able to visit were not easily accessible, with several being located far away from any sizeable town, railway station or road. They also reported that many of the graves were over-grown with grass and scrub, that often they lacked any form of identifying information, and that in some cases the bodies of POWs were indistin-guishable from those of the former enemy.[41] Furthermore, increasing political tensions in the region made travel and communication difficult. Their suggestion was to relocate POW remains to the closest military cemetery.

In the early 1920s, armed with this information, the Imperial War Graves Commission (IWGC) formulated its policy regarding British POW graves in the Ottoman Empire. The IWGC (led by Vice-Chairman Major-General Fabian Ware) was the organisation responsible for com-memorating the sacrifice of all British Empire war dead individually and equally – regardless of rank or race. The IWGC received its royal charter in 1917, and after the war was charged with acquiring land for cemeteries, constructing memorials, making provisions for the upkeep of gravesites, and maintaining burial records and cemetery registers. Their policy regarding the POW graves was straightforward: those located north-west of the Taurus Mountains were to be relocated to Constantinople while those in the south-east – where it was believed the majority of graves were located – would be moved to another nearby Commission-approved cemetery. For various religious and cultural reasons, Indian prisoners were to remain in their original locations.[42] How to deal with deceased POWs whose graves could not be found was the subject of much discus-sion. Eventually the IWGC resolved that, if possible, 'missing' POWs should be commemorated with special memorials in military cemeteries or, if details were too muddy, with the forces they had belonged to before capture.[43]

Concentrating graves and confirming who was to be commemorated on memorials to the missing took some time. Within the Ottoman Empire the work of identifying graves, constructing cemeteries and establishing memorials on the Gallipoli peninsula was given precedence.[44] Moreover, tensions between the allied powers and the growing Turkish nationalist movement made travel – and therefore the identification of grave sites – in the crumbling Ottoman Empire difficult, and the drawing of new borders caused confusion over who was responsible for graves in certain territories. British graves in a Russian cemetery at Kars, a province on the Ottoman–Russian border and the object of years of fighting between the two empires, caused particular consternation. Kars, along with other territories captured by the Russians during the wars of the nineteenth century, had been handed over to the Ottomans under the provisions of the March 1918 Treaty of Brest-Litovsk, the peace agreement between the Central Powers and the Russians.[45]

The relocation of POW graves did not begin in earnest until well into the 1920s. The first to be exhumed and reinterred were the remains of prisoners buried in and around Constantinople, including twelve Australians. In March 1924, the brother of Lance Corporal Francis Easton, who died from pneumonia in November 1916 and was buried in a Catholic cemetery at Ismidt, was informed that Francis' remains had been reinterred at Haidar Pasha Cemetery. This cemetery in the suburb of Haidar Pasha, on the eastern side of the capital, had been given to the British by the Ottomans in 1855 as a place to commemorate the dead of

Haidar Pasha Cemetery, Istanbul, the cemetery of concentration for prisoner-of-war graves from around the Constantinople region. Twelve Australian POWs are buried at Haidar Pasha. (Commonwealth War Graves Commission)

the Crimean War.[46] AIF Base Records, aware of the potentially upsetting nature of such news, assured John Easton that the reburial had been performed 'with every measure of care and reverence' and that a religious service was held.[47] It is clear that the family had fostered a strong connection with Francis' original grave – they had been particularly determined to obtain photographs of the Ismidt grave immediately after the war, and had even requested twenty-four extra copies on top of the three free photographs provided by the government to all next-of-kin.[48] How they felt about the relocation of Francis' remains to a different cemetery is not noted.

A similar process was undertaken for the remains of prisoners buried outside the Constantinople region, although performing this work proved more complicated for IWGC officials. The main issue to be resolved was in which nearby British cemetery these graves would be concentrated. Some IWGC officials argued that all graves should be relocated to Constantinople, but it was pointed out that the cemetery of concentration there, Haidar Pasha, was full. Gallipoli was one suggested alternative, but this was rejected because the majority of POWs captured by Ottoman forces had not been associated with the Gallipoli campaign and, more prudently, because it would have been necessary to transport the remains by sea to get to the peninsula. IWGC staff in London argued that this would set a dangerous precedent in an atmosphere where – despite official rulings that deceased servicemen would not be repatriated – bereaved families were still agitating for the return of their loved ones for burial at home.[49] Smyrna was another possible option, but this was also vetoed, this time by the Turkish Government as they wanted the site for a military and naval base.[50]

In 1926 Iraq, or more precisely Baghdad, was chosen as the site of concentration for these POW graves. At the time, Baghdad seemed to be the best option. A large British cemetery had been established there in April 1917 when the Indian Expeditionary Force took the city from Ottoman troops. It had lots of room for new burials, there were plenty of staff to facilitate the construction of graves and memorials, and, importantly, it was closer to where the majority of the POW graves were believed to be – meaning that transportation of remains could be undertaken by road or rail rather than sea.[51] Baghdad was also outside the new Turkish republic, which minimised any potential diplomatic problems. In a message from Lieutenant-Colonel Cyril Hughes, Deputy Controller of IWGC Eastern District (and former director of graves work on Gallipoli), to Fabian Ware, Hughes flagged the sensitive nature of the British presence in the new republic. 'I have had an informal discussion with Chukri

Bey [Turkish government's representative to the Commission],' he wrote, 'and I can clearly see the Turks do not want a cemetery anywhere in the interior.'[52]

IWGC workers eventually began the grim task of combing through the cemeteries that were identified as holding POW remains. Three teams, including an IWGC official and an interpreter on each, were deployed to cover all the necessary ground. The IWGC estimated that there were ninety-seven sites to visit and 1763 graves to find. Between them, the three teams needed to cover approximately 2500 miles of railway and 560 miles of road, and it was expected that the work would be completed within two months at a total cost of £1162.[53] Almost immediately, however, the IWGC workers encountered difficulties. The new Turkish government placed certain restrictions on where and when the teams could travel, and the cemeteries they did find were in an even worse state than in 1919: some had disappeared entirely, while others had been built on and turned into rubbish heaps. Complaints were made to the Turks and, according to Hughes, 'those responsible have been severely taken to task'. However, Hughes was quick to state that Chukri Bey was not to blame, and that he had provided as much help as possible to the IWGC teams. Chukri Bey's position as 'an Old Turk' was somewhat delicate – as Hughes explained to Ware, 'Angora [i.e. the Turkish nationalist government] are ruthless and if he did not do as Angora desired he stated he is only putting a rope around his neck.'[54]

Despite these constraints, the IWGC teams successfully identified and relocated the remains of hundreds of British POWs to Baghdad North Gate Cemetery. Brendan Calcutt was one of several Australians moved during this process. Calcutt's grave at Hadjikiri in the Taurus Mountains was deemed 'unsuitable for permanent retention', and in 1927 his remains were relocated to Baghdad.[55] Calcutt's parents, who had also lost another son on Gallipoli, were informed of the reinterment and assured that the process, although regretful, was necessary to 'ensure the future mainten-ance and upkeep' of Brendan's grave.[56] Like the Eastons, the Calcutts were guaranteed that 'the work of re-burial has been carried out carefully and reverently' and that their son could now be permanently commemorated.[57]

Of course, complete reburials were not always possible. As with many of the graves found on the former battlefields of Europe and the Middle East, prisoners' remains became tangled with other bodies, and over the months and years identifying marks, papers and uniforms were damaged or degraded. In these instances, the identification of individual men was not feasible and collective burials were necessary. The bodies of three Australians buried at Adana, south-east of the Taurus Mountains – Francis Adams, William Lord and Charles Smith – were recovered for reinterment, but their individual remains could not be identified. Their families were notified of the exhumation of the original graves and were informed that the collective remains were buried in three graves at Baghdad North Gate. In keeping with procedures for similar cases in Europe, each grave was marked by a headstone inscribed with the name and particulars of one of the men, and the words 'buried near this spot'.[58]

Headstone of Air Mechanic Francis Adams, Baghdad North Gate Cemetery, 2009. Adams was one of three Australian POWs recovered from an original burial site at Adana in 1927. Their individual remains could not be identified so each grave is marked 'buried near this spot'. (Commonwealth War Graves Commission)

Distressing as exhumation and reburial might have been, these families at least knew that their loved one had a permanent grave. Twenty-five thousand Australians who died during the First World War were never identified and were instead listed as missing.[59] The bodies of several prisoners were never recovered from their original burial sites. In early 1928, relatives of eleven Australians buried in the Armenian Cemetery at Angora were informed that the IWGC's efforts to locate their graves had failed and, in keeping with Commission policy, these men were to be commemorated on a memorial in Baghdad North Gate Cemetery. Trooper Andrew Day's mother received a letter informing her that as no identifying markings of her son's original grave at Angora could be traced, his name and regimental particulars would be inscribed on a 'special Kipling memorial'. These memorials, so called because they featured an inscription prepared by British poet-author and IWGC official Rudyard Kipling, were designed to honour British Empire servicemen whose original graves were known to be in a particular location but for various reasons could not be located after the war. At Baghdad, the Angora Memorial was to commemorate the lost POWs: 'To the memory of these 265 soldiers and sailors of the British Empire who died as P. of. W. and were buried at the time in the cemetery at Angora, Ada Bazar, Bozanti, Islahin and Nisibin but whose graves are now lost. "Their glory shall not be blotted out."'[60] It would seem, however, that this memorial was never actually built. The Angora POWs are commemorated in Baghdad North Gate with individual headstones that specify 'buried in Angora cemetery' across the top, but there is no record of an associated memorial on archival layout diagrams of the cemetery.

In other cases, prisoners whose bodies could not be found were added to general memorials for the missing. One such memorial was constructed at Basra, southern Iraq, and was unveiled in March 1929. The Basra Memorial commemorates 40 500 'missing' British Empire servicemen who died primarily in the Mesopotamian theatre during and immediately after the First World War, including seven Australian prisoners: Troopers Sydney Crozier, George Donnison, Claude Redman and Norman Sherwin, Private Richard Stripling, Corporal Thomas Soley and Air Mechanic Leo Williams.[61] Three Australian POWs captured on Gallipoli whose bodies could not be recovered after the war – Privates Alan Campbell, Elvas Wilson and William Warnes – were listed alongside nearly 5000 of their fellow Anzacs on the Gallipoli Lone Pine Memorial.

The treatment and ongoing maintenance of Australian graves on the different fronts caused anxiety at home. Bereaved families assumed that the care of graves on the former Western Front was essentially guaranteed – the Australians were buried in European soil, and fellow Christians maintained the gravesites – yet the appropriate respect that Australian graves in the former Ottoman Empire would be afforded was more of a cause for concern.[62] Would the Islamic Turks neglect the Christian cemeteries? Would locals desecrate the graves? At Cape Helles, evidence of British burial sites having been tampered with seemed to bear out these worries.[63] Similar concerns preyed on the minds of the families of deceased POWs, and many of those whose relative's grave had been successfully relocated to an IWGC cemetery expressed gratitude and relief. The brother of Allan Kimber, whose remains were, along with several other Australians, moved from Nidge camp cemetery to Baghdad North Gate in 1927 was pleased that Allan's final resting place was not in Turkish territory. Kimber's remains could not be individually identified, but his brother explained to AIF Base Records that he and his family were 'quite satisfied that everything possible has been done in order to perpetuate his memory', adding that 'it is a great consolation to know my Brother is now buried in British territory'.[64] Although the Kimbers were unlikely ever to visit Allan's grave in Baghdad, knowing that his body rested in what Bart Ziino calls 'some distant extension of Australia or England' brought comfort to the family.[65] Some of the families of POWs who could not be identified appear to have struggled with the knowledge that their loved one would forever lie in Turkish soil. *AE2* submariner Michael Williams' body was never located after the war, which caused his mother great distress. Mrs Williams wrote an anguished letter to Prime Minister Hughes outlining her grief, and explaining that 'my son was buried as A Turk which is hard on true Britishers'.[66]

Along with identifying, relocating and commemorating the dead and missing, the Australian Government and military authorities also acknowledged the grief of the bereaved by honouring their lost loved ones. Like the families of all Australians killed in action, the families of deceased prisoners were eligible to receive specific commemorative items including brass memorial plaques, a memorial scroll and message from the King, a register of all British and Dominion war graves in the cemetery in which their loved one was buried or commemorated, and service medals. These treasured items, together with the deceased's personal effects such as jewellery, clothing and bibles, helped facilitate what historian Tanja Luckins calls the transition from the experience of loss to the process of memory-making.[67] But not all next-of-kin were interested in mementoes of their loved one's service. The wife of Bert Wood, who died of his wounds soon after his capture on Gallipoli in August 1915, renounced her claim to Bert's war medals in favour of his mother. Mrs Wood had also lost two brothers and a nephew in the war, and told Base Records: 'I do not think I need anything more to remind me of that cursed war.'[68] Tangible evidence of their loss, as Luckins notes, sometimes brought distress for the bereaved rather than comfort.[69]

In mid-1928 Hughes wrote to Ware that it was unlikely that the remains of any other British prisoners of the Ottomans would be recovered.[70] Ten years after the end of the war and eight years after the publication of *Where the Australians Rest*, the search for POW graves in the former Ottoman Empire was over.

Pushing for prosecution

For some POW families, the distress of losing a loved one in captivity was expressed as a desire to punish the perpetrators of their grief. Maude Jennings Green, 'haunted' by what her brother Edgar must have felt before his death from pneumonia just before the Armistice, explained to Chomley that she was angry that 'no one can ever make up to him for all he has suffered'.[71] Francis Adams' father was similarly outraged at the treatment his son endured during the long march from Kut before his death at a staging camp in Adana. In early 1919 he wrote to AIF Base Records about the possibility of prosecuting the Ottomans for the mistreatment of POWs. 'Can you tell me if any action is to be taken in regard to the inhuman treatment these men received,' he wrote, 'as I considered they were murdered.'[72] Adams was not alone in calling for the prosecution of the former enemy for their treatment of prisoners of war. In November 1918, the Executive Committee of the Prisoners in Turkey Committee passed a resolution pushing the War Office to demand the Ottoman Government compensate the families of deceased prisoners and that 'guilty individuals be punished'.[73]

The prosecution of those accused of violations of international law – the term 'war crimes' gained traction only in the mid- to late 1920s – was a key aspect of the 1919 Paris Peace Conference and the post-war treaties established between the Central Powers and the allies. In the immediate aftermath of the war, some 860 Germans were accused by the allies of breaking international law, and in what historian Alan Kramer calls 'a test of Germany's good will', several members of the German military were tried by the German Government at the Supreme Court in Leipzig in 1921.[74] Of the forty-five cases heard in Leipzig, three junior officers were found guilty of crimes related to POWs and sentenced to short periods of imprisonment.[75] The evidence given at the trials by British ex-prisoners and others led to a wave of new negative ideas and rhetoric regarding the former enemy, and the seemingly lenient sentences sparked outrage and protest in Great Britain, France and the United States.[76] But British delegates in Leipzig argued that the trials were in fact a significant victory for the allies. As historian Daniel Segesser states, the trial and conviction of supposed German war criminals by a German court carried more weight in Germany than would any trials conducted by an allied court.[77]

The prosecution of Ottomans accused of similar crimes was complicated by Great Power politics and internal division in the empire. Government reports regarding British POWs in the Ottoman Empire produced immediately after the war openly condemned the treatment they received, particularly those prisoners captured at Kut. Alongside allegations of the massacres of Armenians in the empire, these accusations formed the basis of the push for trials of those accused of violations of the laws of war.[78] The new Ottoman Government – many of the wartime Young Turk leaders had fled overseas immediately at the cessation of hostilities – investigated and took steps towards prosecuting the accused through special courts-martial convened under Ottoman law in Constantinople. But the British, frustrated by the slow process and low conviction rate, moved a group of the accused to Malta in May 1919 to face a possible international tribunal. These prisoners were later released after the British were accused by the Ottoman Government of infringing its sovereignty, and as a result of increasing pressure from the rival Ankara-based Turkish nationalist government – which had set up its own parliament in April 1920 – including the taking of twenty-nine British soldiers as hostages.[79] The Ankara nationalists assured the British that the prisoners from Malta – some of whom had been specifically accused of crimes against POWs – would be tried upon their return; such trials never eventuated, and several of the detainees assumed roles in the nationalist government.[80]

The signing of the Treaty of Sèvres by delegates of the Ottoman Government in 1920 escalated internal tensions in the empire. The Turkish nationalists rejected the provisions of the treaty – which included territorial, financial and military restrictions as well as the trial of those accused of violations of the laws of war by international tribunals – and they continued to fight against its terms and those who imposed them. Bitter conflict between the nationalists and the former allies continued during the years of the Turkish War of Independence, until a new treaty, the Treaty of Lausanne, replaced Sèvres in 1923. With it, the Ottoman Empire ceased to exist and the republic of Turkey, headed by Mustafa Kemal Ataturk from the new capital of Ankara, was formally recognised. There were no provisions in the Lausanne treaty for the continued prosecution of those accused of violations of international law during the First World War. The general reciprocal amnesty outlined in the treaty meant that accusations of crimes against Armenians and POWs were dropped.[81]

The aftermath of the Armistice, then, brought with it further challenges for those affected by captivity in the Ottoman Empire. The former

POWs, their families, and allied government and military authorities experienced relief, excitement, frustration, happiness and heartache. Repatriated prisoners were welcomed warmly in Egypt and England but also had to face the public recognition of the difference of their experiences. Identifying the remains of those who perished as POWs was a difficult task for IWGC officials operating in a crumbling empire riven by internal conflict and political discord, and bereaved families faced long waits before they learned how their loved one was to be commemorated. As time went on, the longer-term consequences of captivity emerged, and the former POWs and others intimately and more broadly entangled in their experiences had to navigate the legacy of their imprisonment.

CHAPTER | 7

'REPAT' AND REMEMBRANCE

In his short memoir of captivity, published soon after the end of the war, George Handsley claimed that he had returned to Australia 'little the worse for my terrible experiences while prisoner of war in Turkey'.[1] But for many other prisoners returned from the Ottoman Empire, captivity left a far more indelible impression – on their physical and psychological health, on their families and their careers, and on their sense of belonging within the developing national memory of the First World War. For these men and their families, adjusting to the aftermath of captivity proved difficult and, as they came to realise, the effects of wartime imprisonment reverberated long after the war ended.

DEALING WITH 'THE REPAT'

The Repatriation Department, colloquially known as 'the Repat', is the precursor of the Department of Veterans' Affairs. The Repat was established in 1917 in response to the growing number of Australian veterans and families affected by war service. As soon as war was declared in 1914, the Australian Government set out to estimate the cost of establishing a war pension scheme. Paying pensions or a form of special grant to disabled soldiers – or the families of soldiers who died on active service – was common practice in Britain at the turn of the twentieth century. Fuelled by a growing recognition that citizen soldiers who served their nation deserved some recompense, the Australian Government followed suit. The Commonwealth Statistician calculated that, based on an expected annual mortality rate of 5 per cent of a force of 20 000 – a figure reached by assessing annual death rates for various combatant forces over the previous hundred years – Australia would have to provide death benefits and pensions for more than 1600 men at an estimated cost of £230 000 per year.[2] These figures would prove woefully inadequate, but at the time they were accepted, and in December 1914 the War Pensions Act passed parliament. Australian soldiers who were wounded during the war, or their families in the case of their death, would be eligible for financial assistance.

Initially these pensions were funded by the government, and were supplemented by private money raised through charitable and patriotic organisations (patriotic funds had been the main source of funds for Australian veterans of the Boer War). But by 1917, the realisation had dawned that providing for wounded soldiers and the families of the dead was a much bigger problem than originally anticipated. Australian soldiers were dying in the thousands, while medical and surgical advances meant that many injured and ill servicemen who in previous wars would most likely have perished from their wounds or disease were surviving. The families of the dead would need ongoing support, as would the ever-growing number of wounded and sick. Australians around the country, including the Premier of New South Wales, William Holman, argued that it was the responsibility of the state to coordinate, fund and administer this complex task effectively and efficiently.[3] In 1917 the federal government passed the first Repatriation Act – technically the Australian Soldiers' Repatriation Act – and appointed Senator Edward Millen as the Minister for Repatriation.

Further amendments to the Act widened the scope of the government's role in assisting returned soldiers and their families. Aside from the pension scheme, the Repat would assist veterans with continuing health problems: medical care would be provided to the wounded and sick; artificial limbs would be made for amputees; and places in special hostels and homes would be reserved for the totally incapacitated. For returned servicemen who could return to civilian employment, the Repat provided loans to purchase tools and equipment necessary to resume work, offered vocational training to those whose apprenticeships or education was disrupted by war service, and instituted rehabilitation training for the disabled. Schemes to settle returned men on the land were also introduced, as well as a system of employment preference for veterans in the Commonwealth public service. The emphasis was firmly on ensuring that ex-servicemen would have productive post-war lives.

Of the approximately 140 ex-prisoners of the Ottomans who returned to Australia, fifty-six have been identified as having Repat case files that detail some form of contact with Repatriation authorities. Other former POWs undoubtedly also had dealings with the department, but Repatriation files were often destroyed upon a beneficiary's death, and their cases are lost. It is possible also that some returned prisoners did not engage with the Repat, perhaps wishing to put the war years behind them and move on with their lives on their own terms. The identified files provide a snapshot of the diverse ways in which support was offered to returned servicemen in post-war Australia. Some files outline assistance regarding vocational training. D'Arcy Armstrong applied to the department in July 1919, less than a month after his discharge, for help securing training in accountancy. Repat officials offered Armstrong, who had worked as a clerk for three years before enlistment, a job at the Brisbane Repatriation offices and, under the Vocational Training Scheme, provided him with a position in a training course at the Central Technical College in Brisbane.[4] Other case files detail the provision of loans to enable the purchase of equipment and goods necessary for the resumption of pre-war occupations. Edgar Hobson, for example, had worked as a wool-classer before the war and, after obtaining similar work on a sheep station in Queensland's Western Downs, required a loan of ten pounds from the department to purchase a tent, work clothes, boots, blankets and other supplies he would need for his new position.[5] Several files offer insights into the Soldier Settlement Scheme, an ambitious program created by the federal and state governments to provide returned servicemen with a career on the land. William Vincent Kelly successfully applied for a parcel of land through the scheme on which he grew maize and potatoes. As was the story with so many soldier settlers, however, Kelly vacated his block in July 1925 owing to the failure of his crops.[6]

The majority of the ex-prisoners entered into correspondence with the Repat regarding health and pension matters. Each applicant claimed that his problems were the result of time spent on active service and in captivity, and requested medical care and financial assistance. The correspondence and medical records contained within these files must be used with care – remembering historian Stephen Garton's warning about the inherent agenda of the applicants – yet they provide important insights into the longer-term health effects of wartime imprisonment and the way the ex-prisoners constructed captivity for those who held significant influence over the success or failure of their claims. Returned servicemen and their families who applied for Repat assistance had to demonstrate that any illness, injury or incapacity they were suffering was directly linked to war service.[7] Some cases were straightforward: amputees, men with visible scars from bullets and shrapnel, the blinded and the gassed all could readily prove how their disability was the result of their service. Others, such as men suffering from chronic disease or psychological issues like 'shell shock', often found it much more difficult to prove the link. One way regular ex-servicemen could demonstrate the validity of their claims was through medical records kept by casualty clearing stations, field hospitals and bigger base hospitals, both overseas and in Australia. But for ex-prisoners claiming for incapacities suffered as a consequence of captivity, similar documentation was impossible to produce. Ottoman records could be requested, but this was often a long drawn-out, fruitless procedure. The link between captivity and continuing ill health was difficult to prove to officials who had not experienced capture and imprisonment themselves, particularly when evidence was limited.

To emphasise the legitimacy of their applications, the ex-prisoners followed similar patterns as other returned servicemen with regard to the language and rhetoric of their claims. Good health before the war was emphasised in nearly all applications, as were ideas of coping with the consequences of war service independently for extended periods. One former POW, when asked why his first application to the Repat was lodged some twenty years after the end of the war, explained that 'my only reason for not applying before was solely because I felt I could "paddle my own canoe"'.[8] The ex-prisoners also tapped into those impressions of captivity made popular during the latter years of the war – poor quality and insufficient rations, substandard accommodation and health care, physically demanding work, and exposure to disease – to portray their experiences of imprisonment as a time of great suffering that necessitated compensation. In many instances, their supporters (wives, family friends, fellow ex-POWs and local doctors) did the same.

Malaria was one of the most significant problems for the ex-POWs in the post-war period. The mosquito-borne disease was endemic to many of the regions in which Australians served, including Egypt, Gallipoli, the Sinai desert, Palestine and Mesopotamia.[9] In 1931, the department recorded that malaria accounted for 1647 pensions awarded to ex-AIF members.[10] Malaria was also, as we have seen, a problem in the interior of the Ottoman Empire. Many ex-prisoners believed that limited treatment of the disease in captivity led to continued health complications and argued that recurrent malarial attacks left them weak and unable to work. Former light horseman George Gilbert was one of twenty-three ex-POWs from the identified group in receipt of a pension for malaria after discharge. Gilbert initially received 25 per cent of the full pension rate until his payments were reduced to 12.5 per cent in 1923 (the 100 per cent pension rate in 1920 was 42 shillings per week, or approximately A$140 in 2016; claimants could also receive extra payments for dependants).[11] He continued to receive this rate of pension until the late 1930s, when a medical investigation determined that he was suffering from post-malarial debility rather than malaria itself, and stabilised his pension at the fortnightly rate of 18 shillings and eight pence.[12] Gilbert was fortunate to have had his pension stabilised. Colin Campbell was told in May 1932 that 'the state Repatriation Board has decided that you are no longer suffering from malaria, or any effects thereof, and your entitlement for treatment and war pension for this condition is accordingly cancelled'.[13] The cancellation of Campbell's pension perhaps had more to do with cost-cutting measures implemented in the 1930s by an increasingly financially stretched government rather than the reality of his physical condition and continued malarial attacks.

Dysentery and gastric troubles were another key problem, with fifteen ex-prisoners from the identified group pensioned for digestive conditions in the post-war period, including chronic diarrhoea, stomach pain and vomiting. Like malaria, dysentery was a common complaint in the wartime Ottoman Empire. Lack of treatment upon initial infection could lead to a chronic form of the disease, which caused intermittent periods of constipation and diarrhoea, abdominal pain, vomiting, and anorexia, often for many subsequent years. George Roberts endured debilitating stomach problems throughout the 1920s and early 1930s. He applied to the department for medical and pension assistance in January 1936, complaining of pain in the stomach, constipation, and feeling ill after eating. Roberts told Repat officials that he had suffered from food that was 'bad and scarce and sometimes uneatable' in captivity, and that lack of clothing and blankets to protect against the elements had left him susceptible to dysentery, as well as typhus and malaria.[14] Roberts stated in his claim that disease was so prevalent and medical care so limited in the Ottoman POW camps that 'it was die or get over it the best way you could'.[15] His claim was initially rejected but, on appeal, the Melbourne Commission's senior medical officer argued it was 'reasonable' to attribute his condition to war service and captivity.

Problems associated with 'nerves' were also a considerable concern for the former POWs. Twenty ex-prisoners from the group claimed Repat assistance for nervous troubles in the aftermath of the war. Foreshadowing what those who endured captivity at the hands of the Japanese and

Germans would report in the years after the Second World War, these former prisoners told Repat medical officers that they suffered from insomnia, nightmares, depression, inability to concentrate, anxiety and extreme nervousness.[16] Several linked their digestive complaints to nervous conditions.[17] In 1934 William Mackay applied to have his nervous troubles assessed by the department. Dr S. McDonald's post-examination report on Mackay paints a picture of a man in severe psychological distress:

> This man is in a state of nervous strain the whole time ... There is constant tremor of the hands which he tries to control with only partial success. There is an occasional facial tic and his expression suggests that he is far from normal ... His voice is loud and expressionless. I should say that his neurosis is fairly severe.[18]

Mackay was not alone in being diagnosed as 'far from normal'. Military medical historian Michael Tyquin suggests that about 8 per cent of all Australian servicemen were believed to have suffered from psychological problems during the war. A 1931 Australian Repatriation Department report indicated that 829 applications had been received from returned servicemen claiming 'shell shock' – an umbrella term applied to those who presented with symptoms including tremors, paralysis, mutism, extreme emotional responses and other so-called 'hysterical' reactions to life in the trenches and its attendant stresses. A further 5138 applications were received from men claiming for neurasthenia, another noted 'nerve'-related problem characterised by chronic feelings of fatigue and weakness rather than hysteria.[19]

Constructing captivity as a period of intense suffering could also be of benefit in claims related to nervous trouble. William Mackay explained to Repat officials that 'the treatment meted out to prisoners of war in Turkey did not improve my constitution'.[20] His nervous problems were, he believed, the result of being 'knocked about a lot'.[21] However, the senior medical officer at the Brisbane department believed that Mackay's health concerns were not particularly incapacitating, and instigated an investigation into his work and social habits to ensure that he was not embellishing his problems. Eventually, a diagnosis of neurosis was added to Mackay's previous claims for wounds, and he was pensioned at the rate of 75 per cent.[22] In his (eventually successful) claim for 'nerves', Maurice Delpratt and his wife also highlighted the features of POW life that they believed led to Maurice's condition. In 1937 Mary Delpratt wrote to the Repat explaining that her husband's time in imprisonment had been a 'nerve-wracking [sic] experience'. She added that it was 'a wonder they [ex-POW] are not permanently mad'.[23] Mary's testimony indicates that she had also become a casualty of captivity: as Betty Peters discovered in her work with the wives of former POWs of the Japanese, the psychological troubles suffered by ex-prisoners also exacted a toll on partners and relationships.[24] Delpratt himself argued that 'the everlasting drag and the fear and uncertainty' of captivity had played on his mind, adding that 'the bugs, the lice, the funerals' and other privations, coupled with the beating he received at Hadjikiri, had left him feeling depressed and anxious.[25] Ernest Ingram's application for nervous trouble was also framed around his experiences of captivity. His claim was accepted in April 1936, after a doctor's report suggested Ingram's health concerns – particularly 'loss of self-control' – were directly linked to his time as a prisoner of war. 'Such privation and apparently hopeless outlook during his captivity,' wrote Dr L. Bond, 'must inevitably cause serious nervous trauma in one so young at the time.'[26]

Although a successful claim for 'nerves' meant access to medical and financial assistance, some ex-prisoners felt the stigma of diagnoses related to psychological trouble. Lancelot Lightfoot was diagnosed with neurosis in the late 1930s, linked to what one doctor later stated was the 'not inconsiderable rigours of life as a POW in Turkish hands'.[27] Twenty-five years later, after he was admitted to a Repatriation hospital for treatment and was placed in a psychiatric ward, Lightfoot wrote an angry letter to the department, claiming that his diagnosis as a 'neurotic' had 'coloured' his relationship with the Repat.[28] His letter was forwarded to the hospital with a covering note from Repat authorities: 'He has a thing about psychiatric wards (stigma etc) and feels very strongly that admission to a ward of this sort is a reflection on his integrity and an indication that he is mad. "How could he explain such a thing to his grandchildren, friends, and fellow members of the T&PI Association?" is the theme he labours.'[29]

Before the war, mental illness carried a long tradition of social stigma and was seen as a typically feminine condition. But with the advent of industrial-scale warfare during the First World War and the widespread carnage it brought, the numbers of servicemen suffering from a multitude of nervous troubles increased dramatically. There was a persistent undercurrent of non-believers, who argued that those with psychological disorders were effeminate cowards or malingerers with a pre-disposition to mental weakness, yet sufferers' perceived unmanly behaviour was made somewhat more socially acceptable by the fact that it was usually connected to direct combat experience.[30] Although they suffered from similar complaints, the ex-prisoners did not share that experience of prolonged exposure to bombardment and shellfire, and their troubles could therefore not be made more acceptable by linking them to the dynamic, hyper-masculine world of combat. That Lightfoot's neurosis was never attributed to combat experience was another possible factor behind his obvious discomfort with his diagnosis and subsequent treatment.

As the returned prisoners aged, health concerns such as ulcers, arth-ritis, hernias and heart disease became more prevalent. Like their regular service counterparts, many of the former POWs lodged speculative or rather hopeful claims to the Repat – although the ex-prisoners argued that these multiple health problems were the result of increased susceptibility caused by a weakened constitution brought about by captivity. In some instances, drawing on narratives of suffering as a POW to explain such health problems worked. George Paltridge first approached the Repat in 1936 claiming a history of chronic ill health stretching back to his days as a prisoner. He argued that his time in captivity left him prematurely debilitated and unable to work. After years of examinations and rejections, another medical assessment in 1948 diagnosed that Paltridge suffered from avitaminosis as a prisoner, and stated that his symptoms were the result of debility 'caused by conditions during time as POW'.[31] Emphasising his ex-POW status eventually worked in his favour, and Paltridge was pen-sioned at the rate of 50 per cent – although it is interesting to note that this diagnosis and acceptance of claim for pension correlates with the return of the prisoners of the Japanese, many of who suffered from similar nutri-tional diseases as a result of their captivity in the Second World War, and the distribution of material to Repat doctors about the kinds of health troubles with which they might present.[32] In 1963 Fred Haig, aged 68, applied to have a hiatus hernia (a bulging of the stomach into the dia-phragm) accepted as a war disability. A pilot during the war, Haig successfully argued that his multiple war-related health problems – includ-ing his crash-landing in 1918, the removal of a hydatid cyst contracted while in captivity, his 'weakened state while a prisoner' and Spanish influenza also contracted in the Ottoman Empire – contributed to the deterioration of his diaphragm muscles and therefore his hernia.[33]

The Repat also considered applications from the relatives of veterans who died after the war from illness or disease believed to be related to war service. The families of several ex-prisoners who passed away applied to have the death officially recognised by the department; success in such claims would mean that the bereaved family would be eligible for ongoing pension benefits. Common causes of death among the ex-POW group included cancers and problems associated with heart or vascular disease, such as heart attacks, stroke and myocarditis. Tuberculosis killed several, two men died in accidents, and another two committed suicide. The deaths of ten of the identified group of ex-POWs were officially attributed to their war service and, as the case of Joseph O'Neill demonstrates, the suffering inherent in captivity was a key theme in these applications.[34] O'Neill died in December 1937 at the age of 45 when his gastric ulcer haemorrhaged. With two small children to provide for, his widow Violet approached Repat authorities to argue that her husband's death be ascribed to his experiences during the war. Her first application was refused, but Violet appealed and, with a supporting statement from O'Neill's doctor, which emphasised the continued constitutional effects of captivity – 'the deficient treatment and insufficient nutrition whilst prisoners greatly undermined their resistance ... Many Australians suffered severely from malaria and intestinal diseases and emaciation in some cases extreme' – her claim was accepted.[35]

However, applications for health problems or death associated with experiences of captivity were not always successful. Former light horseman Matthew Sloan suffered from recurrent attacks of malaria for several years after the end of the war. He first applied to the Repat in October 1935, claiming that he had been 'a victim' to the disease ever since his captivity, and was unable to continue working on his dairy farm.[36] Enquiries were made of Turkish authorities regarding records of Sloan's medical treatment as a prisoner – their response was that all POW records had been lost – and Sloan was asked to provide a report outlining the reasons he believed his ill health was related to his time in captivity.[37] His angry statement draws on the impressions of imprisonment that circulated towards the end of the war:

> On the 1st May 1918 I was captured by the Turks during the Es Salt fighting. Their treatment of prisoners was brutal. With next to no clothing we slept on the bare ground, not even a handful of straw to lie on, no shelter of any kind over us. Rain or fine I never had even an old bag to put over me at night. Food – you could not call it food at all, a respectable pig would not eat what was given to us. Broken in health and body and well neigh [sic] broken in spirit.[38]

Sloan buttressed his claim with letters of support from family members, friends and persons of influence in his town, including the local reverend and justice of the peace. Each firmly stated that captivity clearly had a deleterious effect on Sloan's health. Nevertheless, his application was rejected, as were his subsequent appeals, after medical officials stated that 'the evidence does not support a claim that conditions found on investigation are related to W/S [war service]'.[39]

Other ex–POWs also had their applications rejected. At the same time that Haig lodged his successful claim for hiatus hernia, Ron Austin applied to have Parkinson's disease accepted as brought on by his war service. Diagnosed with the degenerative disease in the late 1950s, Austin argued that his time in captivity had caused its onset. In the early 1960s his local doctor wrote a letter of support:

> This condition has gradually progressed until now he needs a lot of help. The burden of his care is becoming more than can be arranged for. We apply for consideration of his case as due to, or aggravated by, privations suffered while a prisoner. I think it very probable, but we have few who might have suffered similar treatment as prisoners under the conditions which he suffered.[40]

Despite this supporting documentation – which demonstrates that doctors were complicit in portraying captivity as an experience of suffering that had the potential to cause legitimate health concerns – Repat officials rejected Austin's claim, arguing that Parkinson's could not have been caused by war experiences more than forty years ago.[41]

Applications for death of a former prisoner as attributable to captivity were also rejected.[42] In May 1933 Mary Earnshaw applied to have her husband's sudden death from heart failure related to carcinoma of the stomach attributed to his war service. Mary wrote to the Repat in late June that year, arguing that Frederick's health had been adversely affected by his POW experiences. Owing to her 'poor circumstances', Mary requested financial assistance in the form of a war widow's pension.[43] Several other doctors and family friends supported her claim, including one man, Mr P. Gallagher, who drew on a narrative of suffering to explain Earnshaw's declining health upon his return from the war:

> He [Earnshaw] was never the same man after he came back. Before going to the war he was as hardy and healthy a man as you could find anywhere. He gradually went back [downhill] till the last 2 years he was practically an invalid. He never said much but at times he would mention that his constitution was ruined by what he went through.[44]

Nevertheless, in October 1933, the Repat rejected Mary's claim, stating that 'carcinoma of the stomach is a constitutional condition and could have no possible relationship to war service'.[45] Amy Stormonth's claim to have her husband's death by suicide in September 1935 recognised as owing to war service was also rejected. The cause of Stewart Stormonth's suicide was never fully understood: officially it was attributed to financial stress, but there was some suggestion from family friends that he had an underlying nervous problem related to his experiences of the war. In a letter to fellow ex-POW Thomas White, Amy expressed her grief and guilt over her husband's death. 'I'm afraid until too late,' she wrote, 'we did not realise how ill Stormy was.'[46] For these applicants, former POW status and the construction of captivity as an experience of suffering bound to have inevitable consequences on health and well-being did not guarantee a positive outcome.

Rejected claims, suspicion over late applications and lack of documentary evidence, and close investigation of bodies, minds and sometimes lifestyles led to a sense of bitterness among some former POWs towards the Repat. However, there is no evidence to suggest that the ex-prisoners were subject to more scrutiny, or suffered more rejection, than other returned servicemen. Indeed, as Marina Larsson and other scholars of repatriation in Australia note, feelings of anger and discontent about Repat authorities' rulings were a popular discourse among ex-servicemen and their families.[47] *Smith's Weekly*, a patriotic newspaper popular among members of the AIF, even dubbed the Repat the 'cyanide gang', and made it a priority to critique the rulings of Repatriation authorities and promote cases of perceived injustice.[48] Nevertheless, and despite the fact that many ex-POWs had their claims approved largely because of their history of captivity, there was a feeling among some of the former prisoners that they had been badly done by. Matthew Sloan, for example, strongly believed that his many applications were rejected because officials and doctors had not properly taken into consideration his time in captivity.[49]

In a 1947 speech to the House of Representatives regarding the proposal of a 'three shillings a day' payment to Australians held captive by the enemy during the Second World War, Thomas White, then Member for Balaclava, also stressed what he felt was an ambivalent response from the Repat to ex-POWs of the First World War. 'As prisoners of war they disappeared from the face of the earth,' White argued. 'They were lost souls. When they returned to civil life they were Rip Van Winkles ... The position of men who have disappeared for a long time is not understood by repatriation officials.' Drawing on his own experiences, and those of his fellow former prisoners, White claimed that 'the sufferings that men underwent as prisoners of the enemy countries have imprinted on them a mark that will not become apparent for years'.[50] He pushed for the formation of a special government board to ensure that Second World War POWs were adequately compensated for any continuing health problems related to their imprisonment – something he clearly felt he and his fellow ex-POWs had been denied upon their return from captivity a war earlier.

INTERWAR MEMORY AND MARGINALISATION

White's feelings towards the Repat – and those of other ex-POWs like Matthew Sloan – can be attributed to the seeming public reinforcement of the prisoners' feelings of inferiority and sense of difference from other returned servicemen. As we have seen, capture and imprisonment made many POWs question their contribution to the war. Involvement in the war effort took on particular currency in post-war Australia, when the fighting spirit and martial prowess of the Anzacs were celebrated throughout the country and the returned serviceman was held up as the epitome of manly success. Some ex-prisoners felt they had fallen short of the expectations of the Australian soldier and had failed to meet the prescription for contemporary masculinity. John Halpin expressed these feelings in his memoir, writing that the prisoners had not only surrendered their bodies to the Turks but had also 'surrendered manhood'.[51] Instead of suffering in the trenches of the Western Front or participating in the victories in the Middle East, the POWs had finished the war in isolated prison camps, where many had worked for the enemy. Such obvious differences between their war and those of their counterparts perpetuated a sense of shame and guilt among many of the ex-prisoners for, as Michael Tyquin writes, 'despite the much-vaunted larrikinism and casualness of the Australian psyche, in reality there was little room for personal failure in war'.[52]

Maurice Delpratt's embarrassment at becoming a POW was clear throughout his time in captivity. But, as his 1937 statement to the Brisbane Repatriation Department suggests, underlying feelings of shame and inadequacy continued to haunt him long after the war ended. 'I worry and brood continually on the fact I had failed so badly to serve my country,' he wrote, 'and had, in fact, served my country's foe by helping to build a railway to be used against my own mates.'[53] Delpratt's wife Mary argued that his awkwardness about his former POW status led Delpratt to develop what she described as a 'distinct inferiority complex' and made him reluctant to discuss his experiences of the war.[54] Amy Stormonth explained that she had also noticed her husband's hesitation at talking about his war service, and tried to speak to him about it on several occasions. 'But he always replied "don't worry about me, I am quite alright",' she wrote in a statement to the Repat, 'and that was all I could ever get out of him.'[55]

Such private concerns were reinforced by an apparent lack of public awareness of, or interest in, the prisoners' experiences. As we have seen, newspapers printed articles during the war about the prisoners in Germany and the Ottoman Empire, and many Australians helped raise funds to ensure the continued work of welfare agencies on behalf of the captives. But this broader public engagement with captivity was quickly overwhelmed in the aftermath of the war by the stories of servicemen returned from victory in France and, to a lesser extent, the Middle East. Historian Alon Rachamimov writes that the Western Front was always going to garner the most attention in the post-war period as it was where the main belligerents deployed the majority of their troops. It was also the site of the newest and most exciting war experiences – industrialised warfare and technologically advanced weaponry called for new tactics that diverged from traditional battlefronts – and it was where the majority of allied casualties (aside from the Russians) were sustained.[56] Other fronts, and other experiences, quickly became viewed as 'side-shows' and, just as Joy Damousi argues in relation to bereaved mothers losing the primacy of their position in the years after 1918, different forms of sacrifice and suffering that had genuine currency during the war – such as captivity – lost their legitimacy.[57] This was something former POW William Randall experienced first-hand in his Victorian hometown. Randall accepted an invitation to a local convention for returned servicemen in early 1919, and was placed last on the list of speakers. The organiser of the event justified Randall's position by explaining that, although 'Private Randall was equally as good as the others', the rest of the guests 'had been in France'.[58] An obvious hierarchy of experiences operated at this event in which those who fought on the Western Front occupied the top rung, publicly emphasising the lustre of the combat experience and reinforcing any sense of inferiority or awkwardness Randall might have felt.

The marginalisation of captivity was a phenomenon common among many nations in the aftermath of the war. Heather Jones suggests that ex-prisoners in Britain and Germany were victims of a 'historical amnesia' in the period between the end of the First World War and the outbreak of the Second, as POW experiences and issues were glossed over in favour of reconciliation between the former belligerents.[59] Other European states ignored, and sometimes openly attacked, their former POWs. French prisoners returned from captivity in Germany were accused of disloyalty, while Austro-Hungarian POWs repatriated from Russia were the subjects of intense scrutiny and surveillance by a government that feared they had been exposed to Bolshevism or indoctrinated in anti-Habsburg beliefs.[60] Russian POWs returning to the new Soviet state were openly dismissed, as they were largely pre–Red Army forces who were seen, as historian Reinhard Nachtigal writes, to have 'fought on the side of reaction'.[61] In a terrible irony some Italian POWs repatriated from Austria were charged with mass defection and interned in Italian gaols and prison camps. The particularly hard line taken by the Italian Government against its POWs was due to suspicions that they had surrendered to escape fighting – the decision to go to war against Austria–Hungary was not popular among Italians, and the harsh conditions experienced by Italian troops in the alpine regions were not well known to the Italian military authorities.[62] When placed in this international context, William Randall's experience of rejection seems relatively benign, but it was still there.

Public reinforcement of the prisoners' sense of inferiority was also expressed in unit and battalion histories. These accounts were a popular publishing phenomenon in the post-war period and contributed to the burgeoning literature related to Australian participation in the First World War. However, they also helped perpetuate the lack of recognition of the experiences of POWs. With few exceptions battalion and regimental histories rarely mentioned those of their members who became prisoners, except in footnotes or columns of statistics. The author of the 15th Battalion's history wrote that his unit was 'proud of their record of never any large numbers of prisoners being lost to the enemy' when, in reality, the 15th had the second highest number of men taken POW by Ottoman forces.[63] Such statements offer further evidence of the low regard in which prisoners of war were held.

Memoirs of former POWs also – somewhat paradoxically – contributed to the marginalisation of captivity in the interwar period. Nine Australian former prisoners of the Ottomans published accounts of their captivity in the form of memoirs. The majority were published in the late 1920s and the 1930s, including perhaps the best known, Thomas White's *Guests of the Unspeakable* (1928). These early memoirs received some critical attention. A 1933 review of White's memoir called it a 'record of remarkable adventure and disregard of danger', while *Reveille* claimed of John Halpin's *Blood in the Mists* (1934) that 'no member of the AIF has written a more magnificently dramatic story'.[64] But captivity memoirs did not have the same public resonance as the plethora of books produced by soldiers who fought in Europe. First World War POW memoirs lack the 'edge and urgency' of battle memoirs and, as Robin Gerster has commented, they are often characterised by a 'blend of humility and querulousness'.[65] Moreover, the experiences of suffering outlined in vivid detail in many POW memoirs – lack of food, overcrowding, hard labour and disease – were, as Alon Rachamimov notes, familiar forms of adversity for many readers who had lived through pre- and post-war economic depression, and were rather dull in comparison to rousing stories of barbed wire, flame-throwers, gas attacks, machine guns and trench life told by those who had fought in France and Belgium.[66] POW memoirists therefore tended to sensationalise their stories by telling daring tales of escape – despite the fact that escape, as we have seen, reflected the stories of only a very limited number of former prisoners – or by attacking their former captors through the lens of race.[67] In doing so the former prisoners highlighted the differences between their experiences and those of their counterparts who had remained on the battlefront, differences that ensured they were relegated to 'an inferior place' in the hierarchies of commemoration that developed after the war.[68]

Shifting Australian perceptions of the former Ottoman enemy in the interwar period fed into a lack of awareness of the POWs' experiences, too. Before the war, as we have seen, ideas of the ethnic Turks were based on their supposedly inherent barbarism and lack of civilised culture. But there was another element to these Australian impressions that gathered momentum after Gallipoli. In defending their homeland, the Ottoman soldiers demonstrated resourcefulness, stoicism and fighting prowess, qualities the Australian troops both admired and identified with. Such admiration was reflected in the changing language used by the Australians to describe their enemy, who went from 'unspeakable' to 'Johnny' Turk, 'Abdul' or 'Jacko'. The changing sentiment of the soldiers was reported at home in such newspapers as the Melbourne *Argus*, which in November 1915 published an article that presented the Ottoman enemy as a stubborn yet ultimately worthy opponent:

> The Turk is a sport! Every Australian soldier at Anzac will tell you that, and perhaps in homely phrase he will also remark that 'Abdul is a white man!' It is neither athletic ability nor colour, however, that the Commonwealth soldier takes into consideration in sizing up the men who are opposed to him, but he has an unbounded admiration for anyone who plays the game, and in this respect the Turks has sprung something of a surprise. The Australians went to Gallipoli expecting that their dead would be mutilated ... and that every rule

of 'civilised' war would be broken, but they admit that they have been agreeably disappointed.[69]

In proving their sportsmanship and adherence to the rules of 'civilised' warfare, the enemy had earned the respect of the Australian troops – although, it must be noted, this did not prevent the Australians from continuing to fight and kill Ottoman soldiers.

Impressions of the Ottoman enemy as a gentlemanly opponent were given further currency with the publication of *The Anzac Book* in 1916. Originally conceived as a Christmas–New Year special to boost morale on the peninsula, the book evolved into a commemorative account of the Gallipoli experience after the evacuation in late 1915. Charles Bean, as editor, selected and rejected all material for *The Anzac Book*, allowing him to craft a highly stylised image of the Australian troops on Gallipoli based on quintessential Anzac ideals and values drawn from frontier bushman mythology, British military history and allusions to the classical world. Many of the supposed characteristics of the Australian soldier and the foundations of the Anzac myth are evident in the book; there are multiple tales of stoicism, bravery, larrikinism and irreverence, and draw-ings and cartoons portray the 'average' Anzac. One poem, titled 'Abdul', depicts the changed Australian attitude towards the enemy soldier:

> So though your name be black as ink
>> For murder and rapine,
> Carried out in happy concert
>> With your Christians from the Rhine
> We will judge you Mr Abdul
>> By the test by which we can –
> That with all your breath, in life, in death,
>> You've played the gentleman.[70]

'Abdul' was written by Charles Bean and, as historian David Kent points out, it is one of very few contributions to the book to express such glowing ideas of the enemy. Indeed, Kent argues that Bean was the initial driving force behind the idea of the Ottomans as a worthy foe – for specific reasons.[71] By emphasising the stoicism and fighting prowess of the defenders on the peninsula, and stressing the relationship between enemies as one of mutual respect, Bean not only portrayed the fighting as noble – important when there had been such high casualties for little gain – but also legitimised the allied withdrawal. As media scholars Antje Gnida and Catherine Simpson write in their analysis of representations of former enemies in Australian film, 'the portrayal of the noble Turk as respectful of Australian fighting qualities put the Anzacs on a pedestal as courageous and heroic fighters, who had to withdraw in Gallipoli because they had encountered a "worthy opponent"'.[72] In this regard, then, the enemy became the beneficiary of attempts to explain Australian and British failures on Gallipoli.

Bean's claims of positive Anzac attitudes towards the enemy and ideas of the Turks as a noble foe became part of the developing mythology of Gallipoli as *The Anzac Book* spread through the troops, reinforcements in training camps and, eventually, to Australians at home. By mid-1916, the publishing house had sold nearly 104 500 copies as thousands of soldiers purchased the book and sent it to family and friends. The book was received with 'unanimous enthusiasm and laudatory reviews', and its many messages, including that of the Ottoman enemy as a noble opponent, became part of the growing understanding of the war for Australians both in battle and at home.[73]

Despite public anxiety in the early 1920s over the care of graves on Gallipoli – mollified by reports from IWGC workers and inspectors who emphasised that the Turks were acting as 'trustworthy stewards' of the sacred ground – the compassionate narrative linking Australians and Turks continued into the interwar period.[74] Officials of the Turkish Government participated in Anzac Day events on Gallipoli in the 1930s, and pilgrims who travelled to the peninsula told of the warm reception they received from the former enemy. The leader of the Turkish nation, Mustafa Kemal Ataturk, sent several messages to Australia emphasising the martial prowess of the Anzacs, which were often published in the press. But these expressions of gratitude and praise for the old enemy angered at least one ex-POW. In 1934 – the same year Ataturk allegedly made his famous, and now fiercely contested, speech about 'those heroes who have shed their blood and lost their lives' – John Halpin wrote a scathing letter to the editor of *Reveille* about the willingness of Australians to praise the former enemy.[75] Published under the headline 'Praise of the Turks: A captive in reply', Halpin asked: 'May I give comment on a matter which has become of nation-wide interest – on the sentiments of admiration expressed . . . to Kemal Pasha, and all the Turks . . . as generous foes, splendid fellows, etc etc.' He called for his fellow returned servicemen to acknowledge the experiences of all those who fought the Ottomans, including POWs:

> Let those who wish to publicly express their appreciation of our
> erstwhile foes weigh the experiences of comrades in this conflict as

a whole, and not overlook the dead who fell, not as victims of the cleanly bullet or bayonet, but before unleashed savagery, brutality, and bestiality, and the onslaughts of which they were helpless to oppose ... Hate does not enter into the matter, neither does undeserved admiration. We can all forgive, but in the silence of our hearts, forget? No, that is impossible.[76]

Halpin's rather melodramatic letter demonstrates his sense of disconnection between the prisoners' experiences of the war and the public emphasis on the honour of his former captors.

These instances of the public reinforcement of any private sense of inferiority or difference felt by the former prisoners, and the collective 'forgetting' of their experiences, goes some way to explain the prevalence of nervous disorders among their group in the interwar period. Historian Eugene Michail notes that tension between individual and collective memory was a common problem for veterans of the First World War. The fact that this was the first 'total war' involving multiple fronts and multiple levels of mobilisation meant that more people were able to claim connections with the war effort, but conversely, because of the patterns of press coverage during the war and commemorative efforts in its aftermath, those with more peripheral roles or experiences were relegated to the sidelines. According to Michail, who studied the British Army on the Salonika Front, their exclusion from the collective memory of the war 'negated for them the chance to construct their own positive memory of their personal experiences'.[77]

Christina Twomey has also explored the potential ramifications of being overlooked in collective memory. She argues in relation to civilian internees of the Japanese during the Second World War that those who have endured unusual experiences within a specific historical episode need to express their story in order for the experience to become 'integrated into the life history' of the subject.[78] If their different experiences are not recognised within the broader historical narrative – if there is no 'receptive audience for the tale' – the trauma of the difference can cause recurrent problems for those involved.[79] Alistair Thomson's work on Australian veterans of the First World War – and the inability of individuals to reconcile their experiences with the collective memory of an event leading to a sense of alienation – is important here, too.[80]

Thomson, Michail and Twomey's insights can be applied to the former prisoners of the Ottomans: the lack of public space within which to articulate their distinctive experiences of the war meant that any personal sense of shame or difference ex-POWs like Maurice Delpratt might have felt was compounded, to the potential detriment of their health and well-being.[81]

CONTEMPORARY UNDERSTANDINGS OF THE POWS

First World War POWs were pushed even further back in Australian public consciousness after the Second World War, during which some 30 000 Australians were held as prisoners by the Italians, Germans and Japanese. Captivity had been the fate of only a minority during the First World War; however, it was far more of a familiar experience during the Second, and POWs eventually assumed a greater prominence in Australian memory of that war. The prisoners of the Japanese, in particular, also came to dominate broader Australian conceptions of wartime imprisonment. Any impressions of the POWs of the Ottomans as victims of a brutal captivity were eclipsed after the liberation of the Japanese prison camps in Asia and the Pacific. The prisoners of the Japanese also experienced an inversion of the perceived racial hierarchy, but the horror of their captivity was more corporeal. Their accounts of the murder of POWs – both men and women – slave labour, brutal physical and psychological punishments, and the privation of the prison camps horrified and fascinated Australians, who continued to despise their former captors well after the war. Indeed, there was no attempt to promote a positive narrative about the Japanese in the aftermath of the Second World War, and POWs remained a source of tension in Australia–Japan relations for decades after.

The tone of two memoirs written after the Second World War by former prisoners of the Ottomans – Leslie Luscombe's *Story of Harold Earl* (1970) and C.W. Hill's *The Spook and the Commandant* (1975) – reflects a seeming acceptance of the dominance of the POWs of the Japanese in Australian ideas of wartime captivity. Historian Jennifer Lawless notes that these publications, particularly Luscombe's, present a 'moderate, good-humoured, and balanced assessment' of life as a POW, and offers this as evidence that the prisoners' time in the Ottoman Empire was not as bad as earlier memoirs made out.[82] However, the more restrained tone of Luscombe's account could also be attributed to his recognition that the POWs of the Ottomans no longer resonated in the public consciousness of captivity, influenced as it was by those who endured imprisonment under the Japanese.

The significance of the prisoners of the Japanese is also reflected in commemorative efforts dedicated to POWs. The publication of memoirs and other accounts of captivity in the Asia-Pacific region generated intense interest in these POWs, but public awareness has also been fostered more recently by the creation of memorials dedicated to their experiences. For many years after the war, the former prisoners of the Japanese worked to be treated as ex-servicemen (and women) rather than ex-POWs, and the RSL and Repatriation Department also pushed for their integration into general commemorative practices and events. By the mid-1980s, however, feminist and pacifist critiques of war led to increasing interest in the individual's experience of conflict, while new ideas about trauma encouraged a focus on the horror, suffering and deprivation of war, and the stories of the prisoners of the Japanese assumed greater currency.[83] In what historian Ken Inglis calls 'a spirit of amendment', memorials to these POWs were constructed in Australia and at their former sites of captivity.[84] There are now many different examples of memorials dedicated to the prisoners of the Japanese, including a series commemorating Australians who died in Borneo on the Sandakan Death Marches – such as the memorials in Sydney's Burwood Park, Brisbane's New Farm Park and at Sandakan itself – a stone tablet marking the spot of the Bangka Island massacre (the killing of Australian nurses by the Japanese in 1942), and a memorial and museum at the notorious Hellfire Pass cutting on the former Burma–Thai Railway in Kanchanaburi, Thailand.[85]

The first official national memorial dedicated to Australian prisoners of war from all conflicts, the Changi Chapel, located in the grounds of the Royal Military College, Duntroon, Canberra, also demonstrates the centrality of the POWs of the Japanese to Australian understandings of wartime captivity. Erected in 1988, the memorial was constructed from the remains of a chapel built by allied prisoners in the Changi prison camp in Singapore. As a memorial to all Australian POWs, the Changi Chapel is limited. It is situated in the grounds of a military college – making access something of a problem – and it has clear links to the prisoners of the Japanese.[86] It was largely this lack of recognition of other Australian POWs that drove the construction of the Australian ex-POW Memorial in Ballarat, Victoria. Unveiled in 2004, this memorial wall, 130 metres long, has the names of more than 37 000 Australians who experienced captivity in conflicts from the Boer War to Korea inscribed upon its black granite. The Ballarat memorial cost an estimated $1.8 million, of which $200 000 was provided by the Department of Veterans' Affairs.[87] In September 2008, after years of debate over the legitimacy of its claim to being a 'national' memorial, the Ballarat memorial was attributed official national status.[88] Aside from a stained-glass window in the Garden Island

Naval Chapel in Sydney, dedicated to the memory of those who lost their lives after the submarine HMAS *AE1* disappeared off the cost of New Guinea in 1914 and which also mentions the capture of the crew of the *AE2*, the Ballarat monument is the only Australian memorial on which the POWs of the Ottomans are commemorated as a distinct group.

POWs have not really made much impression in more recent Australian understandings of the First World War, either. They are, according to historian Peter Stanley, practically 'invisible in the Australian story of the war'.[89] Again, numbers must be taken into account. The experiences of fewer than 200 men in Ottoman captivity continue to be overwhelmed by the focus on the thousands who died on Gallipoli and the Western Front. But lack of awareness of the POWs in contemporary commemoration and memory of the war can also be attributed to the ways in which Australian society today understands the First World War. From the 1980s onwards, increasing research into the war experiences of grandfathers and great-grandfathers by family historians and new understandings of trauma resulted in something of a shift in the way Australians thought of war and of those who fought in it.[90] No longer were soldiers symbols of militarism and warmongering; instead former servicemen came to be seen as victims and war as, above all else, a tragedy – particularly the First World War, with its popular portrayals of the senseless slaughter of thousands, the incompetence of generals at the expense of the rank and file, and the ravaged landscapes of northern France and Belgium. This expanded rubric of First World War memory could have included POWs, for many had suffered great hardships and misery in captivity; however, their 'victimhood' was not of the same level as, for example, those who endured the hardships and misery of the Somme. Captivity, according to Alon Rachamimov, has 'at best a marginal place' in understandings of the First World War as the '*Urkatastrophe* [seminal catastrophe]' of the twentieth century.[91]

Although the prisoners continue to reside on the margins of Australian history and memory of the war, commemoration of their former captors has boomed. In return for the official renaming of Anzac Cove by the Turkish Government on the seventieth anniversary of the Gallipoli landings in 1985, a memorial dedicated to the first president of the Turkish republic, Mustafa Kemal Ataturk, was established at the top of Anzac Parade in Canberra (as well as in Wellington, New Zealand). Unveiled on Anzac Day 1985, the Canberra memorial, situated diagonally opposite the entrance to the Australian War Memorial, consists of a bronze likeness of Ataturk's head and a plaque on which the famous speech is inscribed on a curved concrete wall. At the same time as the Canberra memorial was dedicated, a stretch of water in Lake Burley Griffin was named 'Gallipoli Reach', and at Albany in Western Australia, the site of departure for the first convoys of the AIF in 1914, the body of water linking King George Sound and Princess Royal Harbour was named 'Ataturk Channel' (in 2001, a life-sized statue of Ataturk was also unveiled at Albany). These are the only memorials in Australia to represent a former enemy commander and are a tangible testament to the cultivation of an idea of special friendship between the two nations – although, as David Stephens argues, it was the Turks who initially did much of the 'heavy lifting' in this regard.[92]

Other representations of the First World War, including those on film, have continued to omit POWs while simultaneously privileging the position of their former captors. The idea of the honourable enemy has been a strong discourse in Australian cinema; Charles Chauvel first portrayed the formidable but noble Turk in the 1940 film *Forty Thousand Horsemen*, and these themes were also a significant aspect of Peter Weir's 1981 film, *Gallipoli*. Catherine Simpson writes that *Gallipoli*, made during a period of revival of the Australian film industry, fed renewed ideas of Australian nationalism centred on anti-British sentiment.[93] *Gallipoli* positioned the enemy as comrade more than foe, and emphasised the fact that both the Australians and the Turks were victims of their respective imperial overlords. Weir's film spawned a renewed interest in the Anzacs and their experiences on the peninsula, and inspired a number of other documentaries, TV series and feature films.

One recent film, Russell Crowe's *The Water Diviner*, released in late 2014, is significant in that it makes explicit reference to allied prisoners in Ottoman captivity. Set in the immediate aftermath of the war, Joshua Connor, played by Crowe, travels to Gallipoli to locate the bodies of his three dead sons, but while there learns that one was taken prisoner. Connor rather fancifully finds his son at his former site of confinement – becoming embroiled in the conflict between the Greeks and the nationalist Turks on the way – but there is no discussion of his son's experiences as a POW or his feelings about imprisonment. The captivity element is useful in advancing the narrative arc of the film, but it is an underwhelming and underplayed theme. What is emphasised, however, as in Weir's *Gallipoli*, is the sense of a special relationship between two nations birthed in the crucible of war.

Indeed, this idea of a special relationship is key to contemporary Australian commemorative events. A Turkish presence (in some form) is now common at Anzac Day services throughout the country, often through the reading of Ataturk's ode. Turks have participated in the annual Anzac Day parade in Melbourne since 1996 and, although the then President of the Victorian branch of the RSL, Bruce Ruxton, initially opposed their involvement, they were later permitted to establish a Turkish subbranch of the RSL. This decision was ostensibly based on the fact that the two nations had fought together during the Korean War, but historian Kevin Fewster suspects that this was more of a technicality than a measure of real feeling.[94] After officially welcoming descendants of the Turks who fought on Gallipoli into the RSL fold in 2006, Victorian President Major-General David McLachlan made it clear that this ruling was not extended to descendants of other wartime enemies, nor would it likely be in future. As McLachlan told the *Age*, 'I could never ever see ... Japanese veterans of the Second World War marching in an Anzac Day march ... [T]hey were a dreaded enemy that was despised by the Australian veterans.'[95] The *Age* 's commentator Mark Baker, under the headline 'Our favourite enemies', argued that the rebadging of the Turks 'as some kind of ersatz ally' and the privileging of their presence in commemorative events came at the expense of the sense of goodwill developed with other former enemies of Australia, and of understanding the realities and complexities of human conflict.[96]

Ken Inglis and Jock Philips have written that contemporary Australian willingness to commemorate the Turks could be read as 'acts of atonement or gratitude to the enemy without whom there would be no ANZAC'.[97] Indeed, the continuity of Gallipoli commemorations, and Anzac more broadly, rests in part on the idea of 'the noble Turk' and the special friendship narrative. As historians Mark McKenna and Stuart Ward argue, 'The stories of Turkish–Australian friendship at Gallipoli are repeated endlessly today as a means of ennobling the campaign for a generation uneasy with older myths of martial valour.'[98] Such romanticised understandings of the conflict on Gallipoli and subsequent relations between the two nations also helps to manage any potential issues that come with the influx of Australians travelling to Turkey every April to, as McKenna and Ward state, reoccupy the ground conceded in late 1915.[99] Although there have been moments of diplomatic tension, such as the construction of roads at Anzac Cove in 2005, the special friendship interpretation of the Gallipoli campaign is of continued benefit to both Australia and Turkey. According to Catherine Simpson, 'Australia has an important need to whitewash Turkey, because in whitewashing Turkey it, by association, whitewashes itself and makes its formative national narrative ... more simplistic and complete.'[100] Any critique of Turkish actions during the war, including the deportation and massacre of Armenians and, indeed, the issue of prisoners of war, complicate this 'whitewashing', which perhaps also explains the continued silencing of POW experiences in contemporary Australian memory of Gallipoli, of the fighting in the Middle East from 1916 to 1918, and of the First World War more broadly.

In exploring the aftermath of captivity in the Ottoman Empire, we can see how its challenges continued well into the post-war period. The physical and psychological effects of imprisonment exacted a toll on ex-POWs' health, relationships and careers, and some continued to feel the stigma of surrender as the developing national narratives of the war marginalised their experiences and stories. Many of the former prisoners and their families, along with such official bodies as the Repat, struggled to deal with the legacy of the POW experience and to comprehend and incorporate captivity into their understanding of the war. As the prisoners continue to be sidelined in Australian commemoration of the First World War and of understandings of captivity more broadly, today, it seems, so too do we.

CONCLUSION

Of the nearly 4000 Australians held as POWs during the First World War, 198 were captured and confined in prison camps in the Ottoman Empire. For these men, captivity was an unexpected outcome of their volunteering to fight for the war effort, and it brought with it significant challenges. For the Australian military authorities, the government, the prisoners' families, patriotic organisations, Australians at home, the Imperial War Graves Commission, the Repatriation Department and others, the extended captivity of Australian servicemen at the hands of a radically different enemy also posed certain constraints, ambiguities and difficulties. In scrutinising these particular challenges, this book has revealed that, for all it involved or affected, captivity in the Ottoman Empire necessitated new responses in order to successfully manage, adjust to and cope with this unanticipated consequence of war.

Assessing the Australians' reactions to capture illustrates that becoming a POW involved more than formal definitions suggest. The transition from combatant to captive was particularly galling, and many new prisoners felt angry, ashamed and frustrated by their status and their immediate treatment behind Ottoman lines. Coming to terms with their identity as POWs proved the first significant challenge in their lives as captives and the first step in adjusting to captivity.

Exploring how the prisoners reacted to the circumstances of their confinement demonstrates that they were not passive, powerless recipients of the experience but that they sought to manage their conditions and treatment actively and so shape their imprisonment to best suit their needs. Internal division and external threats, underdeveloped trade, communication, transport and medical infrastructure, and an army still suffering from the effects of defeat in the Balkans inevitably affected the Ottomans' ability to administer POWs. Alongside the difficulties of their physical environments and the emotional strain generated by the restrictions of prolonged confinement, the prisoners also felt the effects of culture clash. As products of a society that reflected generally accepted beliefs about social Darwinism and racial hierarchies, being held prisoner by a supposedly 'inferior' people represented a humiliating inversion of this perceived natural order. By modifying their accommodation, food, work practices and health care, the prisoners were able to normalise – to an extent – their conditions, implementing formal strategies such as sports and educational schemes as well as more informal means of escapism such as mess parties offered ways to beat the effects of 'barbed wire disease', while asserting Britishness, aligning with the Germans and reproducing traditional cultural practices meant that the POWs could reassert their sense of racial superiority and, when necessary, mitigate the intrusion of death into the camp environment.

Expanding the focus from the prisoners themselves to include the perspectives and voices of others affected by their captivity reveals how significant were its reverberations and ramifications. The Australian Government relied on the British to determine the scale of official relief efforts, and administer and implement such relief through the protecting powers. The Americans and later the Dutch assumed the role of intermediary between the belligerents, which often placed them in an invidious position. Providing welfare to the POWs was also a challenge for the Australian Red Cross POW Department; War Office restrictions, limited communication with the men in the camps and, initially at least, inadequate premises and staff made the daily operations of the department difficult. Nevertheless, this network of official support worked in tandem to manage, as well as possible, the provision of welfare to the POWs.

Examining the ways in which the prisoners were portrayed at home demonstrates the discourses about captivity that circulated in the public sphere during the war. Initially captivity was believed to be a tolerable if monotonous existence, yet by the end of the war the dominant impression was that it was a miserable life of neglect and cruelty. With little meaningful interaction between the prison camps and home, the government and the Red Cross had something of a monopoly over the ways in which the captivity experience was presented. Each portrayed prisoners of war in such a way as to encourage increased enlistment and more donations from

war-weary Australians. The response to these ideas of wartime imprisonment – through critique of perceived government inaction and donations
to and work for the RCPF – indicates how ordinary Australians engaged
with this extraordinary situation.

The ripple effects of captivity were felt particularly strongly by the
prisoners' families. Emotive correspondence between the mothers, fathers,
siblings, extended family and friends of the POWs and the Red Cross
POW Department in London testifies to the intense anxiety felt by those at
home. Families found it difficult to foster imagined connections with their
captive loved ones, which intensified fears over their physical and emotional well-being. To alleviate these concerns, the prisoners' families
developed an intimate network of fictive kin among whom information
and news of the prisoners was shared. In developing such a network the
POW families demonstrated that, like the men in the camps, they too
sought to manage and cope with the specific hardships of wartime imprisonment that they faced.

The aftermath of captivity continued to pose significant challenges.
The relocation of the remains of deceased POWs, although believed to be
necessary by the families involved, was a delicate operation that tested
the diplomatic skills of IWGC employees working in the new nation
of Turkey, while attempts to prosecute those alleged to have breached
international law with respect to the treatment of POWs – along with
those accused of the deportation and massacre of Armenians – proved
difficult in the face of political machinations within the empire and
ongoing conflict between the new nationalist government and the Great
Powers. As the former POWs restarted their civilian lives, many experienced health problems, which they argued were a direct consequence of
their time in captivity. Constructing claims for medical and pension
benefits around the misery and hardships of their imprisonment worked
for some, but not all. As well as dealing with physical and psychological
health concerns, the stigma of captivity and the marginalisation of POW
experiences compounded lingering personal feelings of inferiority and
inadequacy.

The theme of 'coping', 'managing' or 'adjusting' is not new in
Australian histories of the First World War but, for those who felt the
effects of captivity in the Ottoman Empire, this aspect of their stories has
long been unexplored. As symbols of defeat or failure, POWs do not easily
fit into the scope of traditional military history and, for various reasons –
ranging from the glorification of the battlefield experience, the dominance
of the POWs of the Japanese in Australian understandings of captivity,

and the development of a positive, compassionate narrative surrounding Australians and Turks – the prisoners of the Ottomans remain on the very edge of First World War history and memory. Perhaps more than anything, however, the stories of such a relatively limited number of men made little impression in the aftermath of the war, and they continue to be relegated to the margins as centenary commemorative efforts focus squarely on the suffering and sacrifice of the thousands of battlefield dead. It is 'the big numbers that pull out the emotional stops' yet, as David Stephens points out, this obsession with great numbers in Australian remembrance of the First World War comes at the expense of understanding the complexities of Australians' wartime experiences, and obscures the stories of individuals and families as well as the resonances of war at home and in the years after.[1]

Understanding how Fred Ashton, John Halpin, Thomas White, Maurice Delpratt, Patrick O'Connor and other POWs felt about their capture and responded to the various challenges of their imprisonment is a central aim of this book. Exploring their attitudes towards becoming prisoners of war, their feelings towards their captors, their anxieties and worries about families at home, their gratitude towards the Red Cross and other providers of aid and, for some, their bitterness upon return, reveals the complex and textured nature of their experiences. In moving beyond the POWs themselves to explore the totality of captivity, the book also brings into the picture the stories of others who became entangled in imprisonment: the diligent American Ambassador Abram Elkus; the indomitable Mary Elizabeth Chomley of the Red Cross POW Department; the dedicated Maude Jennings Green, sister of Edgar; the helpful but cautious Chukri Bey, the Turkish representative attached to the IWGC; and the heartbroken Esther Curran, mother of deceased POW David – and demonstrates that the consequences of captivity in the Ottoman Empire spread much wider and deeper than the group of 198 men it directly affected.

APPENDIX I

POWS BY SERVICE

The following list of 198 identified Australian POWs was compiled after cross-examination of several sources including: individual service records, government and military reports held by the National Archives of Australia; Red Cross Wounded and Missing Bureau and POW Department case files at the Australian War Memorial; and personal papers, letters and diaries.

HMAS *AE2* Submarine, Royal Australian Navy*

Name	Rank	Date of capture	Place of capture
Bray, Cecil	Petty Officer	29/30 April 1915	Sea of Marmara
Cullen, James	Stoker	29/30 April 1915	Sea of Marmara
Falconer, William	Telegrapher	29/30 April 1915	Sea of Marmara
Gwynne, Ernest	Able Seaman (*E7*)	4 September 1915	Dardanelles
Harding, Horace	Stoker	29/30 April 1915	Sea of Marmara
Jenkins, William	Stoker	29/30 April 1915	Sea of Marmara
Kerin, John	Leading Stoker	29/30 April 1915	Sea of Marmara
Kinder, Henry	Stoker/Petty Officer	29/30 April 1915	Sea of Marmara
Mitchell, Reuben	Able Seaman (*E14*)	28 January 1918	Dardanelles
Nichols, Albert	Able Seaman	29/30 April 1915	Sea of Marmara
Suckling, Charles	Stoker	29/30 April 1915	Sea of Marmara
Wheat, John	Able Seaman	29/30 April 1915	Sea of Marmara
Williams, Michael	Stoker	29/30 April 1915	Sea of Marmara
Wilson, Archibald	Leading Stoker (*E7*)	4 September 1915	Dardanelles

* Due to a lack of trained personnel, several British Royal Navy submariners (officers and ratings) were loaned to the RAN for service on board the *AE2*. They are not included in the total.

Australian Flying Corps

Name	Rank	Date of capture	Place of capture
Adams, Francis	Air Mechanic	29 April 1916	Kut-el-Amara
Austin, Ronald	Captain	19 March 1918	Kerak, near Dead Sea
Challinor, Ronald	Lieutenant	1 May 1918	between Es Salt and Amman
Curran, David	Air Mechanic	29 April 1916	Kut-el-Amara
Haig, Frederick	Lieutenant	1 May 1918	between Es Salt and Amman
Hancock, Fred	Lieutenant	20 January 1918	Kalkilleh, near Nablus
Heathcote, Leonard	Lieutenant	9 March 1917	near Gaza
Hudson, Keith	Air Mechanic	29 April 1916	Kut-el-Amara
Lee, Oliver	Lieutenant	19 March 1918	Kerak, near Dead Sea
Lord, William	Air Mechanic	29 April 1916	Kut-el-Amara
McElligott, Joseph	Lieutenant	1 May 1918	between Es Salt and Amman
Munro, James	Air Mechanic	29 April 1916	Kut-el-Amara
Parkinson, Vincent	Lieutenant	4 January 1918	Jenin
Poole, Alfred	Lieutenant	20 January 1918	Kalkilleh, near Nablus
Rayment, William	Air Mechanic	29 April 1916	Kut-el-Amara
Rutherford, Douglas	Captain	1 May 1918	between Es Salt and Amman
Sloss, James	Acting Flight Sergeant	29 April 1916	Kut-el-Amara
Soley, Thomas	Corporal	29 April 1916	Kut-el-Amara
Smith, Laurence	Lieutenant	27 June 1918	Katrana
Treloar, William	Lieutenant	September 1915	Es-Sinn
Vautin, Claude	Lieutenant	8 July 1917	near Gaza
White, Thomas	Captain	November 1915	near Baghdad
Williams, Leo	Air Mechanic	29 April 1916	Kut-el-Amara

Australian Light Horse/Imperial Camel Corps

Name	Rank	Date of capture	Place of capture
Angus, John	Private	19 April 1917	Gaza
Armstrong, D'Arcy	Driver	1 May 1918	Es Salt
Blechynden, Reuben	Private	19 April 1917	Gaza
Brennan, Martin	Trooper	1 May 1918	Es Salt

(cont.)

Name	Rank	Date of capture	Place of capture
Briant, Benjamin	Private	I May 1918	Es Salt
Brockhurst, Henry	Private	I May 1918	Es Salt
Cahill, Timothy	Lance Corporal	14 December 1917	Jerusalem
Carlin, Cyril	Private	30 November 1917	near Jaffa
Campbell, Colin	Trooper	19 April 1917	Gaza
Carr, Charles	Trooper	I May 1918	Es Salt
Clarke, George	Private	I May 1918	Es Salt
Clarke, John	Private	8 August 1916	Mageibra
Clarke, Roy	Private	28 March 1918	Amman
Crockett, Alexander	Private	28 March 1918	Amman
Crozier, Sydney	Trooper	28 March 1918	Amman
Currie, Clyde	Corporal	19 April 1917	Gaza
Day, Andrew	Driver	4 August 1916	Romani
Delpratt, Maurice	Sergeant	28 June 1915	Gallipoli
Dodd, Joseph	Private	19 April 1917	Gaza
Donnison, George	Trooper	28 March 1918	Amman
Drysdale, George	Sergeant	4 August 1916	Romani
Duffy, Patrick	Private	19 April 1917	Gaza
Earnshaw, Frederick	Sapper	14 December 1917	Jerusalem
Easton, Francis	Lance Corporal	4 August 1916	Romani
Farley, Harold	Private	28 March 1918	Amman
Flatt, Charles	Private	19 April 1917	Gaza
Fooks, Phillip	Private	19 April 1917	Gaza
Gannon, Frederick	Private	26 March 1918	Amman
Gilbert, George	Private	19 April 1917	Gaza
Gilman, Ellis	Private	I May 1918	Es Salt
Halliday, Thomas	Private	19 April 1917	Gaza
Halpin, John	Sergeant	I May 1918	Es Salt
Handsley, George	Private	4 August 1916	Romani
Hebbard, Herbert	Private	I May 1918	Es Salt
Hewitson, Archibald	Lance Corporal	28 March 1918	Amman
Hobson, Edgar	Private	4 August 1916	Romani
Ingram, Ernest	Private	19 April 1917	Gaza
Jeffery, Frederick	Private	19 April 1917	Gaza
Jones, Daniel	Private	19 April 1917	Gaza
Kelly, James	Private	4 August 1916	Romani
Kelly, William	Lance Corporal	14 December 1917	Jerusalem

(*cont.*)

Name	Rank	Date of capture	Place of capture
Kelly, William V.	Private	1 May 1918	Es Salt
Kennett, Victor	Trooper	4 August 1916	Romani
Kimber, Allan	Lance Corporal	19 April 1917	Gaza
King, Walter	Sergeant	28 March 1918	Amman
Lambert, Leslie	Trooper	1 April 1918	Amman
Littler, Wilson	Private	4 August 1916	Romani
McColl, Robert	Private	4 August 1916	Romani
McPherson, John	Sergeant	2 November 1917	near Beersheba
Maguire, Robert	Driver	19 April 1917	Gaza
Mathews, Francis	Driver	1 May 1918	Es Salt
May, Herbert	Trooper	19 April 1917	Gaza
Merson, John	Sergeant	1 May 1918	Es Salt
Miller, George	Driver	1 May 1918	Es Salt
Mitchell, Ernest	Driver	1 May 1918	Es Salt
Moll, Walter	Private	28 March 1918	Amman
Newton, Edwin	Second Lieutenant	11 October 1917	Palestine
O'Hare, Phillip	Private	19 April 1917	Gaza
O'Neill, Joseph	Private	2 November 1917	near Beersheba
Otway, Charles	Private	19 April 1917	Gaza
Paltridge, George	Sergeant	19 April 1917	Gaza
Patten, Charles	Trooper	4 August 1916	Romani
Peters, Robert	Private	4 August 1916	Romani
Picton, Edward	Corporal	28 March 1918	Amman
Redman, Claude	Trooper	28 March 1918	Amman
Richardson, Duncan	Trooper	4 August 1916	Romani
Roberts, George	Private	4 August 1916	Romani
Romaro, John	Private	3 December 1917	near Jaffa
Rose, Edwin	Private	4 August 1916	Romani
Savill, Frederick	Sergeant	19 April 1917	Gaza
Scroop, Percy	Lance Corporal	4 August 1916	Romani
Sherrie, Noel	Trooper	19 April 1917	Gaza
Sherwin, Norman	Trooper	28 March 1918	Amman
Simmons, William	Private	19 April 1917	Gaza
Simms, William	Corporal	1 May 1918	Es Salt
Skyring, Lowes	Private	1 April 1918	Amman
Seaton, Robert	Private	1 May 1918	Es Salt

(*cont.*)

Name	Rank	Date of capture	Place of capture
Sloan, John	Driver	1 May 1918	Es Salt
Sloan, Matthew	Driver	1 May 1918	Es Salt
Smith, Charles	Acting Corporal	28 March 1918	Amman
Smith, Egbert	Sergeant	3 May 1918	Es Salt
Smith, Leslie	Private	1 May 1918	Es Salt
Sommerville, James	Corporal	4 August 1916	Romani
Spencer, Cecil	Trooper	28 March 1918	Amman
Stripling, Richard	Private	28 March 1918	Amman
Sullivan, Harold	Sergeant	4 August 1916	Romani
Talbot, George	Private	4 May 1918	Es Salt
Thompson, Arthur	Driver	1 May 1918	Es Salt
Thorneycroft, Henry	Lance Corporal	2 November 1917	near Beersheba
Tierney, Arthur	Lance Corporal	19 April 1917	Gaza
Vidler, Harold	Private	19 April 1917	Gaza
Ward, John	Trooper	4 August 1916	Romani
Weidenhofer, Diedrich	Private	1 April 1918	Amman
Young, James	Private	28 March 1918	Amman

Infantry

Name	Rank	Date of capture	Place of capture
Allen, William	Private	28 June 1915	Gallipoli
Ashton, Frederick	Private	25 April 1915	Gallipoli
Bailey, William	Sergeant	8 August 1915	Gallipoli
Beattie, John	Private	8 August 1915	Gallipoli
Boyle, David	Lance Corporal	9 August 1915	Gallipoli
Brooke, Vivian	Lance Corporal	late April/early May 1915	Gallipoli
Brown, Harry	Private	8 August 1915	Gallipoli
Cahir, Keith Joseph	Private	8 August 1915	Gallipoli
Calcutt, Brendan	Private	8 August 1915	Gallipoli

(*cont.*)

Name	Rank	Date of capture	Place of capture
Campbell, Alan	Private	8 May 1915	Gallipoli
Carpenter, Alfred	Private	10 August 1915	Gallipoli
Carter, Alfred	Private	10 August 1915	Gallipoli
Chalcroft, Thomas	Private	8 August 1915	Gallipoli
Cliffe, William	Corporal	8 May 1915	Gallipoli
Creedon, Daniel	Private	28 June 1915	Gallipoli
Davern, John	Private	8 August 1915	Gallipoli
Dowell, Thomas	Private	8 August 1915	Gallipoli
Drake, Sydney	Private	8 August 1915	Gallipoli
Dunne, Bernard	Private	8 August 1915	Gallipoli
Elston, William	Lieutenant	25 April 1915	Gallipoli
Foster, Edwin	Private	8 August 1915	Gallipoli
Foxcroft, Harry	Private	8 August 1915	Gallipoli
Francis, David	Private	8 August 1915	Gallipoli
Goodwin, Shirley	Lieutenant	December 1915	Gallipoli
Green, Edgar	Corporal	8 August 1915	Gallipoli
Griffiths, Robert	Private	8 August 1915	Gallipoli
Hennessy, John	Private	8 August 1915	Gallipoli
Hodges, Louis	Private	8 August 1915	Gallipoli
Hodsdon, Charles	Corporal	8 August 1915	Gallipoli
Jenkins, Albert	Private	8 August 1915	Gallipoli
Jones, William	Private	8 August 1915	Gallipoli
Jordan, Stanley	Second Lieutenant	28 June 1915	Gallipoli
Kelly, Joseph	Private	8 August 1915	Gallipoli
Kerr, George	Corporal	8 August 1915	Gallipoli
Kerrigan, Robert	Private	8 August 1915	Gallipoli
Kilmartin, Hugh	Sergeant	8 August 1915	Gallipoli
King, George	Private	28 June 1915	Gallipoli
Leyden, James	Private	8 August 1915	Gallipoli
Lightfoot, Lancelot	Private	8 August 1915	Gallipoli
Luscombe, Leslie	Lieutenant	8 August 1915	Gallipoli
Lushington, Reginald	Private	25 April 1915	Gallipoli
McDonald, Ronald	Captain	25 April 1915	Gallipoli
Mackay, William	Private	10 August 1918	Gallipoli
McLean, Charles	Private	8 August 1915	Gallipoli
Masterton, James	Private	8 August 1915	Gallipoli
Mathers, Chapman	Private	8 August 1915	Gallipoli

(cont.)

Name	Rank	Date of capture	Place of capture
Matthews, Charles	Private	28 June 1915	Gallipoli
Nelson, Alfred	Private	8 August 1915	Gallipoli
New, Leonard	Private	8 August 1915	Gallipoli
Neyland, Niven	Private	8 August 1915	Gallipoli
O'Callaghan, John	Private	28 June 1915	Gallipoli
O'Connor, Patrick	Private	8 August 1915	Gallipoli
Passmore, James	Private	8 August 1915	Gallipoli
Randall, William	Private	8 August 1915	Gallipoli
Rawlings, Alfred	Sergeant	late April/early May 1915	Gallipoli
Samson, Harold	Private	8 August 1915	Gallipoli
Shelton, Harold	Private	8 August 1915	Gallipoli
Sherlock, Thomas	Private	2 May 1915	Gallipoli
Stormonth, Stewart	Lieutenant	8 August 1915	Gallipoli
Stringer, William	Private	8 August 1915	Gallipoli
Thomas, John	Private	8 August 1915	Gallipoli
Troy, Martin	Private	4 May 1915	Gallipoli
Warnes, William	Private	8 August 1915	Gallipoli
Wiffen, Arthur	Private	8 August 1915	Gallipoli
Williams, Walter	Private	8 August 1915	Gallipoli
Wilson, Elvas	Private	8 August 1915	Gallipoli
Wood, Bert	Private	8 August 1915	Gallipoli

Australians in British forces (not included in total)

Name	Rank	Date of capture	Place of capture
Brown, James	Lieutenant Royal Army Medical Corps	April 1916	Katia
Hackman, Trevor	Flight Commander Royal Naval Air Service	February 1917	Constantinople
Hill, Cedric	Lieutenant Royal Flying Corps	May 1916	Palestine
Piper, Thomas	Lieutenant Royal Naval Air Service	February 1917	Constantinople

POW DEATHS

Details of POW deaths were obtained from several sources including: individual service records, government and military reports and Repatriation Department case files held by the National Archives of Australia; Red Cross Wounded and Missing Bureau and POW Department files at the Australian War Memorial; records of the Commonwealth War Graves Commission; and personal papers, letters and diaries.

Name	Date, place and cause of death	Buried/commemorated
Adams, Francis	August/November 1916 Adana Malaria and dysentery	Baghdad North Gate
Allen, William	December 1916 Belemedik Malaria and dysentery	Baghdad North Gate
Angus, John	November 1917 Nidge Enteritis	Baghdad North Gate
Brooke, Vivian	After capture Gallipoli Wounds	Ari Burnu, Gallipoli
Calcutt, Brendan	December 1916/January 1917 Hadjikiri Septicaemia	Baghdad North Gate
Campbell, Alan	After capture Gallipoli Wounds	Lone Pine Memorial, Gallipoli
Creedon, Daniel	February 1917 Angora Enteritis and typhus	Angora Memorial, Baghdad North Gate

(*cont.*)

Name	Date, place and cause of death	Buried/commemorated
Crozier, Sydney	After capture Amman Reportedly bayoneted	Basra Memorial
Curran, David	August 1916 Nisibin Malaria and exposure	Nisbin Memorial, Baghdad North Gate
Day, Andrew	February 1917 Angora Tuberculosis	Angora Memorial, Baghdad North Gate
Donnison, George	After capture Amman Wounds	Basra Memorial
Drysdale, George	April 1917 Angora Typhus	Angora Memorial, Baghdad North Gate
Easton, Francis	November 1916 Ismidt Typhus/pneumonia/ dysentery	Haidar Pasha

Francis, David	After capture
	Court of Enquiry
	  determined 'Killed
	  in Action' but Francis'
	  remains were identified
	  after the war in a
	  Constantinople cenetery
		Haidar Pasha

Green, Edgar	October 1918 Yozgad Spanish 'flu	Baghdad North Gate
Hennessy, John	December 1915 Constantinople Wounds and dysentery	Haidar Pasha
Hodges, Louis	After capture Gallipoli Wounds	Haidar Pasha
Hodsdon, Charles	January 1916 Constantinople Wounds	Haidar Pasha

(*cont.*)

Name	Date, place and cause of death	Buried/commemorated
Jeffery, Frederick	November 1917 Nidge Dysentery	Baghdad North Gate
Jenkins, Albert	January 1916 Constantinople Wounds and pneumonia	Haidar Pasha
Jones, William	January 1917 Afyonkarahissar Dysentery	Baghdad North Gate
Kelly, Joseph	August 1915 Constantinople Wounds	Haidar Pasha
Kennett, Victor	February 1917 Ismidt Tuberculosis	Haidar Pasha
Kerrigan, Robert	February 1917 Afyonkarahissar Malaria	Baghdad North Gate
Kimber, Allan	November 1917 Nidge Dysentery and malaria	Baghdad North Gate
King, George	August 1918 Afyonkarahissar Disease (unknown)	Baghdad North Gate
Leyden, James	August 1915 Constantinople Wounds	Haidar Pasha
Lord, William	November 1916 Adana Suspected malaria	Baghdad North Gate
Mathers, Chapman	February 1917 Angora Enteritis and typhus	Angora Memorial, Baghdad North Gate
May, Herbert	November 1917 Nidge Dysentery	Baghdad North Gate
Munro, James	October 1916 Adana Dysentery and abscess	Baghdad North Gate

(*cont.*)

Name	Date, place and cause of death	Buried/commemorated
Nelson, Alfred	November 1916 Angora Disease (unknown)	Angora Memorial, Baghdad North Gate
New, Leonard	May 1916 near Belemedik Work accident	Baghdad North Gate
O'Callaghan, John	January 1917 Angora Enteritis	Angora Memorial, Baghdad North Gate
Patten, Charles	February 1917 Angora Malaria	Angora Memorial, Baghdad North Gate
Rayment, William	November 1916 Adana Nephritis	Baghdad North Gate
Redman, Claude	May/November 1918 Damascus Suspected cholera	Basra Memorial
Savill, Frederick	November 1917 Nidge Beri-beri	Baghdad North Gate

Scroop, Percy	December 1916
	Angora
	Dysentery and rheumatic
	    fever
		Angora Memorial,
		    Baghdad North Gate

Shelton, Harold	September 1915 Constantinople Wounds	Haidar Pasha
Sherlock, Thomas	June 1915 Constantinople Wounds	Haidar Pasha

Sherrie, Noel	June 1917
	Damascus
	Wounds
		Damascus
		    Commonwealth War
		    Cemetery

Sherwin, Norman	After capture Amman Reportedly shot	Basra Memorial

(*cont.*)

Name	Date, place and cause of death	Buried/commemorated
Skyring, Lowes	August 1918 Afyonkarahissar Pneumonia	Baghdad North Gate
Smith, Charles	September 1918 Adana Disease (unknown)	Baghdad North Gate
Soley, Thomas	June/July 1916 Nisibin Unknown	Basra Memorial
Sommerville, James	April 1917 Angora Typhus	Angora Memorial, Baghdad North Gate
Stripling, Richard	May 1918 Gelebek Work accident	Basra Memorial
Sullivan, Harold	February 1917 Angora Chronic enteritis	Angora Memorial, Baghdad North Gate
Ward, John	March 1917 Angora Pneumonia	Angora Memorial, Baghdad North Gate
Warnes, William	After capture Gallipoli Wounds	Lone Pine Memorial, Gallipoli
Williams, Leo	July/August 1916 Adana Unknown	Basra Memorial
Williams, Michael	September 1916 Bagtchi Dysentery	Bozanti Memorial, Baghdad North Gate
Wilson, Elvas	May 1916 Yozgad Typhoid	Lone Pine Memorial, Gallipoli
Wood, Bert	August 1915 Constantinople Wounds	Haidar Pasha

Notes

Introduction

1 Repatriation Statement of Frederick Ashton, AWM30, B1.1, Australian War Memorial, Canberra (hereafter AWM).

2 Stanley, 'Introduction', in Department of Veterans' Affairs/Australian War Memorial, *Stolen Years*, p. 4. Officially, the number of Australian soldiers taken prisoner by the Boers is stated as 100, although one historian has put the figure as high as 224. See Smith, *Australian Prisoners of War – Boer War 1899–1902*.

3 Beaumont, 'Prisoners of war: Asia Pacific, 1941–45', in *Australian Defence*, ed. Beaumont, p. 340.

4 Recent publications include: Alon Rachamimov, *POWs and the Great War*; Jones, *Violence Against Prisoners of War*; Yanikdag, *Healing the Nation*; and Feltman, *The Stigma of Surrender*.

5 Robertson, 'Prisoners of the Turks', pp. 213–23; Lawless, 'Starvation, cruelty and neglect?', pp. 40–56; Ariotti, '"I'm awfully fed up with being a prisoner"', pp. 276–90; Ariotti, '"At present everything is making us most anxious"', pp. 57–74.

6 See McKernan, *This War Never Ends*; Bomford, 'Fractured lives'; Twomey, 'Compensating prisoners of war of Japan in post-war Australia', pp. 254–75. Barbara Hately-Broad has written about the effects of captivity on British families during the Second World War. See Hately-Broad, *War and Welfare*.

7 Lyons, 'French soldiers and their correspondence', pp. 81–2.

8 Roper, *The Secret Battle*, p. 64.

9 White, *Guests of the Unspeakable*; Austin, *My Experiences as a Prisoner*; Lushington, *A Prisoner with the Turks 1915–1918*; Foster, *Two and a Half Years a Prisoner of War in Turkey*; Halpin, *Blood in the Mists*.

10 Woolley, *From Kastamuni to Kedos*.

11 Gerster, *Big-noting*, p. 144.

12 Garton, *The Cost of War*, p. 86.

Chapter 1 Becoming prisoners of war

1 Halpin, *Blood in the Mists*, pp. 86–8.

2 Repatriation Statement of Edward Picton, AWM30, B2.7.

3 Richardson, *History of the 7th Light Horse Regiment AIF*, p. 86.

4 Repatriation Statement of Martin Troy, AWM30, B1.3; Repatriation Statement of Charles Flatt, AWM30, B2.14.

5 Repatriation Statement of Charles Carr, AWM30, B2.4.
6 Repatriation Statement of D'Arcy Armstrong, AWM30, B2.12.
7 Repatriation Statement of Ernest Ingram, AWM30, B2.14.
8 Repatriation Statement of John Charles Romaro, AWM30, B2.14.
9 Chatway, *History of the 15th Battalion*, pp. 85–8.
10 'Hand-Written Account by Lieut. Treloar', 9, Letters, Serial, Leaflets of
   Lieutenant W.H. Treloar, 1st Half Flight, AFC World War 1914–18, AWM,
   PR84/24. See also Cutlack, *Australian Flying Corps*, p. 12.
11 'Extract from a Statement of Prisoner of War Captain Muhammad Ali,
   105th Turkish Infantry, Basrah, 13 October 1915', B2455 TRELOAR
   WILLIAM HAROLD, National Archives of Australia (hereafter NAA),
   Canberra.
12 Repatriation Statements of Claude Vautin, Frederick Hancock and Arthur
   Poole, AWM30, B3.3.
13 Stoker, *Straws in the Wind*, p. 138.
14 Repatriation Statements of John Merson and Martin Brennan, AWM30,
   B2.10. See also John Merson, 'Behind the Turkish lines', in Hammond,
   History of the 11th Light Horse Regiment, pp. 160–4.
15 Challinor to Traill, 7 July 1918, B2455, CHALLINOR RONALD T., NAA.
16 Ibid.
17 Repatriation Statement of Vincent Parkinson, AWM30, B3.3. See also
   Cutlack, *Australian Flying Corps*, p. 96.
18 Brown, *Turkish Days and Ways*, pp. 36–7.
19 Halpin, 'A captive of the Turks – Episode one', pp. 25–6.
20 Blair, *No Quarter*, pp. 14–16.
21 Pegram, 'Informing the enemy', p. 170; Blair, *No Quarter*, p. 16.
22 For discussion of Australians and the mistreatment of enemy POWs see Blair,
   No Quarter, and Stanley, *Bad Characters*.
23 Bean, *The Story of ANZAC*, p. 258.
24 Chatway, *History of the 15th Battalion*, p. 3.
25 Luscombe, *The Story of Harold Earl*, pp. 40–1.
26 Wheat, 'Unpublished manuscript', p. 13, John Harrison Wheat Papers,
   John Oxley Library, State Library of Queensland, Brisbane (hereafter SLQ);
   Captain Ali Riza's excerpt in *Beneath the Dardanelles*, p. 136.
27 Cutlack, *Australian Flying Corps*, p. xviii.
28 Repatriation Statement of Harry Norman Brown, AWM30, B1.5; Repatriation
   Statement of Diedrich Weidenhofer, AWM30, B2.12; Repatriation Statement
   of Edward Picton, AWM30, B2.7.
29 Repatriation Statement of Frederick Ashton, AWM30, B1.1; Repatriation
   Statement of Robert Griffiths, AWM30, B1.16.
30 See Blair, *No Quarter*, p. 50, and Stanley, *Bad Characters*, pp. 112–16.
31 Repatriation Statement of Patrick O'Connor, AWM30, B1.27.
32 Repatriation Statement of John Charles Romaro, AWM30, B2.14.
33 Repatriation Statement of Timothy Joseph Cahill, AWM30, B2.8; Repatriation
   Statement of Matthew Black Sloan, AWM30, B2.12.
34 Repatriation Statement of John Merson, AWM30, B2.10.
35 Halpin, 'A captive of the Turks – Episode one', pp. 25–6.

36 Repatriation Statement of John Beattie, AWM30, B1.3.
37 Repatriation Statement of Patrick Duffy, AWM30, B2.2.
38 Examples of prisoners' responses to such interrogations can be read in Tetik, Demirtas and Demirtas, *Prisoners of War at the Canakkale Battles*. For discussion of Australian POWs being interrogated by the Germans, see Pegram, 'Informing the enemy', pp. 171–5.
39 Repatriation Statement of Duncan Richardson, AWM30, B2.4; Repatriation Statement of Harold Vidler, AWM30, B2.14. For an example of a POW being threatened, see Repatriation Statement of D'Arcy Armstrong, AWM30, B2.12.
40 Beaumont, 'Rank, privilege and prisoners of war', pp. 67–94.
41 Barker, *Behind Barbed Wire*, p. 44.
42 Halpin, 'A captive of the Turks – Episode two', p. 48.
43 Repatriation Statement of John Beattie, AWM30, B1.3.
44 Luscombe, *The Story of Harold Earl*, p. 44.
45 Repatriation Statement of Clyde Currie, AWM30, B2.14.
46 Repatriation Statement of D'Arcy Armstrong, AWM30, B2.12.
47 Foster, *Two and a Half Years*, p. 17.
48 K.L. Hudson, 'Report on the Treatment of Prisoners from Kut-ell-Amarah', pp. 4–5, Records of Air Mech. K.L. Hudson, AFC 1914–1918, 3DRL/3325.
49 White, *Guests of the Unspeakable*, p. 149. See also 'Report from American Ambassador to British Secretary of State for Foreign Affairs, 2 February 1917', Prisoners of War in Turkey, A11803, 1917/89/377, NAA, Canberra.
50 Major-General Sir C. Melliss to Rt Hon. David Lloyd George, 1 February 1918, Prisoners of War in Turkey – Mortality Among, A11803, 1918/89/724, NAA, Canberra.
51 Repatriation Statement of James McKenzie Sloss, AWM30, B3.1.
52 Wheat, 'Unpublished manuscript', p. 14; Repatriation Statement of John Beattie, AWM30, B1.3.
53 Wheat, 'Unpublished manuscript', p. 14; Repatriation Statement of Ernest Ingram, AWM30, B2.14.
54 Jones, 'Encountering the enemy', pp. 133–62.
55 Lushington, *A Prisoner with the Turks*, pp. 11–2.
56 Foster, *Two-and-a-half Years*, p. 20; Repatriation Statement of Leslie Lambert, AWM30, B2.6.
57 Repatriation Statement of John Davern, B2455, DAVERN J, NAA, Canberra.
58 Repatriation Statement of Patrick O'Connor, AWM30, B1.27.
59 Repatriation Statement of Walter Williams, AWM30, B1.32; Repatriation Statement of John Davern, B2455, DAVERN J, NAA, Canberra.
60 Repatriation Statement of Walter Williams, AWM30, B1.32.
61 Repatriation Statement of Patrick O'Connor, AWM30, B1.27.
62 Repatriation Statement of Ellis Gilman, AWM30, B2.10; Repatriation Statement of Edward Picton, AWM30, B2.7. See also Repatriation Statement of Archibald Hewitson, AWM30, B2.6.

63 Repatriation Statement of Ellis Gilman, AWM30, B2.10; Repatriation Statement of Edgar Hobson, AWM30, B2.1; Repatriation Statement of Vincent Parkinson, AWM30, B3.3.

64 Lunden, 'Captivity psychoses among prisoners of war', p. 726.

65 Ibid.

66 Halpin 'Captives of the Turk – Episode two', 48; Halpin, *Blood in the Mists*, p. 103.

67 Merson, 'Behind Turkish lines', p. 162.

68 Ibid.

69 Jordan to friend, 15 July 1915, Australian Red Cross (hereafter ARC) Wounded and Missing Bureau Case File of Stanley Rupert Jordan, 1DRL/0428.

70 Jones to mother, 10 March 1918, ARC Wounded and Missing Bureau Case File of Daniel Jones, 1DRL/0428.

71 White, *Guests of the Unspeakable*, pp. 41–2.

72 Delpratt to family, 12 July 1915, ACC. 28115 Maurice George Delpratt Correspondence (hereafter MGDC), SLQ.

73 Repatriation Statement of Harry Norman Brown, AWM30, B1.5.

74 Feltman, 'Letters from captivity', p. 104.

75 Gullett, *The Australian Imperial Force in Sinai and Palestine, 1914–1918*, pp. 184–5.

76 Delpratt to family, 12 July 1915, MGDC.

77 Lushington, *A Prisoner with the Turks*, p. 6. This response was not unique to Australians. Brian Feltman writes how the German *Heldentod* myth – the heroic veneration of those who died in service of the nation – excluded those who surrendered, and left German POWs feeling shame and guilt at their capture. See Feltman, 'Letters from captivity', p. 90.

78 Twomey, 'Emaciation or emasculation', pp. 299–300.

Chapter 2 *The circumstances of confinement*

1 Article 7 of 'Annex to the Convention: Regulations Respecting the Laws and Customs of War on Land (Hague IV). October 18, 1907', Hague Convention, Yale Law School, <http://avalon.law.yale.edu/20th_century/hague04.asp> (retrieved 3 August 2017).

2 Stanley, '"He was black, he was a white man, and a dinkum Aussie"', p. 221.

3 Brugger, Australians and Egypt, p. 34; White, 'Sun, sand, and syphilis', pp. 57–60.

4 Hancock to father, 24 December 1914 and 17 January 1915, Papers of Lt F. Hancock 1ALH and No. 1 Sqd AFC, AWM 2DRL/530.

5 White, 'Sun, sand, and syphillis', p. 57; Brugger, *Australians and Egypt*, p. 29.

6 Jupp, *The Australian People*, p. 709; Knibbs, *Statistician's Report*, p. 85.

7 Salt, 'Britain, the Armenian question, and the cause of Ottoman reform', p. 308.

8 Salt, 'Johnny Turk before Gallipoli', pp. 22–3.

9 Gladstone, *Bulgarian Horrors and the Question of the East*, p. 10.

10 Ibid.

11 H. Richard, quoted in Salt, 'Johnny Turk before Gallipoli', p. 23.

12 See Said, *Orientalism*, pp. 7–8, 31–73.

13 'Turkey: Germany's catspaw', *Warwick Examiner and Times*, 9 November 1914; 'Turkey joins the war', *Kalgoorlie Miner*, 2 November 1914.

14 'War with Turkey', *Sydney Morning Herald*, 7 November 1914.

15 Carr, 'The faceless POW', p. 89.

16 'Usera Hakkinda Talimatname Mat-baa-I [Manual Regarding Prisoners of War]', in Lawless, *Kismet*, pp. 233–7.

17 Diamadis, 'Precious and honoured guests of the Ottoman Government', p. 169; Babkenian and Stanley, *Armenia, Australia and the Great War*, pp. 84–101.

18 Repatriation Statement of William Elston, AWM30, B1.13.

19 Rifki Bey Report, 'Prisoners of War in Turkey – Allowances to', 12 April 1918, A11803, 1918/89/453, NAA, Canberra.

20 Keith Hudson, 'Report on the Treatment of Prisoners from Kut of Air Mech. K.L. Hudson, AFC, AWM 3DRL/3325.

21 Repatriation Statement of D'Arcy Armstrong, AWM30, B2.12.

22 Rifki Bey Report, 12 April 1918, A11803, 1918/89/453, NAA, Canberra.

23 Lushington, *A Prisoner with the Turks*, p. 38.

24 Jones, 'A missing paradigm?', p. 28.

25 Ibid., p. 29. The British were slower to mobilise POW labour, largely owing to the fears of trade unions that wages of British workers would be undercut.

26 Coombes, *Crossing the Wire*, pp. 185–8.

27 McMeekin, *The Berlin–Baghdad Express*, p. 241.

28 Ibid., p. 44.

29 Diary entries, 10 and 12 February 1916, in Kerr, *Lost Anzacs*, pp. 161, 163.

30 Delpratt to E. White, undated, MGDC; Repatriation Statement of Arthur Tierney, AWM30, B2.14.

31 Repatriation Statement of John Beattie, AWM30, B1.3.

32 'Report on the Treatment of British Prisoners of War in Turkey', cd. 9208, (London: HMSO, 1918), p. 12.

33 Charles Suckling, 'Unpublished manuscript', 34, Papers of Charles Suckling, Submariner, 1914–1918, AWM 3DRL/6226; Lambert to M. Chomley, 21 July 1918, ARC POW Dept Case File of (hereafter ARC PWD) Leslie Lambert, AWM 1DRL/0428, Box 113.

34 Lushington, *A Prisoner with the Turks*, p. 35.

35 Erickson, *Ordered to Die*, pp. 16–9.

36 Bean, *Gallipoli Mission*, p. 317.

37 Keeling, *Adventures in Turkey and Russia*, p. 43.

38 Ozdemir, *Ottoman Army 1914–1918*, pp. 30–3.

39 Lushington, *A Prisoner with the Turks*, p. 13.

40 'Copy of Diary Written by D.B. Creedon', 13, D.B. Creedon Diary 1915, SLQ.

41 Suckling, 'Unpublished manuscript', p. 33.

42 Erickson, *Ordered to Die*, p. 6.

43 'Copy of Diary Written by D.B. Creedon', 13.

44 Statement made at Aleppo, 20 November 1918, ARC PWD Edwin Rose, AWM 1DRL/0428, Box 179.
45 Repatriation Statement of Maurice Delpratt, B2455, DELPRATT MAURICE, NAA, Canberra; Repatriation Statement of William Mackay, AWM30, B1.21; Repatriation Statement of Edgar Hobson, AWM30, B2.2; Repatriation Statement of John Romaro, AWM30, B2.14.
46 H. Kinder, 'Unpublished manuscript', p. 34, Papers of Kinder, HJE (Stoker, Petty Officer), AWM PR01466.
47 Ibid., p. 38.
48 American Ambassador to Secretary of State for Foreign Affairs, 9 January 1917, Prisoners of War in Turkey, A11803, 1917/89/377, NAA, Canberra.
49 Wheat, 'Unpublished manuscript', p. 14.
50 Melanie Schulze-Tanielian, 'Disease and public health (Ottoman Empire/ Middle East)', in 1914–1918-online. International Encyclopedia of the First World War, ed. Ute Daniel and others, issued by Freie Universität Berlin. doi: 10.15463/ie1418.10466.
51 Foster, Two and a Half Years, p. 42.
52 Repatriation Statement of John Merson, AWM30, B2.10; Brown, Turkish Days and Ways, p. 255.
53 Ozdemir, Ottoman Army 1914–1918, pp. 84, 98, 100.
54 Repatriation Statement of Niven Neyland, AWM30, B1.26.
55 Ozdemir, Ottoman Army 1914–1918, p. 40; Erickson, Ordered to Die, p. 8.
56 Freidrich Kress von Kressenstein, quoted in Ozdemir, Ottoman Army 1914–1918, pp. 140–1.
57 E.B. Harran to Sir H. Rumbold, 15 January 1917, A11803, 1917/89/377, NAA, Canberra.
58 Ozdemir, Ottoman Army 1914–1918, p. 84.
59 Delpratt to E. White, 24 May and 4 August 1917, MGDC.
60 Ozdemir, Ottoman Army 1914–1918, p. 148.
61 Repatriation Statement of Edgar Hobson, AWM30, B2.2.
62 Repatriation Statement of Ron McDonald, AWM30, B1.22.
63 Repatriation Statement of Stanley Jordan, AWM30, B1.17.
64 Vischer, Barbed Wire Disease, pp. 30–1.
65 Diary entry, 21 April 1916, in Kerr, Lost Anzacs, p. 180.
66 Brown, Turkish Days and Ways, p. 214.
67 Reid and Michael, Prisoner of War, p. 157.
68 White, Guests of the Unspeakable, p. 132.
69 Vischer, Barbed Wire Disease, pp. 36–7.
70 Diary entry, 11 January 1916, in Kerr, Lost Anzacs, pp. 145–6.
71 Green to M.J. Green, 26 October 1916, ARC PWD Edgar Green, AWM 1DRL/0428, Box 79.
72 Delpratt to E. White, 4 August 1917, MGDC.
73 Lyons, 'French soldiers and their correspondence', pp. 79–95.
74 Delpratt to E. White, 26 July 1918, MGDC.
75 Delpratt to E. White, 16 September 1916, MGDC.
76 Lyons, 'French soldiers and their correspondence', pp. 89, 90.

77 Becker, 'Art, material life, and disaster', p. 27.
78 Skyring to A.L. Grant, 19 May 1918, ARC PWD Lowes Skyring, AWM 1DRL/0428, Box 190.
79 O'Hare to Chomley, 28 June 1918, ARC PWD Phillip O'Hare, AWM 1DRL/0428, Box 156.
80 Repatriation Statement of John Beattie, AWM30, B1.3.
81 Repatriation Statement of Richard Griffiths, AWM30, B1.16.
82 Delpratt to E. White, undated, MGDC.
83 Halpin, *Blood in the Mists*, p. 184.
84 Randall to Wangemann, 27 May 1918, Papers of Trooper E. Randall 6th ALH and Pte W. Randall 14Bn, AWM 3DRL/7847; Vautin to Harold, 8 July 1918, ARC PWD Claude Vautin, AWM 1DRL/0428, Box 213.
85 Woolley, *From Kastamuni to Kedos*, p. 17.
86 Wheat, 'Unpublished manuscript', p. 25.
87 Gammage, *The Broken Years*, pp. 117–20.
88 Diary entry, 8 May 1916, in Kerr, *Lost Anzacs*, p. 188.
89 *Avoca Free Press*, 2 December 1916, Randall Family Papers, Heritage Collections Library, State Library of Victoria.
90 Cliffe to brother, 30 October 1916, ARC PWD William Cliffe, AWM 1DRL/0428, Box 39.
91 Halpin, *Blood in the Mists*, p. 234.
92 B. Butler to V. Deakin, 28 May 1918, ARC PWD Noel Sherrie, AWM 1DRL/0428, Box 187.

Chapter 3 Shaping camp life

 1 L.H. Smith, 'Experiences of a prisoner of war in Turkey', p. 1, AWM PR83/100.
 2 Luscombe, *The Story of Harold Earl*, p. 61.
 3 Ibid., p. 65.
 4 Ibid.
 5 Iris Rachamimov, 'Camp domesticity', pp. 295–8. For more on the significance of decorative items in POW accommodation, see Becker, 'Art, material life and disaster', pp. 29–30.
 6 Brown, *Turkish Days and Ways*, p. 180.
 7 Ibid., pp. 22, 255. See also Repatriation Statement of Leslie Lambert, AWM30, B2.6.
 8 White, *Guests of the Unspeakable*, p. 143.
 9 Repatriation Statement of John Beattie, AWM30, B1.3.
10 Ibid.
11 Lushington, *A Prisoner with the Turks*, p. 38; Delpratt to E. White, 17 March and 2 June 1918, MGDC.
12 Diary entry, 6 February 1916, in Kerr, *Lost Anzacs*, p. 160.
13 Roper, *The Secret Battle*, pp. 121–5.
14 Repatriation Statement of D'Arcy Armstrong, AWM30, B2.12.
15 Becker, 'Art, material life, and disaster', p. 27.

16 Brown, *Turkish Days and Ways*, p. 175. James Beattie also commented that the guards were equipped with 'old-fashioned Snider rifles dated 1866': Repatriation Statement of James Beattie, AWM30, B1.3.
17 Lushington, *A Prisoner with the Turks*, p. 97.
18 Delpratt to E. White, 21 July 1917, MGDC.
19 Hill, *The Spook and the Commandant*, p. 94.
20 Ibid., p. 113.
21 For a colourful account of White's escape, see *Guests of the Unspeakable*.
22 Pegram, 'Bold bids for freedom'.
23 Some analyses of the importance of sport to Australian prisoners of the Japanese have been published recently. See Kevin Blackburn, *Sportsmen of Changi* (Sydney: New South Publishing, 2012); and Roland Perry, *The Changi Brownlow* (Sydney: Hachette Australia, 2010). For the significance of sport for the prisoners of the Ottomans, see Kate Ariotti and Martin Crotty, 'The role of sport for Australian POWs of the Turks during the First World War', *International Journal of the History of Sport* 31, no. 18 (2014): 2362–74.
24 Delpratt to E. White, 1 April 1918, MGDC.
25 Andrews, *The Anzac Illusion*, pp. 172–4.
26 Thomson, 'Steadfast until death?', p. 476.
27 Delpratt to E. White, 16 December 1917, MGDC.
28 Yanikdag, *Healing the Nation*, pp. 51, 53.
29 Foster, *Two and a Half Years*, p. 33.
30 Jones, *Violence Against Prisoners of War*, pp. 103–5.
31 Jones, 'Imperial captivities', pp. 187–9.
32 Delpratt to E. White, 1 May 1918, MGDC.
33 Repatriation Statement of Edgar Hobson, AWM30, B2.2.
34 McMeekin, *The Berlin–Baghdad Express*, pp. 301–17.
35 Repatriation Statement of D'Arcy Armstrong, AWM30, B2.12; White, *Guests of the Unspeakable*, p. 73.
36 Keeling, *Adventures in Turkey and Russia*, p. 25.
37 Smith, 'Experiences of a prisoner of war in Turkey', p. 4, Letters of Lt Laurence Smith, No. 72 Sqdn, AFC, AWM PR83/100, AWM; Repatriation Statement of Douglas Rutherford, AWM30, B3.3.
38 Repatriation Statement of Harry Foxcroft, AWM30, B1.15; Repatriation Statement of Bernard Dunne, AWM30, B1.12.
39 Captain Jones to Delpratt, 10 November 1919, MGDC.
40 Diary entry, 1 January 1916, in Kerr, *Lost Anzacs*, p. 141.
41 Lushington, *A Prisoner with the Turks*, p. 81.
42 Ibid., p. 77.
43 Roper, *Secret Battle*, p. 50.
44 Makepeace, 'Living beyond the barbed wire', p. 167.
45 Diary entry, 7 January 1916, in Kerr, *Lost Anzacs*, p. 144.
46 White, *Guests of the Unspeakable*, p. 130.
47 Diary entry, 17 December 1915, in Kerr, *Lost Anzacs*, p. 128.
48 Diary entries, 3 and 4 March 1916, in Kerr, *Lost Anzacs*, pp. 169–70.
49 'Taken prisoner by the Turks: Sgt G. Paltridge's experiences', *Mount Barker Courier*, 21 February 1919.

50 Diary entry, 25 April 1916, in Kerr, *Lost Anzacs*, p. 184; White, *Guests of the Unspeakeable*, p. 139.

51 Diary entry, 14 July 1916, in Kerr, *Lost Anzacs*, p. 204.

52 Diary entry, 17 March 1916, in Kerr, *Lost Anzacs*, p. 174.

53 'Copy of diary written by D.B. Creedon', p. 15; diary entry, 25 December 1915, 'Diary of Able Seaman Albert Edward Knaggs RAN', p. 12, Papers of A.E. Knaggs, HMAS *AE2*, PR85/96, AWM.

54 Delpratt to E. White, 5 January 1918, MGDC.

55 Ibid.

56 Woolley, *From Kastamuni to Kedos*, p. 95.

57 Ibid., p. 118.

58 Luscombe, *The Story of Harold Earl*, pp. 75–7.

59 Brown, *Turkish Days and Ways*, p. 178.

60 At Angora in 1915 Daniel Creedon witnessed the funeral of an English private, during which the grave was found to be too shallow: 'the grave was about three feet deep and there were men's skulls and bones lying everywhere' (copy of diary written by D.B. Creedon, p. 13).

61 Roberts to Chomley, 20 November 1917, ARC PWD George Roberts, AWM 1DRL/0428, Box 177.

62 Repatriation Statement of Arthur Tierney, AWM30, B2.14.

63 Ziino, *A Distant Grief*, p. 22.

64 L. Doughty-Wylie to Red Cross, 18 February 1920, ARC Wounded and Missing Bureau Case File of George Burdett King, AWM 1DRL/0428.

65 Diary entry, 8 May 1916, in Kerr, *Lost Anzacs*, p. 188.

66 Diary entry, 15 June 1916, in Kerr, *Lost Anzacs*, pp. 198–9.

67 Bean, *Gallipoli Mission*, p. 318.

68 Lushington, *A Prisoner with the Turks*, p. 65.

69 For discussion about the role of servicemen at the various fronts in facilitating the grief of the bereaved at home and the ways in which such actions helped soothe their own grief, see Jalland, *Changing Ways of Death in Twentieth-Century Australia*, pp. 59–64; Damousi, *The Labour of Loss*, p. 9; Ziino, *A Distant Grief*, pp. 22–9.

70 Secretary, New Zealand Government Offices, London, to Chomley, 30 January 1918, ARC PWD George Roberts, AWM 1DRL/0428, Box 177.

71 Skyring to A.L. Grant, 19 May 1918, ARC PWD Lowes Skyring, 1DRL/0428, Box 190.

72 Delpratt's anxiety over Calcutt's death and the effect it would have on Calcutt's parents is evident in several of the letters Delpratt wrote to his sister. See for example Delpratt to E. White, 24 May 1917, MGDC.

Chapter 4 Outside connections

1 Speed, *Prisoners, Diplomats and the Great War*, p. 3.

2 Yarnall, *Barbed Wire Disease*, p. 9.

3 Speed, *Prisoners, Diplomats and the Great War*, p. 31.

4 Jones, 'A missing paradigm?', p. 26.

5 Speed, *Prisoners, Diplomats and the Great War*, p. 32.

6 'Usera Hakkinda Talimatname Mat-baa-I' ('Manual Regarding Prisoners of War'), in Lawless, *Kismet*, pp. 233–7.

7 Hoffman Phillip to W. Page, 2 June 1916, Prisoners of War in Turkey, A11803, 1914/89/364, NAA, Canberra; W. Page to A. Balfour, 9 January 1917, Prisoners of War in Turkey, A11803, 1917/89/377, NAA, Canberra. Mehmed Talaaf Pasha, the Ottoman Minister for the Interior and later Grand Vizier, emphasised the similarity in treatment of prisoners with Ottoman soldiers in discussions with the American ambassador in Constantinople (American Ambassador to Secretary of State for Foreign Affairs, 9 January 1917, and A. Balfour to W. Page, 13 January 1917, A11803, 1917/89/377, NAA, Canberra). In at least one instance, the British Foreign Office outright rejected the idea that the prisoners received the same treatment as Ottoman troops.

8 See Dodds, *For All Prisoners and Captives*, and Jones, *Violence Against Prisoners of War*, p. 16.

9 Hately-Broad, *War and Welfare*, p. 141.

10 Determined using the Reserve Bank of Australia's 'Pre-decimal Inflation Calculator', which calculates 'the change in cost of purchasing a representative basket of goods and services over a period of time'. 'Pre-decimal Inflation Calculator', Reserve Bank of Australia, <www.rba.gov.au/calculator/ annualPreDecimal.html> (retrieved 3 August 2017).

11 Mordaunt Reid, 'Australian Red Cross Prisoners of War Department – Financial Report', in M.E. Chomley, 'Final report on the Prisoners of War Department of the Australian Red Cross' (hereafter Chomley, 'Final report'), pp. 15–16. See 'Prisoners of War – Pay and Allowances', Prisoners of War – Miscellany, AWM10, 4332/7/30.

12 See 'Encashment of Cheques of Australian Officers Who are Prisoners of War', AWM10, 4332/7/30; and Chomley, 'Final report', p. 16.

13 'Prisoners of War – Turkey and Bulgaria', AWM10, 4332/7/30. The idea of maintenance or subsistence payments (or lack thereof) became a key issue for Australians repatriated from Japanese captivity during the Second World War. See Twomey, 'Compensating prisoners of war of Japan in post-war Australia', pp. 254–75.

14 Foreign Office to Netherlands Minister at Constantinople, 22 January 1918, Prisoners of War in Turkey – Allowances to, A11803, 1918/89/453, NAA, Canberra; Chomley, 'Final report', p. 20. Ottoman lira to pounds sterling conversion taken from Pamuk, *A Monetary History of the Ottoman Empire*, p. 209.

15 Andrews, *The Anzac Illusion*, p. 13.

16 Ibid., pp. 47, 114.

17 Ibid., p. 47.

18 Robertson, *Anzac and Empire*, pp. 215–16. Tension between British and Australian POWs regarding the issue of pay was evident in the camps. Daniel Creedon stated that 'there was a terrible lot of ill-feeling on the part of the Englishmen, apparently because we were being paid more than they. There were several pretty heated discussions about this' ('Copy of Diary Written by D.B. Creedon', p. 14).

19 Australian High Commissioner to Colonial Office, 8 July 1915, MP472/1, 5/19/2520, NAA, Melbourne.

20 Commonwealth Office, London, to Secretary, Department of External Affairs, June 1916, MP472/1, 5/19/2520, NAA, Melbourne.

21 Naval Representative, London to Naval Secretary, Melbourne, 15 November 1915, MP472/1, 5/19/2520, NAA, Melbourne. This avenue was eventually exhausted, and by mid-1916 the Naval Representative sent advances to the prisoners via the International Red Cross Committee in Switzerland.
22 Colonial Office to Australian High Commissioner, 6 July 1915, MP472/1, 5/19/2520, NAA, Melbourne.
23 Naval Representative, London to Naval Secretary, Melbourne, 29 January 1916, MP472/1, 5/19/2520, NAA, Melbourne.
24 Director of Victualling, Admiralty, to Official Secretary, Commonwealth of Australia, London, 23 November 1916, MP472/1, 5/19/2520, NAA, Melbourne; Naval Representative, London, to Naval Secretary, Melbourne, 21 December 1916, MP472/1, 5/19/2520, NAA, Melbourne.
25 Naval Secretary, Melbourne to Naval Representative, London, 8 March 1917, MP472/1, 5/19/2520, NAA, Melbourne.
26 Speed, *Prisoners, Diplomats, and the Great War*, p. 33.
27 Articles 12, 15, 17 and 18, respectively, of 'Agreement between the British and Ottoman Governments Respecting Prisoners of War and Civilians', Prisoners of War – Conference of British and Turkish Delegates, A11803, 1918/89/217, NAA, Canberra.
28 Articles 22 and 23, 'Agreement between the British and Ottoman Governments'.
29 Article 4, 'Agreement between the British and Ottoman Governments'.
30 Article 6, 'Agreement between the British and Ottoman Governments'.
31 Foreign Office to Swedish Minister for Foreign Affairs, 15 August 1918, A11803, 1918/89/217, NAA, Canberra.
32 Foreign Office to British Ambassador to the Netherlands, 14 August 1918, A11803, 1918/89/217, NAA, Canberra.
33 Levie, 'Prisoners of war and the protecting power', p. 376.
34 Morgenthau, *Secrets of the Bosphorus*, pp. 256–67.
35 Elkus to W. Page, 19 December 1916, A11803, 1917/89/377, NAA, Canberra.
36 Ibid. See also Steuer, *Pursuit of an 'Unparalleled Opportunity'*, chapter 15.
37 Elkus to W. Page, 6 February 1917, A11803, 1917/89/377, NAA, Canberra; Repatriation Statement of Ronald McDonald, AWM30, B1.22.
38 Elkus to W. Page, 19 December 1916, A11803, 1917/89/377, NAA, Canberra.
39 Ibid.
40 Repatriation Statement of David Boyle, AWM30, B1.4.
41 In a letter to the American Ambassador in London, Walter Hines Page, to be forwarded to the British Government, an American consular official in Constantinople expressed his frustration at the multifaceted nature of the wartime Ottoman authorities: 'As you know there are five distinct ruling centres here, any one of which may interpose objections to a proposition. There is the Palace Group, and the Sublime Porte Group. Then there is the Military Government. Meshed in these, especially into the second, is the Committee of Union and Progress; this group has special influence in economic affairs. Then in the background is the German rule, potent above all in anything that may affect the military situation, and holding the financial whip

besides. I mention these five Governments to explain in part the difficulty of getting things done. Every official seems to hesitate about assenting to requests for fear that there may be an objection somewhere else.' (Unsigned to W. Page, 13 January 1917, A11803, 1917/89/377, NAA, Canberra)

42 Elkus to W. Page, 23 January 1917, and American Ambassador in Vienna to W. Page, 7 March 1917, A11803, 1917/89/377, NAA.

43 Elkus to W. Page, 15 January 1917, A11803, 1917/89/377, NAA.

44 Ibid. According to an unsigned memo from the American Embassy in Constantinople, dated 13 January 1917, General Townshend reported to the Americans that Indian officers were being well paid by the Ottomans and that they would not be in need of welfare payments. On the basis of this report the Americans initially discontinued their payments, but then believed 'there may be doubts as to the wisdom of this policy'.

45 Jones, 'A missing paradigm?', pp. 26–7.

46 W. Page to A. Balfour, 9 January 1917, A11803, 1917/89/377, NAA, Canberra.

47 A. Balfour to W. Page, 13 January 1917, A11803, 1917/89/377, NAA, Canberra.

48 A. Balfour to W. Page, 16 December 1916, A11803, 1917/89/377, NAA, Canberra.

49 Elkus to Sublime Porte, memorandum, 4 December 1916, A11803, 1917/89/377, NAA. Elkus also tried a different tack to encourage the Turks to permit inspections of the camps. One of Talaat Pasha's close friends had been taken prisoner by the British, and Elkus believed he could be used as a bargaining tool to achieve improved conditions for those in Turkey. Elkus put to the British that if they released Talaat's friend, the Turks might potentially permit embassy officials to visit the prisoners. W. Page to A. Balfour, 9 January 1917, A11803, 1917/89/377, NAA, Canberra.

50 'Notes on visits of Swiss International Red Cross delegates to prisoners camps', A11803, 1917/89/377, NAA, Canberra.

51 Elkus to Sublime Porte, 12 March 1917, A11803, 1917/89/377, NAA, Canberra.

52 Repatriation Statement of David Boyle, AWM30, B1.4; Repatriation Statement of Harry Brown, AWM30, B1.5.

53 Steur, *Pursuit of an 'Unparalleled Opportunity'*, chapter 15.

54 Foreign Office to Willebois, 28 April 1918, A11803, 1918/89/453, NAA, Canberra.

55 Dutch Consul to Willebois, 'Report from Rifki Bey', 12 April 1918, A11803, 1918/89/453, NAA, Canberra.

56 Foreign Office to British Ambassador at the Hague, 29 April 1918, A11803, 1918/89/453, NAA, Canberra.

57 Foreign Office to Willebois, 19 July 1918, A11803, 1918/89/453, NAA, Canberra; Paulus to Dutch Minister for Foreign Affairs, 24 May 1918, A11803, 1918/89/453, NAA, Canberra.

58 'Report by Menten and Spengler', A11803, 1918/89/453, NAA, Canberra.

59 Foreign Office to Willebois, 14 September 1918, A11803, 1918/89/453, NAA, Canberra.

60 V. Herbert to P. O'Connor, 12 October 1916, ARC PWD William Elston, AWM 1DRL/0428, Box 60.
61 'Prisoners of war: Relief measures explained', *West Australian* (Perth), 12 December 1916.
62 Yarnall, *Barbed Wire Disease*, p. 108.
63 'Prisoners of war: Relief measures explained', *West Australian* (Perth), 12 December 1916.
64 Chomley to F.M. Merson, 2 August 1918, ARC PWD John Merson, 1DRL/0428, Box 131.
65 Yarnall, *Barbed Wire Disease*, pp. 109–10.
66 No significant scholarly work has been undertaken on Mary Elizabeth Chomley, so that little is known about her life after the war. For a brief overview, see her entry in the *Australian Women's Register*: Rosemary Francis, 'Chomley, Mary Elizabeth Maud (1872–1960)', *Australian Women's Register*, <www.womenaustralia.info/biogs/IMP0133b.htm> (retrieved 3 August 2017).
67 Chomley, 'Final report', pp. 1–2.
68 Ibid., p. 9.
69 Ibid., p. 4.
70 Ibid., p. 4. Lieutenant William Treloar wrote to Chomley specifically thanking her for a parcel that contained Australian jam, butter and biscuits (W.H. Treloar to Chomley, 15 May 1918, ARC PWD William Treloar, AWM 1DRL/428, Box 210).
71 Reid, 'Australian Red Cross', p. 16.
72 Chomley, 'Final report', p. 6. A brief scan of POW Department case files reinforces Chomley's claim; Alfred Carpenter, for example, acknowledged in October 1917 receipt of the boots that had been sent in January.
73 Chomley, 'Final report', p. 12.
74 Reid, 'Australian Red Cross', p. 20.
75 Chomley, 'Final report', p. 6.
76 Ibid., p. 1.
77 B. Talbot to Chomley, 10 February 1918, ARC PWD Benjamin Talbot, AWM 1DRL/0428, Box 203.
78 Repatriation Statement of Robert McColl, AWM30, B2.2.
79 International Committee of the Red Cross, 'The International Prisoners-of-War Agency: The ICRC in World War One' (Geneva: ICRC, 2007), p. 3, <www.icrc.org/eng/assets/files/other/icrc_002_0937.pdf> (retrieved 18 October 2017).
80 Reid, 'Australian Red Cross', p. 15.
81 White, *Guests of the Unspeakable*, p. 84.
82 Luscombe, *The Story of Harold Earl*, pp. 59–60.
83 White, *Guests of the Unspeakable*, pp. 84, 174–5; Lawless, *Kismet*, pp. 78–9.
84 Dutch Consul to Willebois, 'Report from Rifki Bey', 12 April 1918, A11803, 1918/89/453, NAA, Canberra.
85 Ibid.
86 Keeling, *Adventures in Turkey and Russia*, pp. 235, 177.
87 Prisoners in Turkey Committee, 'Regulations and Notes for the Help of Relatives and Friends'.

Chapter 5 Reactions at home

1 Williams, *Anzacs, the Media and the Great War*, p. 75.
2 'Turks claim victory', *Daily News* (Perth), 29 April 1915. Similar articles were published in the Melbourne *Argus*, the *Brisbane Courier* and the Adelaide *Register*.
3 Cth, Parliamentary Debates, House of Representatives, vol. 26, 30 June 1915, 4452; Cth, Parliamentary Debates, House of Representatives, vol. 28, 16 July 1915, 5024; Cth, Parliamentary Debates, House of Representatives, vol. 33, 19 August 1915, 5915.
4 McCallum and Putnis, 'Media management in wartime', p. 21.
5 'Prisoners in Dardanelles', *Argus* (Melbourne), 28 June 1915.
6 See for example 'British prisoners at Pretoria', *Sydney Morning Herald*, 7 December 1899. For reports of bad camps, see 'The Boer War: Starving British prisoners', *Brisbane Courier*, 11 July 1900, and 'The war: Sufferings of British captives', *Camperdown Chronicle*, 10 May 1900.
7 'Prisoners at Pretoria', *Queenslander*, 5 May 1900.
8 'A prisoner of war: Somewhere in Asia Minor', *Queenslander*, 2 October 1915.
9 'Held by the Turks: Letter from an officer', *Argus* (Melbourne), 13 September 1915.
10 'Prisoners of war', *Argus* (Melbourne), 27 July 1916; 'Turks kind to prisoners', *Register* (Adelaide), 29 August 1916.
11 'Australia's duty: The need for recruits', *Leader* (Melbourne), 7 July 1917.
12 Ibid.; Gammage, *The Broken Years*, p. 25.
13 See David Wilson, 'Red Cross or Iron Cross', Imperial War Museum, <www.iwm.org.uk/collections/item/object/205132733> (retrieved 3 August 2017).
14 'Australia's duty: The need for recruits', *Leader* (Melbourne), 7 July 1917.
15 'Australian prisoners in Turkey', *Sydney Morning Herald*, 10 November 1917.
16 'Australian war work in London', *Sydney Morning Herald*, 31 December 1917.
17 'Back from Turkey: Australian prisoners' stories of captivity', *West Australian* (Perth), 25 February 1918. A version of this report also appeared in the *Sydney Morning Herald*, the Hobart *Mercury*, the Melbourne *Argus*, the *Brisbane Courier* and the Adelaide *Register* around the same date.
18 Prime Minister's Department to Governor-General's office, 16 January 1918, 'Prisoners of war in Turkey – treatment of', A11803, 1918/89/50, NAA, Canberra.
19 'Australians in Turkey', *Triad* (Sydney), 10 June 1918.
20 'Prisoners of war: Dealing with repatriated men', *Brisbane Courier*, 26 March 1918.
21 'Australian prisoners in Turkey', *Sydney Morning Herald*, 10 May 1918.
22 Ibid.
23 Ibid.
24 'Our prisoners in Turkey: The need for action', *Advertiser* (Adelaide), 16 October 1918.

25 Rita Hilton, 'Hands across the sea', Hilton (née Duffy) Rita; Luscombe, L.H. (Lieutenant), AWM PR01552.

26 See L. Luscombe to R. Hilton, 24 February 1918, AWM PR01552; and Rutherford, 'The write support', pp. 40–1.

27 Oppenheimer, *All Work, No Pay*, p. 27.

28 'Woman's realm', *Argus* (Melbourne), 8 April 1916.

29 Scott, *Australia During the War*, p. 703.

30 Feltman, 'Letters from captivity', p. 99.

31 Ibid.

32 Delpratt to E. White, 18 August 1917, MGDC.

33 'National funds', *Argus* (Melbourne), 2 October 1916; 'Statement of receipts and disbursements of the New South Wales Division from 1st July 1916 to 30th June 1917', *Sydney Morning Herald*, 31 August 1917.

34 Chomley, 'Final report', p. 15.

35 See for example 'Individual prisoners of war, 9/11/1918', Papers of Chomley, Mary Elizabeth, AWM 1DRL/0615, File 12.

36 'Women's Department: Queensland Women's War Work', *Queenslander*, 1 December 1917.

37 Wallace, *How We Raised the First Hundred Thousand*, pp. 28–9.

38 'Schools War Fund', *Horsham Times*, 8 January 1918.

39 Triolo, *Our Schools and the War*, pp. 69–103.

40 'War Prisoners' Day', *Argus* (Melbourne), 30 November 1917.

41 'War Prisoners Day – A prisoner's mother', *Argus* (Melbourne), 4 December 1917.

42 'Red Cross Button Day', *Register* (Adelaide), 4 September 1917.

43 'Red Cross succour for prisoners: Are you sharing in it?', *Queenslander*, 27 July 1918

44 'Red Cross Appeal', *Daily News* (Perth), 15 May 1918.

45 'Red Cross succour for prisoners: Are you sharing in it?', *Queenslander*, 27 July 1918.

46 Oppenheimer, *All Work, No Pay*, p. 30.

47 'Auburn: Well done', *Cumberland Argus and Fruitgrowers Advocate*, 19 October 1918.

48 'Women's hockey', *Sydney Morning Herald*, 2 September 1918; 'What-Oh Revue', *Daily Observer* (Tamworth), 15 August 1918.

49 'Education Department Fund totals £327 226', *Leader* (Melbourne), 27 July 1918; Triolo, *Our Schools and the War*, p. 40.

50 'Patriotic funds', *Examiner* (Launceston), 22 June 1918; 'Port Adelaide Red Cross Circle', *Register* (Adelaide), 6 November 1918.

51 'Prisoners of war: Who will help them?', *Queenslander* (Brisbane), 19 October 1918.

52 'Prisoners of war', *Queenslander* (Brisbane), Saturday 28 September 1918.

53 'Prisoners of war gift house', *Brisbane Courier*, 23 November 1918.

54 Hunter, 'Captivity', p. 167.

55 Hunter, 'The prisoner of war and his family', p. 31.

56 F. Adams to AIF Base Records, 17 January 1917, B2455, ADAMS FL, NAA, Canberra.

57 M. Jennings to Chomley, 25 January 19– (year unknown), ARC PWD Edgar Green, AWM 1DRL/0428, Box 79.

58 E. White to Delpratt, 12 May 1918, MGDC.

59 Delpratt to E. White, 4 August 1917, MGDC.

60 Larsson, *Shattered Anzacs*, p. 48.

61 E. Ingram to Chomley, 5 October 1918, and E. Ingram to Mother, undated, ARC PWD Ernest Ingram, AWM 1DRL/0428, Box 100.

62 R. Peters to Chomley, 8 September 1918, ARC PWD Robert Peters, AWM 1DRL/0428, Box 163.

63 Roper, *Secret Battle*, pp. 63–4.

64 E. White to Delpratt, 8 March and 12 March 1918, MGDC.

65 V. Elston to Chomley, 25 February 1918, ARC PWD William Elston, AWM 1DRL/0428, Box 60.

66 Such restrictions also caused upset among the families of other Dominion prisoners. As Jonathan Vance writes, the implicit class-based discrimination angered Canadians who wanted to send private parcels to men of the ranks (Vance, *Objects of Concern*, pp. 47–8).

67 Roper, *Secret Battle*, pp. 93–101.

68 M. Gilbert to Chomley, 28 June 1917, ARC PWD George Gilbert, AWM 1DRL/0428, Box 74.

69 Yarnall, *Barbed Wire Disease*, p. 113.

70 Chomley, 'Final report', p. 6.

71 Mrs Flatt to Chomley, 1 July 1918, ARC PWD Charles Flatt, AWM 1DRL/0428, Box 65; Chomley to Capt F.M. Merson, 2 August 1918, ARC PWD John Merson, AWM 1DRL/0428, Box 131.

72 Hunter, 'Captivity', p. 177.

73 F. Ashton to Chomley, 13 January 1917, ARC PWD Frederick Ashton, AWM 1DRL/0428, Box 7.

74 M. Bowry to Chomley, 6 December 1917, ARC PWD Colin Spencer Campbell, AWM 1DRL/0428, Box 32; H. Kimber to Chomley, 4 April 1918, ARC PWD Allan Kimber, AWM 1DRL/0428, Box 112.

75 Winter, 'Kinship and remembrance', pp. 40–60.

76 As well as Winter, see Luckins, *The Gates of Memory*; Larsson, *Shattered Anzacs*; and Stanley, *Men of Mont St Quentin*.

77 Winter, *Sites of Memory*, p. 53.

78 C. Gilman to Chomley, 12 September 1918, ARC PWD Ellis Gilman, AWM 1DRL/0428, Box 75.

79 B. Sherrie to V. Deakin, undated, ARC Wounded and Missing Bureau Case File of Noel Sherrie, AWM 1DRL/0428.

80 Chomley to Mrs Lushington, 20 September 1917, ARC PWD Reginald Lushington, AWM 1DRL/0428, Box 122.

81 Damousi, *The Labour of Loss*, p. 19.

82 Chomley to G.L. Rayment, 22 December 19–, ARC PWD William Rayment, AWM 1DRL/0428, Box 172.

83 Chomley to Mrs Middleton, 16 September 1918, ARC PWD William Falconer, AWM 1DRL/0428, Box 62.

84 L. Hudson to Chomley, 13 June 19–, ARC PWD Keith Hudson, AWM 1DRL/0428, Box 97.

85 Mrs Evans to Mrs Reid, 10 June 1918, ARC PWD Ronald Austin, AWM 1DRL/0428, Box 8.

86 E. White to Delpratt, 16 June 1918, MGDC.

87 Mrs Rawlins to Chomley, undated, ARC PWD Delpratt, AWM 1DRL/0428, Box 52.

88 Chomley to Mrs Rawlins, 5 March 1917, ARC PWD Delpratt, AWM 1DRL/0428, Box 52.

89 V. Deakin to Driver Townley, 18 January 1918, ARC Wounded and Missing Bureau Case File of Harry Foxcroft, AWM 1DRL/0428.

90 Chomley to Cpl Ashton, 19 November 1917, ARC PWD Frederick Ashton, AWM 1DRL/0428, Box 7.

91 M.J. Green to Chomley, 21 November 1917, ARC PWD Edgar Green, AWM 1DRL/0428, Box 79. Emphasis in original.

92 Chomley to Mrs Woods, 15 December 1917, ARC PWD Clyde Currie, AWM 1DRL/0428, Box 48.

93 T. Lusk to Chomley, 7 September 1917, ARC PWD Colin Campbell, AWM 1DRL/0428, Box 32.

94 M. Alexander to Chomley, 21 July 1917, ARC PWD George Drysdale, AWM 1DRL/0428, Box 56.

95 See B2455, REDMAN CLAUDE THOMAS, NAA, Canberra.

96 E. White to Delpratt, 8 March 1918, MGDC.

97 R. Nelson to Chomley, 9 July 1918, ARC PWD Alfred Carpenter, AWM 1DRL/0428, Box 33.

98 E. Curran to Chomley, 3 August 1917, ARC PWD David Curran, 1DRL/0428, AWM, Box 47.

99 Ibid.

100 E. Curran to Chomley, 26 March 1919, ARC PWD David Curran, AWM 1DRL/0428, Box 47.

101 E. Curran to Chomley, 26 February 1918, ARC PWD David Curran, AWM 1DRL/0428, Box 47.

102 Chomley to E. Curran, 26 March 1919, ARC PWD David Curran, AWM 1DRL/0428, Box 47.

103 D. Lambert to Chomley, 4 June 1918, ARC PWD Leslie Lambert, AWM 1DRL/0428, Box 113.

Chapter 6 After the Armistice

1 'Text of the conditions of the Armistice with Turkey, as settled', Armistice Terms with Turkey and with Austria–Hungary, A11803, 1919/89/106, NAA, Canberra. This clause also included the handover of all interned Armenians.

2 Repatriation Statement of Edgar Hobson, AWM30, B2.2; L.H Luscombe, *The Story of Harold Earl*, p. 100.

3 Delpratt to E. White, 3 December 1918, MGDC.

4 Lushington, *A Prisoner with the Turks*, p. 98.

5 Austin, *My Experiences as a Prisoner*, pp. 40–1.

6 Frederick Ashton, 'Typescript of book (unpublished) by Fred Ashton, telling of his experiences during World War I, including a period as a prisoner of war in Turkey', ACC 973A, State Library of Western Australia, pp. 130–1.

7 Keeling, *Adventures in Turkey and Russia*, p. 184. The only exception was the men held at Bor convalescent camp, who left Bor on a train bound for Constantinople approximately two weeks after the Armistice. These men entrained for Itea in Greece, then travelled to Taranto where they followed the same route as those before them, arriving in London on New Year's Day 1919. See Repatriation Statements of Cahill, Campbell, Fooks and Tierney, AWM30.

8 Repatriation Statement of Edgar Hobson, AWM30, B2.2. Keeling was in charge of the transport of POWs from this region. For a description of his return to Turkey in late 1918 to facilitate repatriation of the prisoners, see *Adventures in Turkey and Russia*, pp. 184–90.

9 Woolley, *From Kastamuni to Kedos*, p. 108.

10 Wheat, 'Unpublished manuscript', p. 33.

11 Delpratt to E. White, 3 December 1918, MGDC.

12 Repatriation Statement of Edgar Hobson, AWM30, B2.2.

13 Australian High Commissioner to Major J.L. Treloar, 10 December 1918, Photographs of Repatriated POWs, AWM16, 4375/11/49. It should be noted that the ex-prisoners of the Germans were the main targets of this interest.

14 Ashton, 'Typescript of book', p. 143.

15 F.A. Chaffey to J.L. Treloar, 23 December 1918, AWM16, 4375/11/49.

16 J.R. Browne to J.L. Treloar, 18 December 1918, AWM16, 4375/11/49.

17 Ibid.

18 'Memorandum to all officers, non-commissioned officers, and men returning as prisoners of war from Turkey to Egypt', AWM30, B18.2.

19 Ibid.

20 J.L. Treloar to AIF Headquarters London, 22 February 1918, Enquiries re: Repatriated Prisoners of War, AWM16, 4376/50/2.

21 AIF Headquarters London to Dept of Defence, Melbourne, 5 November 1918, Repatriation, AWM27, 424/28; Dept of Defence to AIF Headquarters, 10 November 1918, AWM27, 424/28. See 'Framed letter from King George V to all returning prisoners of war', Imperial War Museum, <www.iwm.org.uk/collections/item/object/30084510>

22 'AIF Demobilisation Form', Repatriation Case File of George Handsley, J26, M18950 PART 1, NAA, Brisbane; Cahir to Chomley, 21 November 1918, Papers of Chomley, Mary Elizabeth, AWM 1DRL/0615, File 2.

23 White, 'The soldier as tourist', p. 66.

24 Luscombe, *The Story of Harold Earl*, p. 107.

25 Delpratt to E. White, 19 December 1918, MGDC.

26 Chomley, 'Final report', p. 11.

27 Campbell to Chomley, 14 February 1919, ARC PWD Colin Campbell, AWM 1DRL/0428, Box 32.

28 See Kerr, *Lost Anzacs*, pp. 227–31.

29 See Repatriation Case File of Joseph O'Neill, B73/54, R67430, NAA, Melbourne.
30 Chomley, 'Final report', p. 11.
31 Chomley organised introductions between the prisoners and these other significant guests, which included, among others, Generals Birdwood and Brudenell White and Mrs W.M. Hughes. See Chomley, 'Final report', p. 10.
32 Delpratt to E. White, 26 December 1918, MGDC.
33 Ursano and Rundell, 'The prisoner of war', p. 177.
34 Ibid.
35 See 'Casualty Form – Active Service', B2455, INGRAM ERNEST, NAA, Canberra.
36 Lloyd and Rees, *The Last Shilling*, pp. 116–17.
37 Ibid., p. 125.
38 Similar classes were also implemented in France and the Middle East while men awaited repatriation there. Those in the Middle East were eventually transferred to the United Kingdom as problems related to the employment of white Australians alongside 'native' Egyptians were envisaged. See Lloyd and Rees, *The Last Shilling*, p. 125.
39 Ziino, *A Distant Grief*, pp. 85–6.
40 Australian Graves Service, *Where the Australians Rest*, p. 65.
41 Deputy Assistant Director of Graves Registration and Enquiries, EEF to Director-General Graves Registration and Enquiries, War Office, 22 June 1919; Graves of British P. of W. in Turkey, WG436/2, Commonwealth War Graves Commission Archives, Maidenhead (hereafter CWGC); IWGC London to Director Records, 14 June 1922, 'Preliminary Report on POW Graves conducted by Lt Shears in September 1919', Asia Minor – Concentration, WG920/2, CWGC.
42 'Draft Resolution: War Graves in Asia Minor', Asia Minor – Graves In, WG920/1, CWGC.
43 Director of Records to Registrar Memorials to the Missing, 20 February 1923, Memorials to the Missing and Unlocated Graves in Turkey, WG219/20, CWGC.
44 Director of Works to Controller of Administration IWGC, 14 May 1920, WG920/1, CWGC.
45 'Graves in Asia Minor', Asia Minor – Graves In, WG920/1, CWGC.
46 Along with approximately 6000 graves from the Crimean period, the cemetery contains the graves of 407 First World War Commonwealth servicemen. Several casualties of the Second World War, and a memorial to Hindu soldiers of the Indian Army, are also located at Haidar Pasha.
47 Base Records to J.E. Easton, 1 March 1924, B2455, EASTON FP, NAA, Canberra.
48 J.E. Easton to Base Records, 23 August 1921, B2455, EASTON FP, NAA, Canberra. The Eastons received the extra photographs in April 1922.
49 Principal Assistant Secretary to Deputy Director of Works Gallipoli, 14 July 1924, Asia Minor – Concentration, WG920/2, CWGC.
50 Director Works Gallipoli to Ware, 17 March 1926, Asia Minor – Concentration, WG920/2, CWGC.

51 IWGC 88th Meeting, 12 May 1926, Asia Minor – Concentration, WG920/2, CWGC.

52 Hughes to Ware, 27 May 1926, Asia Minor – Concentration, WG920/2, CWGC.

53 Hughes to Ware, 30 May 1926, Asia Minor – Concentration, WG920/2, CWGC.

54 Hughes to Ware, 23 and 31 August 1926, Asia Minor – Concentration, WG920/2, CWGC.

55 Secretary AGS to IWGC, 21 April 1927, B2455, CALCUTT B., NAA, Canberra.

56 Base Records to J.R. Calcutt, 17 June 1927, B2455, CALCUTT B., NAA, Canberra.

57 Secretary AGS to IWGC, 21 April 1917, B2455, CALCUTT B., NAA, Canberra.

58 Secretary AGS to IWGC, 15 August 1927, B2455, ADAMS F.L., NAA, Canberra.

59 Jalland, *Changing Ways of Death in Twentieth-Century Australia*, p. 42.

60 Base Records to C. Day, 3 February 1928, B2455, DAY A, NAA, Canberra.

61 The memorial at Basra had to be moved from its original location on the west bank of the Shatt-al-Arab in 1997 owing to the sensitivity of the site. It is now located near Nasiriyah. See 'Basra Memorial', Commonwealth War Graves Commission, <www.cwgc.org/find-a-cemetery/cemetery/88400/BASRA%20MEMORIAL> (retrieved 3 August 2017).

62 Ziino, *A Distant Grief*, pp. 59–81.

63 Ibid., p. 67.

64 W.C. Kimber to Base Records, 13 November 1927, B2455, KIMBER ALLAN THOMAS, NAA, Canberra.

65 Ziino, *A Distant Grief*, p. 59.

66 M. Williams to W. Hughes, 1 September 1919, Submarine HMAS *AE2* etc, MP472/1, 5/19/2520, NAA, Melbourne.

67 Luckins, *The Gates of Memory*, p. 133.

68 H. Conway to Base Records, 1 March 1921, B2455, WOODS B., NAA, Canberra. In later life Bert's wife evidently changed her mind as she applied for his Gallipoli Medallion in November 1967.

69 Luckins, *The Gates of Memory*, p. 189.

70 Hughes to Ware, April 1928, Asia Minor – Graves In, WG920/1, CWGC.

71 M.J. Green to Chomley, 15 December 1918, ARC PWD Edgar Green, AWM 1DRL/0428, Box 79.

72 F. Adams to Base Records, 5 February 1919, B2455, ADAMS F.L., NAA, Canberra.

73 H. Bentinck, Chairman PITC to Secretary War Cabinet, 5 November 1918, Repatriation for Turkish ill-treatment of Prisoners of War – Copy of Resolution by Executive Committee of Prisoners in Turkey Committee, CAB, 24/69/24, National Archives, Kew (hereafter NAK).

74 Kramer, 'The first wave of international war crimes trials', p. 448.

75 Ibid.

76 Jones, *Violence Against Prisoners of War*, p. 313.

77 Segesser, 'The punishment of war crimes', p. 143. Heather Jones provides interesting background information regarding the trials and the testimony of British ex-POWs. See Jones, *Violence Against Prisoners of War*, p. 295.

78 For a detailed report regarding allegations of mistreatment of POWs by Turkish authorities, see 'Turkish and Turko-German offenders against the laws of war', in *First and Second Interim Reports From the Committee of Enquiry into Breaches of the Laws of War, with Appendices*, 3 June 1915, pp. 169–235, CAB, 24/85/6, NAK.

79 Kramer, 'The first wave of international war crimes trials', pp. 444–5. See also 'Negotiations with the Turkish Nationalists for the mutual release of prisoners of war', CAB, 24/127/71, NAK.

80 Babkenian and Stanley, *Armenia, Australia and the Great War*, p. 184.

81 Kramer, 'The first wave of international war crimes trials', p. 446.

Chapter 7 'Repat' and remembrance

1 Foster, *Two and a Half Years*, p. 64.

2 Garton, *The Cost of War*, p. 77.

3 Ibid., p. 80.

4 Repatriation Case File of D'Arcy Armstrong, BP709/1, M19901 PART 1, NAA, Brisbane.

5 Repatriation Case File of Edgar Hobson, BP709/1, M15754 PART 1, NAA, Brisbane.

6 'Precis of evidence, December 1933', Repatriation Case File of William Kelly, B73/29 H and R41707, NAA, Melbourne. For more on the Soldier Settlement scheme in Australia, see Lloyd and Rees, *The Last Shilling*, pp. 43–61; Lake, *The Limits of Hope*; and Scates and Oppenheimer, *The Last Battle*.

7 Garton, *The Cost of War*, p. 86.

8 Lightfoot to Repat, 27 January 1938, Repatriation Case File of Lancelot Lightfoot, D363/42, M13575, NAA, Sydney. The ex-POWs were not alone in lodging late claims. Marina Larsson notes that the number of applicants for war disability pension increased dramatically during the 1930s – by 1937 just under half of all returned servicemen had applied. That the peak of claims occurred during a period of severe economic depression, when any financial assistance could benefit those facing periods of prolonged unemployment, is one possibility for delayed applications. Less cynically, Larsson suggests that delays were due to the passage of time, and correlate with the transition of the men from youth to middle age and their inevitable decline in health and fitness (Larsson, *Shattered Anzacs*, pp. 215, 209).

9 See Butler, *Gallipoli, Palestine and New Guinea*, pp. 72, 231, 605, 705–11, and Cutlack, *Australian Flying Corps*, p. 8.

10 See table 72 in Butler, *Special Problems and Services*, p. 974.

11 Garton, *The Cost of War*, p. 92; Repatriation Case File of George Ernest Gilbert, B73/77, R57060, NAA, Melbourne. This conversion (and all subsequent conversions) from shillings to dollars are via the Reserve Bank of Australia's Inflation Calculator.

12 Repatriation Case File of George Ernest Gilbert, B73/77, R57060, NAA, Melbourne.

13 Dep. Comm. Repat to C. Campbell, May 1932, Repatriation Case File of Colin Campbell, BP709/1, M40183 PART 1, NAA, Brisbane.
14 'Statement by Roberts, 7 December 1935', Repatriation Case File of George Roberts, C138, H107606 PART 1, NAA, Sydney.
15 Ibid.
16 Studies of the post-war experiences of Australian prisoners of the Japanese – the largest number of Australians to return from a period of wartime captivity – suggest that 46 per cent suffered some form of anxiety-related illness (Hearder, *Keep the Men Alive*, pp. 195–8).
17 At least five ex-POWs – Ellis Gilman, William V. Kelly, Francis Matthews, George Roberts and Leslie Lambert – received pensions for digestive problems related to nervous trouble.
18 'Specialist Report by Dr S.F. McDonald, 3 August 1934', Repatriation Case File of William Mackay, BP709/1, M21112 PART 1, NAA, Brisbane.
19 Tyquin, *Madness and the Military*, p. 13; Butler, *Special Problems and Services*, p. 974.
20 'Form U: Record of Evidence', W. Mackay to Repat, June 1934, Repatriation Case File of William Mackay, BP709/1, M21112 Part 1, NAA, Brisbane.
21 Ibid.
22 C.C. Minty, memorandum, 4 September 1934, Repatriation Case File of William Mackay, BP709/1, M21112 Part 1, NAA, Brisbane.
23 Mary Delpratt to Repat, 17 July 1937, Repatriation Case File of Maurice Delpratt, BP709/1, M32040 Part 1, NAA, Brisbane.
24 Peters, 'The life experiences of partners of ex-POWs of the Japanese'.
25 Delpratt to Repat, 8 October 1937, Repatriation Case File of Maurice Delpratt, BP709/1, M32040 Part 1, NAA, Brisbane.
26 Dr L. Bond to Repat, 3 March 1936, Repatriation Case File of Ernest Ingram, C138, R/M/H84881, NAA, Sydney.
27 Undated doctor's memorandum, Repatriation Case File of Lancelot Lightfoot, D363/42, M13575, NAA, Sydney.
28 Lightfoot to Repat, 10 September 1963, Repatriation Case File of Lancelot Lightfoot, D363/42, M13575, NAA, Sydney.
29 A/Dep. Comm to A/Med. Sup. RGH, 11 September 1963, Repatriation Case File of Lancelot Lightfoot, D363/42, M13575, NAA.
30 For cynical attitudes towards 'shell shock', see Tyquin, *Madness and the Military*, pp. 33–8.
31 'RMO's Report, 3 November 1948', Repatriation Case File of George Paltridge, D363/46, H9587, NAA, Sydney.
32 Lloyd and Rees, *The Last Shilling*, p. 300.
33 F. Haig to Repat, 3 April 1963, Repatriation Case File of Frederick Haig, B73/15, R88740, NAA, Melbourne.
34 These applications related to the deaths of Joseph O'Neill (1937), Roy Clarke (1937), Ellis Gilman (1938), Robert Griffiths (1941), John Halpin (1941), Archibald Hewitson (1954), Leonard Heathcote (1955), Maurice Delpratt (1957), William V. Kelly (1957) and Ron Austin (1965).
35 Dr R.H. Strong to Repat, 15 November 1938, Repatriation Case File of Joseph O'Neill, B73/54, R67430, NAA, Melbourne.

36 M. Sloan to Repat, 24 October 1935, Repatriation Case File of Matthew Sloan, BP709/1, M20001 Part 1, NAA, Brisbane.
37 Turkish Authorities to Australia House, 4 September 1936, Repatriation Case File of Matthew Sloan, BP709/1, M20001 Part 1, NAA, Brisbane.
38 'Form U: Record of Evidence', M. Sloan to Repat, 9 December 1935, Repatriation Case File of Matthew Sloan, BP709/1, M20001 Part 1, NAA, Brisbane.
39 C.C. Minty, memorandum, 29 September 1936, Repatriation Case File of Matthew Sloan, BP709/1, M20001 Part 1, NAA, Brisbane.
40 E. Littlejohn to Repat, 2 May 1963, Repatriation Case File of Ron Austin, B73/0, M118571, NAA, Melbourne.
41 'Repat Report, May 1963', Repatriation Case File of Ron Austin, B73/0, M118571, NAA, Melbourne.
42 Applications regarding the deaths of Frederick Earnshaw (1933), Stewart Stormonth (1935), Frederick Gannon (1937), William Mackay (1941), Edwin Rose (1943), Timothy Cahill (1947), Ernest Ingram (1954), Francis Matthews (1958), Vincent Parkinson (1960), George Paltridge (1961), Matthew Sloan (1963) and William Simms (1973) were all rejected by the Repat as attributable to war service.
43 M. Earnshaw to Repat, June 1933, Repatriation Case File of Frederick Earnshaw, B73/0, M11857, NAA, Melbourne.
44 P. Gallagher to Repat, 25 September 1933, Repatriation Case File of Frederick Earnshaw, B73/0, M11857, NAA, Melbourne.
45 Dr Crowe to Repat, 19 October 1933, Repatriation Case File of Frederick Earnshaw, B73/0, M11857, NAA, Melbourne.
46 A. Stormonth to T. White, 31 January 1936, Repatriation Case File of Stewart Stormonth, BP709, M20283, NAA, Brisbane.
47 Larsson, *Shattered Anzacs*, pp. 217–19.
48 Lloyd and Rees, *The Last Shilling*, pp. 187–208; Garton, *The Cost of War*, p. 96.
49 'Reasons for Appeal', September 1963, Repatriation Case File of Matthew Sloan, BP709/1, M20001 Part 1, NAA, Brisbane.
50 Cth Parliamentary Debates, House of Representatives, vol. 13, 25 March 1947, pp. 1106–7.
51 Halpin, *Blood in the Mists*, p. 122.
52 Tyquin, *Madness and the Military*, p. 9.
53 Delpratt to Repat, 6 October 1937, Repatriation Case File of Maurice Delpratt, BP709/A, M32040 Part 1, NAA, Brisbane.
54 Mary Delpratt to Repat, 17 July 1937, Repatriation Case File of Maurice Delpratt, BP709/A, M32040 Part 1, NAA, Brisbane.
55 'Statement by Mrs A.P.R. Stormonth, 21 September 1935', Repatriation Case File of Stewart Stormonth, BP709/1, M20283 Part 1, NAA, Brisbane.
56 Rachimimov, *POWs and the Great War*, p. 222.
57 Damousi, *The Labour of Loss*, pp. 26–45.
58 'For the Empire: Australia's heroes – Avoca Girls' Patriotic Fund entertains returned soldiers', *Avoca Free Press*, 8 March 1919, Randall Family Papers, Heritage Collections Library, State Library of Victoria.
59 Jones, *Violence Against Prisoners of War*, p. 315.

60 Nachtigal, 'The repatriation and reception of returning prisoners of war, 1918–22', p. 176; Alon Rachamimov, *POWs and the Great War*, p. 193.
61 Nachtigal, 'The repatriation and reception of returning prisoners of war, 1918–22', p. 177.
62 Ibid., p. 176.
63 Chatway, *History of the 15th Battalion*, p. 2.
64 'The World of Books', *Mercury* (Hobart), 24 February 1933; 'Blood in the mists', *Reveille* 7, no. 10 (1934), p. 15.
65 Alon Rachamimov, *POWs and the Great War*, p. 227; Gerster, *Big-noting*, p. 143.
66 Alon Rachamimov, *POWs and the Great War*, p. 227.
67 Wilkinson, 'A fate worse than death?', pp. 36–7; Gerster, *Big-noting*, p. 144. See Lawless, 'The forgotten Anzacs', p. 29 for a discussion of the racial overtones of several memoirs written by ex-POWs of the Ottomans.
68 Alon Rachamimov, *POWs and the Great War*, p. 227.
69 'Turks at close quarters: Australians' impressions', *Argus* (Melbourne), 2 November 1915. Vahe G. Kateb presents an interesting analysis of media coverage related to the Turks during the Gallipoli campaign. In keeping with early impressions that the Turks were a brutal and bloodthirsty opponent, articles such as 'Mutilation of the dead', 'Turks cut bugler's tongue out' and 'Gross Turkish cruelty' appeared in newspapers including the *Age* (Melbourne), the *Sydney Morning Herald* and the *Argus* (Melbourne). Unlike stories of German atrocities, which were usually printed on the main page of newspapers, similar articles about the Turks were instead printed mainly as letters to the editor. Kateb notes that by July, articles sympathetic to the Turks such as 'The Turks – Clean fighters' and 'Turks good fighters' were becoming more common (Kateb, 'Australian press coverage of the Armenian genocide 1915–1923', MA thesis, University of Wollongong, 2003, pp. 128–30).
70 C.E.W.B., 'Abdul', in [C.E.W. Bean, ed.], *The Anzac Book*, pp. 73–4.
71 Kent, '*The Anzac Book* and the Anzac legend', pp. 386–7.
72 Gnida and Simpson, 'Anzac's others', p. 99.
73 Kent, '*The Anzac Book*', pp. 389–90.
74 Ziino, *A Distant Grief*, p. 80.
75 Stephens and Cakir, 'Myth and history', pp. 92–105.
76 Halpin, 'Praise of the Turks', p. 6.
77 Michail, '"A sting of remembrance!"', pp. 242–3, 249.
78 Twomey, '"Impossible history"', p. 157.
79 Ibid. Twomey calls this 'unexpressed history'.
80 Thomson, *Anzac Memories*, p. 216.
81 Oliver Wilkinson makes a similar argument with respect to British POWs of the Germans. See Wilkinson, 'A fate worse than death?', pp. 35–6.
82 Lawless, 'The forgotten Anzacs', p. 33.
83 Bomford, 'Fractured lives', pp. 286–7; Twomey, 'Trauma and the reinvigoration of Anzac', pp. 85–108.
84 Inglis, *Sacred Places*, p. 370.
85 Ibid., pp. 372–4. For the Hellfire Pass Memorial, see 'Hellfire Pass Memorial Museum and Walking Trail', Department of Veterans' Affairs,

<www.dva.gov.au/commemorations-memorials-and-war-graves/memorials/war-memorials/thailand> (retrieved 3 August 2017).

86 Grant, 'What makes a "national" war memorial?', p. 94.
87 Ibid. Australian Ex-Prisoners of War Memorial, 'About the Memorial', <www.powmemorialballarat.com.au/about-the-memorial.php> (retrieved 3 August 2017).
88 Dominic Brine, 'Ballarat Ex-PoW Memorial gets national status', ABC Ballarat, 30 September 2008, <www.abc.net.au/local/stories/2008/09/30/2378198.htm>
89 Stanley, 'Introduction', in Australian War Memorial/Department of Veterans' Affairs, *Stolen Years*, p. 4.
90 Holbrook, 'Adaptable Anzac', pp. 56–7.
91 Alon Rachamimov, *POWs and the Great War*, p. 228.
92 David Stephens, 'Turks did the heavy lifting: A longer look at the building of the Atatürk Memorial in Anzac Parade, Canberra, 1984–85: Parts I and II', *Honest History*, <http://honesthistory.net.au/wp/stephens-david-turks-did-the-heavy-lifting-a-longer-look-at-the-story-of-the-ataturk-memorial-canberra-1984–85-part-i> (retrieved 3 August 2017).
93 Simpson, 'From ruthless foe to national friend', pp. 61–2.
94 Fewster, Basarin and Basarin, *Gallipoli*, p. 19.
95 Quoted in Carolyn Webb, 'Anzac March open to "Johnny Turk"– but that's it', *Age* (Melbourne), 12 April 2006.
96 Mark Baker, 'Our favourite enemies', *Age* (Melbourne), 13 April 2006.
97 Inglis and Phillips, 'War memorials in Australia and New Zealand', p. 191.
98 McKenna and Ward, 'An Anzac myth', p. 46.
99 Ibid.
100 Simpson, 'From ruthless foe to national friend', pp. 62–3.

Conclusion

1 Stephens, 'Anzac and Anzackery', p. 125.

BIBLIOGRAPHY

ARCHIVAL MATERIAL
Australian War Memorial, Canberra
Official records

AWM8	Unit Embarkation Nominal Rolls, 1914–1918 War
AWM10 4332/7/30	Prisoners of War – Miscellany
AWM13 7017/1/34	Comforts for British POWs in Turkey
AWM16 4375/11/49	Photographs of Repatriated POWs
AWM16 4376/50/2	Enquiries re: Repatriated Prisoners of War
AWM18 9982/3/2	Comforts for Prisoners of War in Turkey
AWM18 9982/3/4	Despatches from Netherlands Minister of the Hague regarding P. of. W in Turkey – Forwarded from Foreign Office
AWM27 424/28	Repatriation
AWM27 424/29	Agreement Between the British and Ottoman Governments Respecting Prisoners of War and Civilians
AWM30 B1.1–1.33	Statements of Repatriated Prisoners of War from Turkey (Infantry)
AWM30 B2.1–2.14	Statements of Repatriated Prisoners of War from Turkey (Light Horse and Camel Corps)
AWM30 B3.1–3.3	Statements of Repatriated Prisoners of War from Turkey (Australian Flying Corps)
AWM30 B18.1	Nominal Roll of Prisoners of War in Turkey
AWM30 B18.2	Miscellaneous Statements (Duplicates) Made by Prisoners of War, Particulars of Australians Who Died While Prisoners of War in Germany, and Memorandum to Prisoners of War Returning from Turkey to Egypt
AWM133	Nominal Roll of Australian Imperial Force Who Left Australia for Service Abroad, 1914–1918 War

Australian Red Cross Society records

AWM1DRL/0428	Wounded and Missing Bureau Enquiry Files 1914–18 War
AWM1DRL/0428	POW Department Individual Case Files 1914–1918 War
AWM1DRL/0615	Papers of Chomley, Mary Elizabeth

Personal records

AWMPR83/100	Letters of Lt Laurence Smith, No. 72 Sqdn, AFC
AWMPR84/244	Letters, Serial, Leaflets of Lieut. W.H. Treloar
AWMPR85/96	Papers of A.E. Knaggs, *AE2*
AWMPR01466	Papers of Kinder, H.J.E. (Stoker, Petty Officer)
AWMPR01552	Papers of Hilton (née Duffy), Rita
AWMPR01697	Papers of Sergeant George Richardson Paltridge
AWMPR01708	Papers of Trooper Cecil Spencer
AWM2DRL/530	Papers of Lt. F. Hancock 1st ALH and No. 1 Sqdn AFC
AWM2DRL/0766	Typescript copy diary of Thomas Walter White, November 1915 – December 1918
AWM3DRL/2153	Sgt M.G. Delpratt, Collection of Letters
AWM3DRL/3325	Records of Air Mech. K.L. Hudson AFC 1914–1918
AWM3DRL/6226	Papers of Charles Suckling, Submariner, 1914–1918
AWM3DRL/7847	Papers of Tpr E. Randall 6th ALH and Pte W. Randall 14th Bn

National Archives of Australia
Official records

A11803, 1914/89/364	Prisoners of War in Turkey
A11803, 1917/89/377	Prisoners of War in Turkey
A11803, 1917/89/383	Prisoners of War in Turkey – Repatriation of
A11803, 1917/89/526	Prisoner of War Camps in Turkey
A11803, 1917/89/677	Prisoners of War – Yozgad Turkey
A11803, 1918/89/50	Prisoners of War in Turkey – Treatment of
A11803, 1918/89/217	Prisoners of War – Conference of British and Turkish Delegates
A11803, 1918/89/391	Prisoners of War in Turkey – Remittances etc for
A11803, 1918/89/453	Prisoners of War in Turkey – Allowances to
A11803, 1918/89/724	Prisoners of War in Turkey – Mortality Among
A11803, 1918/89/939	Prisoners of War in Turkey – Release of
A11803, 1919/89/106	Armistice Terms with Turkey and with Austria–Hungary
A11803, 1919/89/298	Prisoners of War in Turkey
A11803, 1919/89/903	Turkish Peace (Conditions for Armistice)
A2939, SC311	Prisoners of War – Agreements with Turkey
B2455	First Australian Imperial Force Personnel Dossiers, 1914–1920
MP16/1, 1915/3/1508	'Turkish Subjects'
MP1565/4	Prisoners of War Australians Captured in Turkey: 'The Shackleton File'
MP472/1, 5/19/2520	Submarine *AE2* etc

Repatriation records
Queensland

J34 C21112	Mackay, William
BP709/1, M13235	Sloan, John

BP709/1, M14301	Simms, William
BP709/1, M15754	Hobson, Edgar
BP709/1, M19901	Armstrong, D'Arcy St George
BP709/1, M20001 Part 1 and Part 2	Sloan, Matthew
BP709/1, M20283	Stormonth, Stewart
BP709/1, M21112	Mackay, William
BP709/1, M32040	Delpratt, Maurice George
BP709/1, M40183, Part 1 and Part 2	Campbell, Colin Spencer
BP709/1, QM13230	Rutherford, Douglas
BP709/1, QM58368	McElligott, Joseph

Victoria

B73, M53760	Earnshaw, Frederick
B73, M85619	Foxcroft, Harry
B73, M87463	Chalcroft, Thomas
B73, M95609	White, Thomas
B73, M118571	Austin, Ronald
B73, M119889	Bailey, William
B73, R41707	Kelly, William Vincent
B73, H41707	Kelly, William Vincent
B73, R41745	McPherson, John
B73, R45911	Cahir, Keith
B73, 41794 Part 1 and 2	Sloss, James McKenzie
B73, R55776	Cahill, Timothy
B73, R57060	Gilbert, George Ernest
B73, R58760	Heathcote, Leonard
B73, R64614	Kelly, William
B73, R67430	O'Neill, Joseph
B73, R86833	Smith, Egbert
B73, R88740	Haig, Frederick
B73, R92248	McLean, Charles
B73, R115248	McDonald, Ronald T.A.

New South Wales

C138, C37969	Gannon, Frederick
C138, C116775	Peters, Robert John
C138, H82284	Poole, Alfred Anderson
C138, H107606	Roberts, George
C138, M40328	Clarke, Roy
C138, M99882	Parkinson, Vincent
C138, M111549	Vidler, Harold
C138, M037992	O'Hare, Phillip
C138, H37992	O'Hare, Phillip
C138, R37985	Lambert, Leslie

C138, R37987   Matthews, Francis
C138, R38914   Griffiths, Robert Wright
C138, R40092   Hewitson, Archibald
C138, R80371   Thompson, Arthur
C138, R83162   Gilman, Ellis Richard
C138, R84881   Ingram, Ernest
C138, M84881   Ingram, Ernest
C138, H84881   Ingram, Ernest
C138, R92258   Halliday, Thomas
C138, R97315   Crockett, Alexander
C138, C97315   Crockett, Alexander
C138, R/C114492   Jeffery, Frederick

Tasmania (held in New South Wales)
P107, M3567   Lee, Oliver Matthew

South Australia (held in New South Wales)
D363, 23987   Briant, Benjamin
D363, H9587   Paltridge, George Richardson
D363, R9588   Rose, Edwin
D363, M13575   Lightfoot, Lancelot
D363, M31773   Carter, Alfred
D363, R11936   Mitchell, Ernest England

National Archives, United Kingdom
CAB 24/69/24   Reparation for Turkish Ill-Treatment of Prisoners of War –
                Copy of Resolution by Executive Committee of Prisoners in
                Turkey Committee
CAB 24/85/6   First and Second Interim Reports from the Committee
                of Enquiry into Breaches of the Laws of War, with
                Appendices
CAB 24/127/71   Negotiations with the Turkish Nationalists for the Mutual
                Release of Prisoners of War

Commonwealth War Graves Commission, Maidenhead
WG219/19 PART 2   Memorials to the Missing – Mesopotamia
WG219/20   Memorials to the Missing – Unlocated Graves in Turkey
WG436/1   Graves of British Prisoners of War – General File
WG436/2   Graves of British P. of W. in Turkey
WG436/3   British Prisoners of War Graves in Palestine, Syria
WG560   Mesopotamia – General File

WG798/11 PART 1   Enemy Graves and Interned Civilians – Egypt, Palestine, Syria
WG920/1   Asia Minor – Graves In
WG920/2   Asia Minor – Concentration
WG1420   Acquisition – Turkey

John Oxley Library, State Library of Queensland
OM64–31/2   John Harrison Wheat Papers
OM90–138   D.B. Creedon Diary 1915
28115   Maurice George Delpratt Correspondence

Mitchell Library, State Library of New South Wales
Richardson War Narrative, 1916–18
Wheat War Diaries and Narratives, February 1914–c. 1920

Heritage Collections Library, State Library of Victoria
Randall Family Papers, 1914–25

State Library of Western Australia
ACC 973A   Ashton, Frederick. 'Typescript of Book (Unpublished) by Fred Ashton, Telling of His Experiences during World War I, Including a Period as a Prisoner of War in Turkey'

OFFICIAL HISTORIES
Bean, Charles. *Official History of Australia in the War of 1914–1918.* Vol. 1: *The Story of Anzac from the Outbreak of War to the End of the First Phase of the Gallipoli Campaign, May 4, 1915.* 11th edn. Sydney: Angus & Robertson, 1941
——*Gallipoli Mission.* Canberra: Australian War Memorial, 1952
Beaumont, Joan, ed. *The Australian Centenary History of Defence.* Vol. 6: *Australian Defence: Sources and Statistics.* Melbourne: Oxford University Press, 2001
Butler, A.G. *Official History of the Australian Army Medical Services 1914–1918.* Vol. 1: *Gallipoli, Palestine and New Guinea.* 2nd edn. Melbourne: Australian War Memorial, 1938
——*Official History of the Australian Army Medical Services 1914–1918.* Vol. 3: *Special Problems and Services.* Canberra: Australian War Memorial, 1943

Cutlack, F.M. *Official History of Australia in the War of 1914–1918*. Vol. 8: *The Australian Flying Corps in the Western and Eastern Theatres of War*. 4th edn. Sydney: Angus & Robertson, 1935

Gullett, Henry. *Official History of Australia in the War of 1914–1918*. Vol. 7: *The Australian Imperial Force in Sinai and Palestine*. 10th edn. Sydney: Angus & Robertson, 1941

Jose, Arthur, *Official History of Australia in the War of 1914–1918*. Vol. 9: *The Royal Australian Navy*. 9th edn. Sydney: Angus & Robertson, 1941

Scott, Ernest. *Official History of Australia in the War of 1914–1918*. Vol. 11: *Australia During the War*. 7th edn. Sydney: Angus & Robertson, 1941

GOVERNMENT RECORDS AND REPORTS

Australian Graves Service. *Where the Australians Rest*. Melbourne: Government Printer, 1920

British War Office. 'Report on the Treatment of British Prisoners of War in Turkey.' cd. 9208. London: HMSO, 1918

British War Office General Staff. *Handbook of the Turkish Army*. 5th edn. 1912

Commonwealth of Australia. *War Precautions Act 1914 and War Precautions Regulations 1914*. Melbourne: Government Printer, 1914

Cth Parliamentary Debates. House of Representatives. Vol. 26. 30 June 1915

Cth Parliamentary Debates. House of Representatives. Vol. 28. 16 July 1915

Cth Parliamentary Debates. House of Representatives. Vol. 33. 19 August 1915

Cth Parliamentary Debates. House of Representatives. Vol. 13. 25 March 1947

Department of Defence. *How the Germans Treated the Australian Prisoners of War: Extracts from Statements Made by Repatriated Australian Prisoners of War, Together with a Copy of a Report to the German Government on the German Concentration Camp at Holdsworthy in Australia*. Melbourne: Government Printer, 1919

Knibbs, G.H., ed. *Census of the Commonwealth of Australia*. Vol. I: *Statistician's Report*. Melbourne, 1917

Millen, E.D. *What Australia is Doing for Her Returned Soldiers*. Melbourne: H.J. Green, 1918

BOOKS

Acton, Carol. *Grief in Wartime: Private Pain, Public Discourse*. Basingstoke: Palgrave Macmillan, 2007

Adam-Smith, Patsy. *Prisoners of War: From Gallipoli to Korea*. Melbourne: Penguin, 1992

Akmese, Handan Nezir. *The Birth of Modern Turkey: The Ottoman Military and the March to World War I*. London: I.B. Tauris, 2005

Andrews, E.M. *The Anzac Illusion: Anglo-Australian Relations During World War I*. Cambridge: Cambridge University Press, 1993

Ashworth, Tony. *Trench Warfare 1914–1918: The Live and Let Live System*. London: Macmillan Press, 1980

Austin, R.A. *My Experiences as a Prisoner*. Melbourne: J. Haase & Sons, n.d. [1918–32]

Babkenian, Vicken, and Peter Stanley. *Armenia, Australia and the Great War.* Sydney: NewSouth, 2016

Barker, A.J. *Behind Barbed Wire.* London: B.T. Batsford, 1974

Basarin, Vecihi, and Hatice Hurmuz. *Beneath the Dardanelles: The Australian Submarine at Gallipoli.* Sydney: Allen & Unwin, 2008

[Bean, C.E.W., ed.], *The Anzac Book,* 3rd edn. Sydney: UNSW Press, 2010

Beaumont, Joan. *Gull Force: Survival and Leadership in Captivity 1941–1945.* Sydney: Allen & Unwin, 1988

——ed. *Australia's War, 1914–18.* Sydney: Allen & Unwin, 1995

——*Broken Nation: Australians in the Great War.* Sydney: Allen & Unwin, 2013

Blair, Dale. *Dinkum Diggers: An Australian Battalion at War.* Melbourne: Melbourne University Press, 2001

——*No Quarter: Unlawful Killing and Surrender in the Australian War Experience 1915–18.* Canberra: Ginninderra Press, 2005

Bou, Jean. *Light Horse: A History of Australia's Mounted Arm.* Melbourne: Cambridge University Press, 2010

Bourke, Joanna. *An Intimate History of Killing: Face-to-Face Killing in Twentieth-Century Warfare.* London: Granta, 1999

Brenchley, Fred, and Elizabeth Brenchley. *Stoker's Submarine.* Sydney: Harper-Collins, 2003

——*White's Flight: An Australian Pilot's Epic Escape from Turkish Prison Camp to Russia's Revolution.* Brisbane: John Wiley & Sons, 2004

Brown, James. *Turkish Days and Ways.* Sydney: Halstead Press, 1940

Brugger, Suzanne. *Australians and Egypt 1914–1919.* Melbourne: Melbourne University Press, 1980

Caulfield, Michael, ed. *War Behind the Wire: Australian Prisoners of War.* Sydney: Hachette, 2008

Chatway, T.P. *History of the 15th Battalion, Australian Imperial Forces, War 1914–1918.* Brisbane: William Brooks, 1948

Cirakman, Asli, *From the Terror of the World to the Sick Man of Europe: European Images of Ottoman Empire and Society from the Sixteenth Century to the Nineteenth.* New York: Peter Lang, 2002

Coombes, David. *Crossing the Wire: The Untold Stories of Australian POWs in Battle and Captivity during WWI.* Sydney: Big Sky Publishing, 2011

Crotty, Martin. *Making the Australian Male: Middle-Class Masculinity 1870–1920.* Melbourne: Melbourne University Press, 2001

Cull, William. *Both Sides of the Wire: The Memoir of an Australian Officer Captured During the Great War,* ed. Aaron Pegram. Sydney: Allen & Unwin, 2011

Damousi, Joy. *The Labour of Loss: Mourning, Memory and Wartime Bereavement in Australia.* Melbourne: Cambridge University Press, 1999

——*Living with the Aftermath: Trauma, Nostalgia and Grief in Postwar Australia.* Melbourne: Cambridge University Press, 2001

Darian-Smith, Kate, ed. *Captive Lives: Australian Captivity Narratives.* London: Sir Robert Menzies Centre for Australian Studies, Institute of Commonwealth Studies, University of London, 1993

Department of Veterans' Affairs/Australian War Memorial. *Stolen Years: Australian Prisoners of War*. Canberra, 2002

Elkus, Abram I. *Memoirs of Abram Elkus: Lawyer, Ambassador, Statesman*. Reading: Taderon Press, 2004

Erickson, Edward. *Ordered to Die: A History of the Ottoman Army in the First World War*. Westport, CT: Greenwood Press, 2001

Feltman, Brian K. *The Stigma of Surrender: German Prisoners, British Captors, and Manhood in the Great War and Beyond*. Chapel Hill: University of North Carolina Press, 2015

Fewster, Kevin. *Gallipoli Correspondent: The Frontline Diary of C.E.W. Bean*. Sydney: Allen & Unwin, 1983

Fewster, Kevin, Vecihi Basarin and Hatice Hurmuz Basarin. *Gallipoli: The Turkish Story*. 2nd edn. Sydney: Allen & Unwin, 2003

Fischer, Gerhard. *Enemy Aliens: Internment and the Homefront Experience in Australia*. Brisbane: University of Queensland Press, 1989

Foster, J.R. *Two and a Half Years a Prisoner of War in Turkey – Related by G.W. Handsley*. Brisbane: Jones & Hambly, 1920

Gammage, Bill. *The Broken Years: Australian Soldiers in the Great War*. Canberra: Australian National University Press, 1974

Garton, Stephen. *The Cost of War: Australians Return*. Melbourne: Oxford University Press, 1996

Gerster, Robin. *Big-noting: The Heroic Theme in Australian War Writing*. Melbourne: Melbourne University Press, 1987

Grey, Jeffrey. *The Centenary History of Australia and the Great War*, Vol. 2: *The War with the Ottoman Empire*. Melbourne: Oxford University Press, 2015

Halpin, John. *Blood in the Mists*. Sydney: Macquarie Head Press, 1934

Hamilton, Patrick M. *Riders of Destiny: The 4th Australian Light Horse Field Ambulance 1917–1918*. Melbourne: Mostly Unsung Military History, 1996

Hammond, Ernest W. *History of the 11th Light Horse Regiment, Fourth Light Horse Brigade, Australian Imperial Forces, War 1914–1919*. Brisbane: William Brooks & Co., 1942

Hately-Broad, Barbara. *War and Welfare: British Prisoner of War Families 1939–1945*. Manchester: Manchester University Press, 2009

Hearder, Rosalind. *Keep the Men Alive: Australian POW Doctors in Japanese Captivity*. Sydney: Allen & Unwin, 2009

Hill, Cedric Waters. *The Spook and the Commandant*. London: William Kimber & Co., 1975

Inglis, Ken. *Sacred Places: War Memorials in the Australian Landscape*. Melbourne: Melbourne University Press, 1998

Jalland, Patricia. *Changing Ways of Death in Twentieth Century Australia: War, Medicine and the Funeral Business*. Sydney: UNSW Press, 2006

Jones, Elias Henry. *The Road to En-dor: An Account of How Two Prisoners of War at Yozgad in Turkey Won Their Freedom*. London: Bodley Head, 1930

Jones, Heather. *Violence Against Prisoners of War in the First World War: Britain, France and Germany 1914–1920*. Cambridge: Cambridge University Press, 2011

Jupp, James, ed. *The Australian People: An Encyclopedia of the Nation, Its People and Their Origins*. Melbourne: Cambridge University Press, 2001

Keeling, E.H. *Adventures in Turkey and Russia*. London: John Murray, 1924

Kerr, Greg. *Lost Anzacs: The Story of Two Brothers*. Melbourne: Oxford University Press, 1997

Lake, Marilyn. *The Limits of Hope: Soldier Settlement in Victoria, 1915–38*. Melbourne: Oxford University Press, 1987

Lake, Marilyn, and Henry Reynolds, eds. *What's Wrong with Anzac? The Militarisation of Australian History*. Sydney: UNSW Press, 2010

Langley, George F., and Edmee M. Langley. *Sand, Sweat and Camels: The Story of the Australian Camel Corps*. Melbourne: Rigby, 1976

Larsson, Marina. *Shattered Anzacs: Living with the Scars of War*. Sydney: UNSW Press, 2009

Lawless, Jennifer. *Kismet: The Story of the Gallipoli Prisoners of War*. Melbourne: Australian Scholarly Publishing, 2015

Lloyd, Clem, and Jacqui Rees. *The Last Shilling: A History of Repatriation in Australia*. Melbourne: Melbourne University Press, 1994

Luckins, Tanja. *The Gates of Memory: Australian People's Experiences and Memories of Loss in the Great War*. Fremantle: Curtin University Books, 2004

Luscombe, L.H. *The Story of Harold Earl – Australian*. Brisbane: W.R. Smith & Paterson, 1970

Lushington, R.F. *A Prisoner with the Turks 1915–1918*. London: Simpkin, Marshall, Hamilton, Kent & Co., 1923

McKernan, Michael. *The Australian People and the Great War*. Melbourne: Thomas Nelson, 1980

——*This War Never Ends: The Pain of Separation and Return*. Brisbane: University of Queensland Press, 2001

McMeekin, Sean. *The Berlin–Baghdad Express: The Ottoman Empire and Germany's Bid for World Power*. London: Allen Lane, 2010

Monteath, Peter. *POW: Australian Prisoners of War in Hitler's Reich*. Sydney: Pan Macmillan, 2011

Morgenthau, Henry. *Secrets of the Bosphorus*. London: Hutchinson & Co., 1918

Morton, Desmond. *Silent Battle: Canadian Prisoners of War in Germany 1914–1919*. Toronto: Lester, 1992

Moynihan, Michael, ed. *Black Bread and Barbed Wire: Prisoners in the First World War*. London: Leo Cooper, 1978

Neave, Denny, and Craig Smith. *Aussie Soldier: Prisoners of War*. Brisbane: Big Sky Publishing, 2009

Oppenheimer, Melanie. *All Work No Pay: Australian Civilian Volunteers in War*. Walcha: Ohio Productions, 2002

Ozdemir, Hikmet. *Ottoman Army 1914–1918: Disease and Death on the Battlefields*. Trans. Saban Kardas. Salt Lake City: University of Utah Press, 2008

Pamuk, Sevket. *A Monetary History of the Ottoman Empire*. New York: Cambridge University Press, 2000

Piper, Thomas Henry. *Prisoner of War in Turkey in World War One: An Autobiography*. Self-published, 1986

Rachamimov, Alon. *POWs and the Great War: Captivity on the Eastern Front*. Oxford: Berg, 2002

Reeson, Margaret. *A Very Long War: The Families Who Waited*. Melbourne: Melbourne University Press, 2000

Reid, Pat, and Maurice Michael. *Prisoner of War: The Inside Story of the POW from the Ancient World to Colditz and After*. London: Hamlyn, 1984

Reynaud, Daniel. *Celluloid Anzacs: The Great War through Australian Cinema*. Melbourne: Australian Scholarly Publishing, 2007

Richardson, J.D. *The History of the 7th Light Horse Regiment AIF*. Sydney: E.N Birks, 1924

Robertson, John. *ANZAC and Empire: The Tragedy and Glory of Gallipoli*. Melbourne: Hamlyn, 1990

Roper, Michael. *The Secret Battle: Emotional Survival in the Great War*. Manchester: Manchester University Press, 2009

Said, Edward. *Orientalism*. 5th edn. London: Penguin Books, 2003

Scates, Bruce, and Melanie Oppenheimer. *The Last Battle: Soldier Settlement in Australia 1916–1939*. Melbourne: Cambridge University Press, 2016

Speed, Richard B. *Prisoners, Diplomats, and the Great War: A Study in the Diplomacy of Captivity*. New York: Greenwood Press, 1990

Stanley, Peter. *Men of Mont St Quentin: Between Victory and Death*. Melbourne: Scribe, 2009

——*Bad Characters: Sex, Crime, Mutiny, Murder and the Australian Imperial Force*. Sydney: Murdoch Books, 2010

Steuer, Kenneth. *Pursuit of an 'Unparalleled Opportunity': The American YMCA and Prisoner of War Diplomacy during World War I*. New York: Colombia University Press, 2009. Gutenberg e-book <www.gutenberg-e.org/steuer/steuer.ch15.html> (retrieved 3 August 2017)

Stevens, Christine. *Tin Mosques and Ghantowns: A History of Afghan Cameldrivers in Australia*. Melbourne: Oxford University Press, 1989

Stockings, Craig, ed. *Anzac's Dirty Dozen: 12 Myths of Australian Military History*. Sydney: NewSouth Publishing, 2012

Stoker, H.G. *Straws in the Wind*. London: Herbert Jenkins, 1925

Thomson, Alistair. *Anzac Memories: Living with the Legend*. Melbourne: Oxford University Press, 1994

Triolo, Rosalie. *Our Schools and the War*. Melbourne: Australian Scholarly Publishing, 2012

Tyquin, Michael. *Gallipoli: The Medical War – The Australian Army Medical Services in the Dardanelles Campaign of 1915*. Sydney: UNSW Press, 1993

——*Madness and the Military: Australia's Experience of the Great War*. Sydney: Australian Military History Publications, 2006

Vance, Jonathan F. *Objects of Concern: Canadian Prisoners of War in the Twentieth Century*. Vancouver: UBC Press, 1994

——ed. *Encyclopaedia of Prisoners of War and Internment*. Santa Barbara: ABC-CLIO, 2000

Wanliss, Newton. *The History of the Fourteenth Battalion, AIF: Being the Story of the Vicissitudes of an Australian Unit during the Great War*. Melbourne: Arrow Printery, 1929

White, Michael. *Australian Submarines: A History*. Canberra: Australian Government Publishing Service, 1992

White, Thomas W. *Guests of the Unspeakable*. Sydney: Angus & Robertson, 1932

Williams, John F. *Anzacs, the Media and the Great War*. Sydney: UNSW Press, 1999

Winter, Jay. *Sites of Memory, Sites of Mourning: The Great War in European Cultural History*. Cambridge: Cambridge University Press, 1995

Woolley, C.L. *From Kastamuni to Kedos: Being a Record of Experiences of Prisoners of War in Turkey 1916–1918*. Oxford: Basil Blackwell, 1921

Wylie, Neville. *Barbed Wire Diplomacy: Britain, Germany and the Politics of Prisoners of War 1939–1945*. Oxford: Oxford University Press, 2010

Yanikdag, Yucel. *Healing the Nation: Prisoners of War, Medicine and Nationalism in Turkey 1914–1939*. Edinburgh: Edinburgh University Press, 2014

Yarnall, John. *Barbed Wire Disease: British and German Prisoners of War, 1914–19*. Stroud, Gloucs: Spellmount, 2011

Ziino, Bart. *A Distant Grief: Australians, War Graves and the Great War*. Perth: UWA Press, 2007

JOURNAL ARTICLES, BOOK CHAPTERS AND OTHER PUBLISHED MATERIAL

Ariotti, Kate. '"At present everything is making us most anxious": Families of Australian prisoners in Turkey.' In *Beyond Surrender: Australian Prisoners of War in the Twentieth Century*, ed. Joan Beaumont, Lachlan Grant and Aaron Pegram, pp. 57–74. Melbourne: Melbourne University Press, 2015

——'"I'm awfully fed up with being a prisoner": Australian POWs of the Turks and the strain of surrender.' *Journal of Australian Studies* 40, no. 3 (2016): 276–90

Barrett, Craig. '"Matters still outstanding": Australian ex-POWs of the Japanese and claims for reparations.' In *Anzac Legacies: Australians and the Aftermath of War*, ed. Martin Crotty and Marina Larsson, pp. 187–210. Melbourne: Australian Scholarly Publishing, 2010

Beaumont, Joan. 'Rank, privilege and prisoners of war.' *War and Society* 1, no. 1 (1983): 67–94

——'Prisoners of war in Australian national memory.' In *Prisoners of War, Prisoners of Peace*, ed. Bob Moore and Barbara Hately-Broad, pp. 185–94. Oxford: Berg, 2005

Becker, Annette. 'Art, material life, and disaster: Civilian and military prisoners of war.' In *Matters of Conflict: Material Culture, Memory and the First World War*, ed. Nicholas J. Saunders, pp. 26–34. Oxfordshire: Routledge, 2001

Blair, Dale. 'The nonsense of universal Australian "fair play" in war.' In *Anzac's Dirty Dozen: 12 Myths of Australian Military History*, ed. Craig Stockings, pp. 112–37. Sydney: UNSW Press, 2012

Bomford, Janette. '"A wife, a baby, a home and a new Holden car": Family life after captivity.' In *Anzac Legacies: Australians and the Aftermath of War*, ed. Martin Crotty and Marina Larsson, pp. 107–25. Melbourne: Australian Scholarly Publishing, 2010

Busuttil, Walter, and Angela Busuttil. 'Psychological effects on families subjected to enforced and prolonged separations under life threatening situations.' *Sexual and Relationship Therapy*, Issue 16 (2001): 207–28

Carr, William K. 'The faceless POW.' *Naval War College Review* (Fall 1977): 88–95

Chomley, M.E. 'Final Report on the Prisoners of War Department of the Australian Red Cross.' n.d.

Cirakman, Asli. 'From tyranny to despotism: The Enlightenment's unenlightened image of the Turks.' *International Journal of Middle East Studies* 33, no. 1 (2001): 49–68

Clissold, Barry. 'Prisoners of Johnny Turk.' *Sabretache* 48, no. 2 (2007): 17–20

Condé, Anne-Marie. 'Capturing the records of war: Collecting at the Mitchell Library and the Australian War Memorial.' *Australian Historical Studies* 37, no. 125 (2005): 134–52

Davis, Gerald H. 'Prisoners of war in twentieth-century war economies.' *Journal of Contemporary History*, Issue 12 (1977): 623–34

Dekel, Rachel, Hadass Goldblatt and Zahava Solomon. 'Trapped in captivity: Marital perceptions of wives of former prisoners of war.' *Women and Health* 42, no. 3 (2006): 1–18

Dent, Owen, and others. 'Prisoner of war experience: Effects on wives.' *Journal of Nervous and Mental Disease* 186, no. 4 (1998): 231–7

Diamadis, Panayiotis. 'Precious and honoured guests of the Ottoman Government.' In *Genocide Perspectives II: Essays on the Holocaust and Other Genocides*, ed. Colin Tatz, Peter Arnold and Sandra Tatz, pp. 162–82. Blackheath: Brandl & Schlesinger/Australian Institute for Holocaust and Genocide Studies, 2003

Dodds, Elliott. *For All Prisoners and Captives: The Work of the Prisoners of War Information Bureau.* London: Wightman & Co., 1917

Duvall, Evelyn Millis. 'Loneliness and the serviceman's wife.' *Marriage and Family Living* 7, no. 4 (1945): 77–81

Feltman, Brian K. 'Tolerance as a crime? The British treatment of German prisoners of war on the Western Front, 1914–1918.' *War in History* 17, no. 4 (2010): 435–58

——'Letters from captivity: The First World War correspondence of the German prisoners of war in the United Kingdom.' In *Finding Common Ground: New Directions in First World War Studies*, ed. Jennifer Keene and Michael Neiberg, pp. 87–110. Leiden: Brill, 2011

Gladstone, W.E. *Bulgarian Horrors and the Question of the East.* New York: Lovell, Adam, Wesson & Co., 1876

Gnida, Antje, and Catherine Simpson. 'Anzac's others: "Cruel Huns" and "noble Turks".' In *Diasporas of Australian Cinema*, ed. Catherine Simpson, Renata Murawska and Anthony Lambert, pp. 93–102. Bristol: Intellect, 2009

Grant, Lachlan. 'What makes a "national" war memorial? The case of the Australian ex-POWs memorial.' *Public History Review*, Issue 12 (2006): 92–102

Halpin, J. 'A captive of the Turks – Episode one', *Reveille*, Issue 7, no. 7 (1934): 25–6

——'A captive of the Turks – Episode two', *Reveille*, Issue 7, no. 8 (1934): 48

——'Praise of the Turks: A captive in reply', *Reveille*, Issue 7, no. 12 (1934): 6.

Hamilton, Paula. 'The knife-edge: Debates about memory and history.' In *Memory and History in Twentieth-Century Australia*, ed. Kate Darian-Smith and Paula Hamilton, pp. 9–32. Melbourne: Oxford University Press, 1994

Hately-Broad, Barbara. '"Nobody would tell you anything": The War and Foreign Offices and British prisoner of war families during World War II.' *Journal of Family History* 27, no. 4 (2002): 459–77

Hawksley, Jen. 'In the shadow of war: Australian parents and the legacy of loss, 1915–1935.' *Journal of Australian Studies* 33, no. 2 (2009): 181–94

Hearder, Rosalind. 'Memory, methodology and myth: Some of the challenges of writing Australian prisoner of war history.' *Journal of the Australian War Memorial*, Issue 40 (2007): n.p.

Hill, Reuben. 'The returning father and his family.' *Marriage and Family Living* 7, no. 2 (1945): 31–4

Holbrook, Carolyn. 'Adaptable Anzac: Past, present and future.' In *The Honest History Book*, ed. David Stephens and Alison Broinoswki, pp. 48–63. Sydney: NewSouth, 2017

Hunter, Edna J. 'Captivity: The family in waiting.' In *Stress and the Family: Coping with Catastrophe*, ed. Charles R. Figley and Hamilton I. McCubbin, pp. 166–83. New York: Brunner/Mazel, 1983

Hynes, Samuel. 'Personal narratives and commemoration.' In *War and Remembrance in the Twentieth Century*, ed. Jay Winter and Emmanuel Sivan, pp. 205–20. Cambridge: Cambridge University Press, 1999

Inglis, Ken, and Jock Phillips. 'War memorials in Australia and New Zealand: A comparative survey.' *Australian Historical Studies* 24, no. 96 (1991): 179–91

Jones, Heather. 'Encountering the enemy: Prisoner of war transport and the development of war cultures in 1914.' In *Warfare and Belligerence: Perspectives on First World War Studies*, ed. Pierre Purseigle, pp. 133–62. Leiden: Brill, 2005

——'A missing paradigm? Military captivity and the prisoner of war, 1914–18.' *Immigrants and Minorities* 26, no. 1–2 (2008): 19–48

——'Imperial captivities: Colonial prisoners of war in Germany and the Ottoman Empire, 1914–1918.' In *Race, Empire and First World War Writing*, ed. Santanu Das, pp. 175–93. Cambridge: Cambridge University Press, 2011

Kent, David A. '*The Anzac Book* and the Anzac legend: C.E.W. Bean as editor and image-maker.' *Historical Studies* 21, no. 84 (1985): 376–90

Kildea, Josephine. 'Bridging the divide.' *Wartime*, Issue 41 (2008): 50–2

Klein, Kerwin Lee. 'On the emergence of memory in historical discourse.' *Representations*, Issue 69 (2000): 127–50

Kramer, Alan. 'The first wave of international war crimes trials.' *European Review* 14, no. 4 (2006): 441–55

Lawless, Jennifer. 'The forgotten Anzacs: Captives of the Turks.' *Southerly: The Journal of the English Association, Sydney* 65, no. 2 (2005): 26–41

——'Starvation, cruelty and neglect? Captivity in the Ottoman Empire, 1915–18.' In *Beyond Surrender: Australian Prisoners of War in the Twentieth Century*, ed. Joan Beaumont, Lachlan Grant and Aaron Pegram, pp. 40–56. Melbourne: Melbourne University Press, 2015

Levie, Howard S. 'Prisoners of war and the protecting power.' *American Journal of International Law* 55, no. 2 (1961): 374–97

Londey, Peter. 'A possession for ever: Charles Bean, the Ancient Greeks, and military commemoration in Australia.' *Australian Journal of Politics and History* 53, no. 3 (2007): 344–59

Lunden, Walter A. 'Captivity psychoses among prisoners of war.' *Journal of Criminal Law and Criminology* 39, no. 6 (1949): 721–33

Lyons, Martyn. 'French soldiers and their correspondence: Towards a history of writing practices in the First World War.' *French History* 17, no. 1 (2003): 79–95

McCallum, Kerry, and Peter Putnis. 'Media management in wartime.' *Media History* 14, no. 1 (2008): 17–34

McKenna, Mark, and Stuart Ward. 'An Anzac myth: The creative memorialisation of Gallipoli.' *Monthly* (December 2015 – January 2016): 40–7

MacKenzie, S.P. 'The ethics of escape: British officer POWs in the First World War.' *War in History* 15, no. 1 (2008): 1–16

Makepeace, Clare. 'Living beyond the barbed wire: The familial ties of British prisoners of war held in Europe during the Second World War.' *Historical Research* 86, no. 231 (2013): 158–77

Manne, Robert. 'A Turkish tale: Gallipoli and the Armenian genocide.' *Monthly* (February 2007): 1–21

Michail, Eugene. '"A sting of remembrance!" Collective memory and its forgotten armies.' In *British Popular Culture and the First World War*, ed. Jessica Meyer, pp. 237–57. Leiden: Brill, 2008

Nachtigal, Reinhard. 'The repatriation and reception of returning prisoners of war, 1918–22.' *Immigrants and Minorities* 26, no. 1–2 (2008): 157–84

Noble, Roger. 'The Australian prisoner of war experience and national identity.' *Australian Defence Force Journal*, Issue 167 (2005): 23–33

Page, Thomas Nelson. *Italy and the World War.* New York: Charles Scribner's Sons, 1920

Pegram, Aaron. 'Informing the enemy: Australian prisoners and German intelligence on the Western Front, 1916–1918.' *First World War Studies* 4, no. 2 (2013): 167–84

——'Bold bids for freedom: Escape and Australian prisoners in Germany, 1916–18.' In *Beyond Surrender: Australian Prisoners of War in the Twentieth Century*, ed. Joan Beaumont, Lachlan Grant and Aaron Pegram, pp. 18–39. Melbourne: Melbourne University Press, 2015

Peters, B. 'The life experiences of partners of ex-POWs of the Japanese.' *Journal of the Australian War Memorial*, Issue 28 (1996): n.p.

Prisoners in Turkey Committee. 'Regulations and Notes for the Help of Relatives and Friends.' 1918

Rachamimov, Iris. 'Camp domesticity: Shifting gender boundaries in WWI internment camps.' In *Cultural Heritage and Prisoners of War: Creativity Behind Barbed Wire*, ed. Gilly Carr and Harold Mytum, pp. 291–305. New York: Routledge, 2012

Rundell, J.R. 'The prisoner of war.' *Military Medicine* 155, no. 4 (1990): 176–80

Rutherford, Diane. 'The write support.' *Wartime*, Issue 30 (2005): 40–2

Salt, Jeremy. 'Johnny Turk before Gallipoli: 19th-century images of the Turks.' In *Before and After Gallipoli: A Collection of Australian and Turkish Writings*, ed. Rahmi Akcelik, pp. 15–27. Melbourne: Australia-Turkish Friendship Society Publications, 1986

—— 'Britain, the Armenian question, and the cause of Ottoman reform 1894–96.' *Middle Eastern Studies* 26, no. 3 (1990): 308–28

Scates, Bruce. 'The unknown sock-knitter: Voluntary work, emotional labour, bereavement and the Great War.' *Labour History* 81 (2001): 29–49

—— 'In Gallipoli's shadow: Pilgrimage, memory, mourning and the Great War.' *Australian Historical Studies* 33, no. 119 (2002): 1–21

Schneider, Eric F. 'The British Red Cross Wounded and Missing Enquiry Bureau: A case of truth-telling.' *War in History* 4, no. 3 (1997): 296–315

Segesser, Daniel Marc. 'The punishment of war crimes committed against prisoners of war, deportees and refugees during and after the First World War.' *Immigrants and Minorities* 26, no. 1–2 (2008): 134–56

Simpson, Catherine. 'From ruthless foe to national friend: Turkey, Gallipoli, and Australian nationalism.' *Media International Australia*, Issue 137 (2010): 58–66

Smith, Neil C. *Australian Prisoners of the Turks 1915–1918*. Gardenvale: Mostly Unsung Military Research and Publications, 1992

Sobocinska, Agneizska. 'The language of scars: Australian prisoners of war and the colonial order.' *History Australia* 7, no. 3 (2010): 58.1–58.19

Stanley, Peter. '"He was black, he was a white man, and a dinkum Aussie": Race and Empire in revisiting the Anzac Legend.' In *Race, Empire and First World War Writing*, ed. Santanu Das, pp. 213–33. Cambridge: Cambridge University Press, 2011

Stephens, David. 'Anzac and Anzackery: Useful future or sentimental dream?' In *The Honest History Book*, ed. David Stephens and Alison Broinowski, pp. 120–33. Sydney: NewSouth, 2017

Stephens, David, and Burcin Cakir. 'Myth and history: The persistent "Ataturk words".' In *The Honest History Book*, ed. David Stephens and Alison Broinowski, pp. 92–105. Sydney: NewSouth, 2017

Tetik, Ahmet, Sema Demirtas, and Y. Serdar Demirtas. *Prisoners of War at the Canakkale Battles: Testimonies and Letters*. Ankara: Genelkurmay Basim Evi, 2009

Thomson, Alistair. 'Steadfast until death? C.E.W. Bean and the representation of Australian military manhood.' *Australian Historical Studies* 23, no. 93 (1989): 462–78

—— 'Anzac stories: Using personal testimony in war history.' *War and Society* 25, no. 2 (2006): 1–21

Twomey, Christina. 'Impossible history: Trauma and testimony among Australian civilians interned by the Japanese in World War II.' In *History on the Couch: Essays in History and Psycholanalysis*, ed. Joy Damousi and Robert Reynolds, pp. 155–65. Melbourne: Melbourne University Press, 2003

—— 'Emaciation or emasculation: Photographic images, white masculinity and captivity by the Japanese in World War Two.' *Journal of Men's Studies* 15, no. 3 (2007): 295–310

——'Trauma and the reinvigoration of Anzac: An argument', *History Australia* 10, no. 3 (2013): 85–108

——'Compensating prisoners of war of Japan in post-war Australia.' In *Beyond Surrender: Australian Prisoners of War in the Twentieth Century*, ed. Joan Beaumont, Lachlan Grant and Aaron Pegram, pp. 254–75. Melbourne: Melbourne University Press, 2015

Ursano, Robert, and James Rundell. 'The prisoner of war', *Military Medicine* 155, no. 4 (1990): 176–80

Vischer, A.L. *Barbed Wire Disease: A Psychological Study of the Prisoner of War* (translated from German). London: John Bale, Sons & Danielsson Ltd, 1919

Wallace, Gilbert M. *How We Raised the First Hundred Thousand: An Account of Two Years' Work for the Education Department's War Relief Fund, Victoria.* Melbourne: Lothian Book Publishing Co., 1917

Ware, Fabian. *The Immortal Heritage: An Account of the Work and Policy of the Imperial War Graves Commission during Twenty Years 1917–1937.* Cambridge: Cambridge University Press, 1937

White, Richard. 'The soldier as tourist: The Australian experience of the Great War.' *War and Society* 5, no. 1 (1987): 63–77

——'Sun, sand, and syphilis: Australian soldiers and the Orient, Egypt 1914.' *Australian Cultural History*, Issue 9 (1990): 49–64

Wilkinson, Oliver. '"A fate worse than death?" Lamenting First World War captivity.' *Journal of War and Culture Studies* 8, no. 1 (2015): 24–40

Yanikdag, Yucel. 'Ottoman prisoners of war in Russia, 1914–22.' *Journal of Contemporary History* 34, no. 1 (1999): 69–85

Ziino, Bart. '"A lasting gift to his descendants": Family memory and the Great War in Australia.' *History and Memory* 22, no. 2 (2010): 125–46

THESES

Barrett, Craig. 'Remembering captivity: Australian prisoners of war of the Japanese.' PhD thesis, University of Queensland, 2011

Bomford, Janette. 'Fractured lives: Australian prisoners of war of the Japanese and their families.' PhD thesis, Deakin University, 2002

Brackenbury, Noel. 'Becoming guests of the Unspeakable: A study of the pre-internment experiences of Australian servicemen captured by the Turks during World War I.' BA (Hons) thesis, Macquarie University, 1983

Kateb, Vahe G. 'Australian press coverage of the Armenian Genocide 1915–1923.' MA thesis, University of Wollongong, 2003

Regan, Patrick Michael. 'Neglected Australians: Prisoners of war from the Western Front, 1916–1918.' MA thesis, Australian Defence Force Academy, University of New South Wales, 2005

NEWSPAPERS AND MAGAZINES

Advertiser (Adelaide)
Age (Melbourne)
Argus (Melbourne)
Barrier Miner (Broken Hill, NSW)

Brisbane Courier
Leader (Melbourne)
Mercury (Hobart)
Register (Adelaide)
Reveille
Sydney Morning Herald
Queenslander
West Australian

WEBSITES

'Annex to the Convention: Regulations Respecting the Laws and Customs of War on Land (Hague IV). October 18, 1907.' Hague Convention, Yale Law School. <http://avalon.law.yale.edu/20th_century/hague04.asp>

Commonwealth War Graves Commission <www.cwgc.org>

Department of Veterans' Affairs <www.dva.gov.au>

International Committee of the Red Cross <www.icrc.org/eng>

Reserve Bank of Australia – pre-decimal inflation calculator <www.rba.gov.au/calculator/annualPreDecimal.html>

INDEX

Entries in bold indicate illustrations

Abbott, Chief Petty Officer Harry, 75
Aboriginal Australians, 32
Absent Without Leave (AWL), 122
accommodation
  bathing facilities, 53
  furniture, 53
  insect infestations, 53–5
  modifications, 52–7
  post-release, 118
  prison camps, 35–6
  sanitation schemes, 53, 55
  transit, 24
Ada Bazar, 37, 63, 110, 129
Adams, Mechanic Francis, 24, 128,
  131
Adams, Mr F. L., 104
Afyon, 35, 38, 46, 53–5, **54**, 59, 65, 67–8,
  88, 97, 116, 118
Afyon hospital, 45
agricultural labour, 37–8
aid organisations, 83–9
alcohol, 64
Aleppo, 44, 79
Alexandria, 118
Ali, Captain Muhammed, 14
Allen, Private William, **69**
American Ambassador to the Ottoman
  Empire, 42, 78–81, 91
American Red Cross, 118
Amman, battle of (1918), 11, 23
Angora, 38, 41, 43, 52–3, 61, 68, 88, 97,
  116, 128
Angora Memorial, 129
The Anzac Book, 149–50
Anzac Cove, 154, 156
Anzac Day, 150–1, 154, 156
Anzac legend, 3–4, 145, 149–50, 156
Armenian cemeteries, 69, 128
Armenians, 17, 33, 93, 132, 157, 160
Armistice, 89, 103, 115–16, 132
  ex-POWs and governments, 118–22
  prosecution attempts, 131–3

release of POWs, 115–18
relocating the dead, 123–31
Armstrong, Driver D'Arcy, 12, 23, 36, 57,
  136
Ashton, Private Frederick, 1, **3**, 18, 107,
  111, 117–18
Ataturk, Kemal, 132, 150–1, 154, 156
Ataturk Channel, 155
auctions, 116–17
Austin, Captain Ronald, 6, 57, 110,
  116–17, 143
Australian Ex-Prisoners of War Memorial,
  Ballarat, 153
Australian film, 150, 155
Australian Flying Corps, 2, 10, 15, 18, 24,
  58
  No. 67 (Australian) Squadron, Royal
    Flying Corps., 11
Australian Government, 74–6, 93–4, 130,
  134–6, 159
Australian Graves Detachment (AGD), 123
Australian Graves Service (AGS), 123
Australian High Commissioner, 74
Australian Historical Mission, 41
Australian Imperial Force (AIF), 10, 16, 28,
  32, 42, 87, 103, 111, 119, 122
  11th Battalion, 1
  15th Battalion, 147
  16th Battalion, 11
  Base Records, 104, 112, 126, 130–1
  No. 14 Australian General Hospital, 118
Australian Light Horse/Imperial Camel
  Corps, 2, 10, 12, 28
  4th Light Horse Field Ambulance, 12, 19,
    23
  7th Light Horse, 11
  9th Light Horse, 12
  11th Light Horse, 14, 16
  12th Light Horse, 11
Australian and New Zealand Army Corps
  (ANZAC), 1
Australian Red Cross, 97–103

Australian Red Cross Prisoner of War
Department, 70, 76, 85, 108, 123,
159
Australian Red Cross Wounded and Missing
Bureau, 50
Australian Soldiers' Repatriation Act
(1917), 135
Australian War Memorial, 154
Australian War Records Section, 119
Australians at home, 90–114
families and emotional strain, 103–14
patriotic work and fundraising, 96–103
press coverage, 90–6
Austria–Hungary, 37, 80, 147

Baghdad North Gate Cemetery, 127–30,
128
Balkan Wars, 17, 31, 34, 38, 43, 159
Bangka Island massacre (1942), 153
barbed wire disease, 45, 159
Barker, A. J., 22
Basra Memorial, 129
Bean, Charles, 17, 40, 69, 149–50
Beattie, Private John, 20, 38, 56
Beaumont, Joan, 4, 21
Becker, Annette, 47, 57
Belemedik, **69**
Belemedik camp, 36–9, **37**, 43–4, 55–6, 60,
64, 68–9
Belfield, Lieutenant-General Sir Herbert, 72
Berlin–Baghdad Railway, 36–9, **37**, **39**, 44,
116
Berne Agreement (1917), 76–7, 83
Blair, Dale, 17
Boer War (1899–1902), 2, 60, 91–2, 97, 135
Bomford, Janette, 4
Booth's Centre for Soldiers' Wives and
Mothers, 108
Bor, 44
Boyle, Lance Corporal David, **3**, 80, 82
Bozanti, 129
Brennan, Trooper Martin, 14
Briant, Private Benjamin, 12
British Government, 33, 38, 42, 44, 80, 89,
94, 99
Australian–British relations, 60–1, 74, 159
Berne Agreement, 76–7
British–Ottoman POW negotiations, 31,
76–83, 91
control of charitable relief, 84
control of parcels, 106
enlistment strategies, 93
Kut siege, 23–4
location of graves, 123–31
military strategies, 9–11
payment to POWs, 73–4
POW departments, 118–19

POW reports, 118–19
push for prosecutions, 132
British Graves Registration Unit, 123
British imperialism, 31
British POWs, 58
British Prisoners of War Book Scheme, 85
British Red Cross Society, 98
Britishness, 59–61, 65, 159
Brockhurst, Private Henry, 12
Brown, Private Harry, 18, 27, 82
Brown, Lieutenant James, 16, 43, 54, 56, 67
Brugger, Suzanne, 32
Bulgarians, 17, 33, 93
Bullecourt, battles for (1917), 3, 93
burials, 68–9, 123, 126
Burma–Thai Railway, 153
button days, 100

Cahill, Lance Corporal Timothy, 19
Cahir, Private Keith, **3**, 120
Calcutt, Private Brendan, 69–70, 112, 127
Calcutt family, 127
camp inspections, 44, 81, 83
Campbell, Private Alan, 129
Campbell, Trooper Colin, 107, 111, 121,
138
Cape Helles, 129
capture, 2, 49
causes, 9–16
responses, 16–17, 26
treatment of POWs, 17–22
Carr, Trooper Charles, 12, 22
Carr, William, 35
Caulfield Repatriation Hospital, 100
celebrations, 49, 65–6
censorship, 5, 76, 88, 91, 104–6
Central Prisoners of War Committee, 84–7
Chalcroft, Private Thomas, **3**
Challinor, Lieutenant Ronald, 15, 23
Changi Chapel, Royal Military College,
Duntroon, 153
Changi prison camp, Singapore, 153
Changri, 41, 55, 58
Chauvel, Charles, 155
cholera, 38, 43–4
Chomley, Mary Elizabeth, 85–7, **85–7**, 104,
106, 108–13, 121, 131
Christian cemeteries, 68, **69**, 123, 129
Christianity, 33
Christmas, 49, 65
Chukri Bey, Hussein, 127
Clarke, Private George, 12
Clarke, Private John, 16
Cliffe, Corporal William, 50
Clifford, Corporal, 57
clothing, 57, 75, 82, 84–5, 87, 107
collection centre stupor, 26

collective memory, 151
Colonial Office, 74, 76
commandants, 49, 57–8, 63, 83, 88, 116
commemoration, 130, 152–7
  film, 155
  memoirs, 152
  memorials, 152–3
  Second World War, 152–3
  of Turks, 155–7
Commission for the Inspection of POW
  Camps in Turkey, 44
Commonwealth Statistician, 134
coping strategies, 52–70
Creedon, Private Daniel, 41, 65
Crimean War, 26, 33, 61, 126
Crozier, Trooper Sydney, 129
Cullen, Stoker James, 46
cultural superiority, 32–5, 57–61
Curran, Mechanic David, 24, 112–13,
  113
Curran, Esther, 112–13
Curran, Samuel, 112–13
Currie, Corporal Clyde, 23, 111
Cutlack, Frederic, 18

Damascus hospital, 26
Damousi, Joy, 70, 146
Dardanelles, 1, 10, 14–15, 22, 27, 41, 90,
  97, 116
Davern, Private John, 21, 77, 94
Day, Driver Andrew, 129
Deakin, Vera, 50
death benefits, 134–5
Delpratt, Mary, 139, 145
Delpratt, Sergeant Maurice, 28, 47, 58, 60,
  105, 116, 120
  Alexandria, 118
  Calcutt family, 70, 112
  capture, 15
  flogged, 42, 104
  Hadjikiri camp, 66
  meets Governor, 121
  response to captivity, 27–8, 48, 99, 110,
    139, 145–6, 152
  work, 38, 62
Department of Defence, 104, 120
Department of Education, 85
Department of Repatriation, 134–45, 153,
  157–8
  death benefits, 141
  employment schemes, 135
  medical care, 135–45
    health–captivity link, 136–7
    malaria, 137–8
    nervous disorders, 138–41
  rejected applications, 142–5
  Soldier Settlement Scheme, 135–6

  tensions with ex-POWs, 144–5
  war pensions scheme, 134–5
Department of Repatriation Act (1917), 135
Department of Veterans' Affairs, 134, 153
Dernancourt, battle of (1918), 3
Directorate of Prisoners of War, 72
disease, 40, 43–5, 50, 54, 57, 68–9, 112,
  137, 141
  See also malaria
Donnison, Trooper George, 129
Drysdale, Edith, 112
Drysdale, Sergeant George, 111
Drysdale family, 113
Duffy, Private Patrick, 20
Duffy, Rita, 96
Dutch, 81–3, 88, 117, 159
dysentery, 24, 138

Earnshaw, Sapper Frederick, 143
Easton, Lance Corporal Francis, 21, 125
Easton family, 126
educational schemes, 68, 122, 159
Effendi, Osman, 65
Egypt, 32–3, 119
Elkus, Abram, 78–81
Elston, Violet, 106
Elston, Lieutenant William, 2, 35, 67, 83,
  91, 106
employment schemes, 135
Enver Pasha, 23, 80
Es Salt, battle of (1918), 11–12, 14, 23, 142
Es-Sinn, battle of (1915), 13
escape attempts, 27, 59, 67, 148
external agencies, 71–89
  aid organisations, 83–9
  government departments, 71–7
  protecting powers, 78–83

Falconer, Telegrapher William, 110
families, 48–9, 150
  communication issues, 104
  death benefits, 141
  emotional strain, 103–14
  parcel concerns, 106–7
  unofficial network, 108–10
Federation, 32, 74
Feltman, Brian, 28, 99
feminism, 153
Fewster, Kevin, 156
film, 150, 155
Fisher, Andrew, 74
Flatt, Private Charles, 12, 107
floggings, 42
food, 42–3, 55–7, 60
Foreign Office, 76, 80
Foreign Office Prisoner of War
  Department, 73

Forty Thousand Horsemen, film, 155
Foxcroft, Private Harry, **3**, 63, 111
French POWs, 57, 60, 146
Fromelles, battle of (1916), 3, 85, 93

Gallipoli, film, 155
Gallipoli campaign, 1, 4, 9–10, 12–13, 15,
    17, 74, 90, 156
    The Anzac Book, 149–50
    Anzac Day, 150–1
    commemorations, 65, 156
    graves, 123–4, 150
    memorials, 129, 154
    mythology, 150
Gallipoli Reach, Canberra, 155
Gammage, Bill, 93–4
Garden Island Naval Chapel, 154
Garton, Stephen, 6, 136
Gaza, battle of (1917), 11–13, 20, 23, 92
Gelebek camp, 36, 38, 57, 69
gender roles, 56
Geneva Convention, 16
German Military Mission, 20, 44
German New Guinea, 74
German Red Cross, 20
Germans, 93, 159, 62
    air engagements, 14–16
Germany, 3, 34, 37, 78, 83, 94
    medical care, 44
    war crimes, 131
Gerster, Robin, 6, 58, 148
Gilbert, Private George, 106, 137
Gilbert, Maud, 106
Gilman, Private Ellis, 26, 108
Gilman family, 108
Gladstone, William, 33
Gnida, Antje, 149
Gough-Calthorpe, Sir Somerset, 116
Government Committee on the Treatment
    by the Enemy of British Prisoners of
    War (1915), 73
Governor-General of Australia, 74, 76
Grant, Corporal Audie, 48
graves, 68–70, 114, 123–31, **128**, 150
Green, Corporal Edgar, 46, 104, 111
Green, Maude Jennings, 104, 111, 131
Griffiths, Private Robert, 19
guards, 57–9, 66
Gullett, Henry, 28

Hadjikiri camp, 38, 42, 56–7, 62, 66, 69,
    99, 110, 127, 140
Hadjikiri camp hospital, 63
Hague Conventions of 1899 and 1907, 9,
    16, 31, 35–7, 71–3, 88–9, 104
Haidar Pasha Cemetery, **125**, 125
Haig, Lieutenant Frederick, 15, 23, 141

Halpin, Sergeant John, 6, 11, 16, 20, 22, 27,
    49–50, 61, 145, 147, 150
Hancock, Lieutenant Fred, 14, 32
Handsley, Private George, 6, 23, 43, 61, 66,
    120, 134
Harbie Military Hospital, 26
Haworth-Booth, Captain Francis, 75–6
Heathcote, Lieutenant Leonard, 14
Hebbard, Private Herbert, 12
Hennessy, Private John, 26
Herbert, Lady Victoria, 83
Hilal, 47
Hill, Lieutenant C.W., 58–9
historical amnesia, 146
HMAS *AE1*, 154
HMAS *AE2*, 10, 14–15, 18, 21, 24, 75–6,
    91, 130, 154
HMAS *Kanowna*, 118
HMS *Agamemnon*, 115
HMS *E15*, 90
Hobson, Private Edgar, 26, 42, 44, 62, 110,
    116, 118, 136
hospitals, 44, 56, 25
Hotel Crocker, 117
Hudson, Mechanic Keith, 24, 36, 110
Hughes, Billy, 76, 122, 130
Hughes, Lieutenant-Colonel Cyril, 126, 130
Hunter, Edna, 103

Immigration Restriction Act (1901), 32
Imperial War Graves Commission (IWGC),
    124–9, 150, 158, 160
Indian POWs, 23, 40, 57, 61, 80, 84, 124
Indian Soldiers Fund, 84
Inglis, Ken, 153, 156
Ingram, Private Ernest, 105, 122, 140
International Committee of the Red Cross
    (ICRC), 81, 88
interrogations, 21
Invalid Comforts Fund, 85
Iraq, 126
Islahin, 129
Islam, 33, 68
Italian Government, 147

Jalland, Pat, 70
Japanese, 3–4, 140–1, 151, 156
Jones, Captain, 57, 63
Jones, Private Daniel, 27
Jones, Elias, 58–9
Jones, Heather, 25, 37, 61, 72, 80, 146
Jordan, Second Lieutenant Stanley, 27, **67**, 100

Kars, 125
Kedos, 66–7, 116
Keeling, Edward, 89, 117–18
Kelly, Private William V., 136

Kent, David, 149
Kerin, Leading Stoker John, 100
Kerr, Corporal George, 38, 45–6, 50, 56, 63–4, 68–9, 121
Kimber, Lance Corporal Allan, 107, 130
Kimber family, 130
Kinder, Stoker/Petty Officer Henry, 42
King, Private G.B., 69, 110
Kipling, Rudyard, 129
Kramer, Alan, 131
Kress von Kressenstein, General Friedrich, 44
Kut-el-Amara siege (1916), 10, 23–4, 40, 57, 61, 65, 81, 89, 95, 104, 131

Lady Mayoress' Patriotic League, 97
Larsson, Marina, 105, 144
Lawless, Jennifer, 4, 152
Lee, Lieutenant Oliver, 110
Leipzig trials, 131
letter-writing, 5, 64, 96, 109
Lightfoot, Private Lancelot, 140
Lloyd George, David, 24
Lone Pine Memorial, 129
Lord, Mechanic William, 24, 128
Luckins, Tanja, 130
Lunden, Walter, 27
Luscombe, Lieutenant Leslie, 9, 17, 22, 52–3, 67, 88, 116, 120, 152
Lushington, Private Reginald, 2, 3, 6, 25, 28, 39–40, 56, 58, 63, 69, 109, 116
Lyons, Martyn, 5, 47

Mackay, Private William, 42, 122, 139
Makepeace, Clare, 64
malaria, 24–5, 43–4, 57, 105, 121, 137–8, 142
Manual Concerning Prisoners of War (1914), 72
marches, 23–4, 40–1, 61, 95
marginalisation of captivity, 2–4, 145–52, 154, 157
Matthews, Driver Francis, 12
McColl, Private Robert, 3, 87
McDonald, Captain Ronald, 2, 45, 91
McElligott, Lieutenant Joseph, 15, 23
McKenna, Mark, 156
McKernan, Michael, 4
McLachlan, Major-General David, 156
McMeekin, Sean, 62
medical care, 25, 43–5, 57, 63, 118, 121
    See also Department of Repatriation
medical repatriation, 77, 95
Melliss, Major General Charles J., 24
memoirs, 6, 147–8, 152
memorials, 113, 123–4, 126, 129, 152–4
memory, 154
mental illness, 140

Mersina, 79
Merson, Sergeant John, 14, 19, 27, 43, 107
Mesopotamia, 2, 10, 13, 18, 22, 25, 27, 40, 61, 116
mess parties, 64, 159
messes, 55–7, 60
Michail, Eugene, 151
Millen, Edward, 122, 135
Miller, Driver George, 12
mobile Kommando work units, 37
Monash, Lieutenant-General Sir John, 74, 122
Morgenthau, Henry, 78
Mudros agreement, 115–16
Munro Ferguson, Lady Helen, 98
Munro Ferguson, Governor-General Sir Ronald, 98
Munro, Mechanic James, 24
Murdoch, Colonel, 94

Nachtigal, Reinhard, 147
Nelson, Private Alfred, 112
Nelson, Hank, 4
Netherlands Ambassador, 82
New, Private Leonard, 69
newspapers, 6–7, 118
    alarmist reports, 94–6, 106
    coverage of captivity, 90–6
    and enlistment strategies, 92–4
    losses of E15 and AE2, 90
Newton, Lord, 73, 76
Neyland, Private Niven, 43
Nidge, 68, 130
Nightingale, Florence, 26
Nisibin, 116, 118, 129

O'Connor, Private Patrick, 19, 26, 77, 94
O'Hare, Private Phillip, 48
officer prisoners, 21, 23, 25, 35, 55, 58, 73, 76
O'Neill, Private Joseph, 121, 142
O'Neill, Violet, 142
Oppenheimer, Melanie, 97
Orientalism, 17, 34
Ottoman Army, xiv, 2, 20, 38, 41–2, 41, 44, 60, 72, 115
Ottoman Empire, 34, 44, 78, 103, 132, 137
    demise, 2, 31, 34, 71–2, 74, 115
    malaria, 138
    transport infrastructure, 40
    See also Turkey
Ottoman Government, 71, 73, 80–1, 89, 93, 132
    Berne Agreement, 76–7
    British–Ottoman POW negotiations, 31, 76–7, 91
    protecting powers, 78–83
Ottoman postal system, 48, 106–7

Ottoman Red Crescent, 36, 82, 88
Ottoman soldiers, 17–18, 20, 95, 148–51, 156
Ottoman War Ministry, 35, 72
Ozdemir, Hikmet, 40, 43

Palestine, 2, 10, 12, 14, 16, 18, 21–2, 25, 27, 115
Paltridge, Sergeant George, 141
parcels, 48, 55, 65, 76, 80–8, 94, 99, 102, 106, 110
Paris Peace Conference (1919), 131
Parkinson, Lieutenant Vincent, 16, 26
parties, 64–6
patriotic funds, 96–103
Patten, Trooper Charles, 12
pay and allowances, 38, 73–6
Pearce, George, 93–6
Pegram, Aaron, 4, 17
Peters, Private Robert, 105
Philip, Hoffman, 80
Philipp Holzmann, construction company, 38
Picton, Corporal Edward, 11
Poole, Lieutenant Arthur, 14
postal services, 47, 76, 80, 87, 94, 104, 106, 109
    See also parcels
Prisoner of War Gift House, 102
Prisoner of War Information Bureau, 73
prisoners from the ranks, 22, 35–6, 39, 42, 55, 73
Prisoners in Turkey Committee, 89, 96, 131
Prisoners of War Department, 73, 76
protecting powers, 78–83
psychological issues, 63–70
    and captivity, 45–52
    coping strategies, 52–70
    families and emotional strain, 103–14
    nervous disorders, 137–41, 151
    responses to capture, 26–30
    responses to release, 121–2

quinine, 44

race, 32–5, 60, 148, 159
Rachamimov, Alon, 146, 148, 154
railway work camps, 39, 43, 62, 79
railways, 36–40
Randall, Private William, 49–50, 146–7
Rauf Bey, 116
Rayment, Mechanic William, 24, 109
Red Cross, 65, 94, 98, 103, 105, 107, 111–13, 159
Red Cross POW Fund (RCPF), 99–103, 160
Red Cross Prisoner of War Department, 89, 104, 107, 109–10, 160

Red Cross Wounded and Missing Bureau, 109
Redman, Trooper Claude, 112, 129
Redman family, 112–13
Regimental Care Committees, 84
Reid, Pat, 46
release, 115–18
    photographs of ex-POWS, 119
    post-war reports, 119–20
    and propaganda, 120
    psychological issues, 121
    routes home, 119–21
Returned and Services League of Australia (RSL), 16, 153, 156
Returned Sailors' and Soldiers' Imperial League of Australia, 16
Richardson, Trooper Duncan, 21
Rifki Bey, Hussein, 36, 88
Roberts, Private George, 68, 70, 138
Romani, battle of (1916), 11, 13, 21, 23, 28, 92
Romaro, Private John, 13, 42
Roper, Michael, 5, 56, 106
Rose, Private Edwin, 12, 42
Royal Australian Navy, 75
    See also HMAS AE2
Royal Military College, Duntroon, 153
Rundell, James, 122
Russia, 9, 33, 61, 118, 125, 147
Russian POWs, 43, 61, 147
Rutherford, Captain Douglas, 15, 23, 63

Said, Edward, 34
Salt, Jeremy, 33–4
San Stefano camp, 3, 38, 63, 117
Sandakan Death Marches, 153
Scheme for British Prisoners of War, 83
Scott, Ernest, 98
Scroop, Lance Corporal Percy, 12
Seaton, Private Robert, 12
Second World War, 3–4, 26, 35, 46, 59, 139, 141, 145, 151, 156
Segesser, Daniel, 131
shell shock, 137, 139
Sherrie, Bessie, 109
Sherrie, Trooper Noel, 50, 94, 109, 111
Sherrie, William M., 94–6
Sherrie family, 114
Sherwin, Trooper Norman, 129
Simpson, Catherine, 149, 155–6
Skyring, Private Lowes, 47–8, 68, 70
Sloan, Driver John, 12
Sloan, Driver Matthew, 12, 19, 142, 144–5
Sloss, Acting Flight Sergeant James, 24
Smith, Acting Corporal Charles, 128
Smith, Lieutenant Laurence, 52, 62–3
Smith's Weekly, 144

Smyrna, 79, 118, 126
Soldier Settlement Scheme, 135–6
Soldier's Aid Society, 100
Soley, Corporal Thomas, 24, 129
Spanish Consul, Aleppo, 82–3
Speed, Richard, 72
Spencer, Trooper Cecil, 69
sports, 59–60, 68, 102, 159
Stanley, Peter, 32, 154
Stephens, David, 155, 161
Stoker, Commander Henry, 14
Stormonth, Amy, 143–5
Stormonth, Lieutenant Stewart, 13, 22, 144–5
Stripling, Private Richard, 39, 70, 129
submariners, 14, 18, 24, 75
Suckling, Stoker Charles, 39, 41
suicide, 142–4
Sullivan, Sergeant Harold, 12
Sultanhisar, 14, 18
Symonds, Philip Warburton, 77
Syria, 116

Talbot, Benjamin, 87
Tasch Durmas railway camp, 36, 56
Tashkishla Barracks Hospital, 26
theft, 19–20
Thomas, Leo, 24
Thompson, Driver Arthur, 12
Thomson, Alistair, 60, 151
Tierney, Lance Corporal Arthur, 38, 68
Townshend, Major General Charles, 23, 115
transportation, 22
Treaty of Brest-Litovsk (1918), 125
Treaty of Lausanne (1923), 132
Treaty of Sèvres (1920), 132
Treloar, Major John, 119
Treloar, Lieutenant William, 14, 25, 67, 119
Triolo, Rosalie, 100
Troy, Private Martin, 3, 11, 46, 83
Turkey, 127, 132, 156, 160
    See also Ottoman Empire
Turkish–Australian relations, 148–51, 155–7
Turkish Government, 131, 150, 154
Turkish War of Independence, 132
Turks, 154–7
Turks in Australia, 33, 156
Twomey, Christina, 4, 29, 151
Tyquin, Michael, 139, 145

United States, 131, 159
    protecting power role, 78–81

Van Bommel, Dirk Johannes, 79, 82–3
Van Spengler, J., 83
Vautin, Lieutenant Claude, 14, 49, 67
Victoria League of Victoria, 97
Victorian Education Department War Relief
    Fund, 100, 102
Vietnam War, 103, 121
Vischer, Adolf, 45, 81
vocational training, 122, 135–6

war crimes, 131–3
War Office, 72, 74, 84–6, 89, 107, 124, 131, 159
war pensions, 134–5
War Pensions Act (1914), 135
Ward, Stuart, 156
Ware, Major-General Fabian, 124, 127, 130
Warnes, Private William, 129
The Water Diviner (film), 155
Weidenhofer, Private Diedrich, 56
Weir, Peter, 155
Western Front, 3, 10, 47, 56, 74, 129, 146, 154
Western Women War Workers' Association, 100
Wheat, Able Seaman John, 17, 24, 42, 49, 118
White, Elinor (Nell), 104–5
White, Richard, 32, 120
White, Captain Thomas, 6, 14, 18, 25, 27, 46, 55, 59, 64, 67, 144, 147
Williams, John, 90
Williams, Mechanic Leo, 129
Williams, Stoker Michael, 130
Wilson, Private Elvas, 129
Winter, Jay, 107
Wood, Private Bert, 130
Woolley, Leonard, 6, 49, 66, 118
work, 36–9, 56
work camps, 39, 42, 44, 55–7, 67–8, 118

Yanikdag, Yucel, 61
Yarbaschi camp, 36, 38
Yarnall, John, 84, 106
Young Men's Christian Association, 78
Yozgad camp, 58

Ziino, Bart, 68, 70, 123, 130